DEVELOPMENT
THEORY

Theory, Culture & Society

Theory, Culture & Society caters for the resurgence of interest in culture within contemporary social science and the humanities. Building on the heritage of classical social theory, the book series examines ways in which this tradition has been reshaped by a new generation of theorists. It also publishes theoretically informed analyses of everyday life, popular culture, and new intellectual movements.

THE TCS CENTRE
The Theory, Culture & Society book series, the journals *Theory, Culture & Society* and *Body & Society*, and related conference, seminar and postgraduate programmes operate from the TCS Centre at Nottingham Trent University. For further details of the TCS Centre's activities please contact:

Centre Administrator
The TCS Centre, Room 175
Faculty of Humanities
Nottingham Trent University
Clifton Lane, Nottingham, NG11 8NS, UK
e-mail: tcs@ntu.ac.uk
web: http//tcs@ntu.ac.uk

Recent volumes include:

Paul Virilio
From Modernism to Hypermodernism
edited by *John Armitage*

Subject, Society and Culture
Roy Boyne

Norbert Elias and Modern Social Theory
Dennis Smith

Occidentalism
Modernity and Subjectivity
Couze Venn

Simulation and Social Theory
Sean Cubitt

The Contradictions of Culture
Cities: Culture: Women
Elizabeth Wilson

DEVELOPMENT THEORY

Deconstructions/Reconstructions

JAN NEDERVEEN PIETERSE

SAGE Publications
London • Thousand Oaks • New Delhi

First published 2001
Reprited 2002

SAGE Publications Ltd
6 Bonhill Street
London EC2A 4PU

SAGE Publications Inc
2455 Teller Road
Thousand Oaks, California 91320

SAGE Publications India Pvt Ltd
32, M-Block Market
Greater Kailash - I
New Delhi 110 048

Published in association with *Theory, Culture & Society*, Nottingham Trent University

British Library Cataloguing in Publication data

A catalogue record for this book
is available from the British Library

ISBN 0-7619-5292-6
ISBN 0-7619-5293-4 (pb)

Library of Congress catalog record available

Typeset by Siva Math Setters, Chennai, India
Printed in Great Britain by The Cromwell Press Ltd,
Trowbridge, Wiltshire

To Lisa, Lara, Kim

CONTENTS

ACKNOWLEDGEMENTS

Most chapters in this book have appeared earlier as articles in journals and books and they have all been revised for this volume. I acknowledge the kind permission of the following publishers and copyright holders:

Institute of Social Studies: 'Dilemmas of development discourse: the crisis of developmentalism and the comparative method', *Development and Change* (22, 1, 1991: 5-29); 'My paradigm or yours? Alternative development, post development, reflexive development', *Development & Change* (29, 2, 1998: 343-73).

Routledge: 'The development of development theory: towards critical globalism', *Review of International Political Economy* (3, 4, 1996: 541-64); 'Trends in development theory', in Ronen Palan (ed.), *Global Political Economy* (London, 2000, pp. 197-214); 'After Post-Development', *Third World Quarterly* (20, 1, 2000: 175-91).

Frank Cass: 'The cultural turn in development: questions of power', *The European Journal of Development Research* (7, 1, 1995: 176-92). 'Growth and equity revisited: a supply-side approach to social development', *The European Journal of Development Research* (9, 1, 1997: 128-49) and in Cristóbal Kay (ed.), *Globalisation, competitiveness and human security* (London, 1997, pp. 128-49). 'Critical holism and the Tao of development', *The European Journal of Development Research* (11, 1, 1999: 75-100).

Zed Books: 'Critical holism and the Tao of development' was the Inaugural Vincent Tucker Memorial Lecture at University College Cork, Ireland, February 1998. A short version appears in Ronaldo Munck and Denis O'Hearn (eds), *Critical development theory: contributions to a new paradigm* (London and New York, 1999, pp. 63-88). The full version is in this book.

'Delinking or globalization?' appeared in *Economic and Political Weekly* (29, 5, 1994: 239-42).

I am indebted of course to many more friends and sources of inspiration than I can acknowledge. Friends and colleagues have commented on different chapters. I cordially thank Lisa Chason, Ranjit Dwivedi, Des Gasper, Ananta Giri, Thomas Blom Hansen, Frank Hirtz, Gerrit Huizer, Sudipto Kaviraj, Cristóbal Kay, W.D. Lakshman, Lily Ling, Gilbert Rist, Melania Portilla Rodriguez, Henk van Roosmalen, Mohamed Salih, Jan Aart Scholte, David Slater, Vincent Tucker, Peter Waterman, W.F. Wertheim and Chris Williams. These essays were written while I was at the Institute of Social Studies, an international graduate school in development studies in The Hague, and I thank the Institute for many lessons learnt. I have been inspired by several generations of students at the Institute of Social Studies, particularly in the Politics of Alternative Development Strategies MA programme. To name only a few, my thanks go to Hanan Abdel Rahman, Michael Chai, Daniel Chavez, Mike Demel,

Fiona Dove, Azza M. Karam, Sergio Lenci, Wangu Mwangi, Edgar Pieterse, Imad Sabi, Albana Shala, Nahda Sh'hada Younis, Kim Scipes, P.L. de Silva, Mukta Srivastava, Stuart Todd, Hasmet Uluorta. The usual disclaimer of course applies.

INTRODUCTION

This book represents my engagement with development studies over many years. To guide the reader, here is a brief overview of the treatment and arguments in the different chapters.

Chapter 1 is the substantive introduction to the book. It problematizes development knowledge and offers a stock taking of major trends in development thinking. Together with Chapter 10 (Futures), Chapter 1 (Trends) ties a ribbon around the book.

Chapters 2 to 7 mainly consist of critical treatments of different approaches to development. Chapters 2 and 3 discuss the career of development thinking in the mode of discourse analysis. Chapter 2 focuses on the deep legacies of Eurocentrism in developmentalism. Chapter 3 addresses the zigzag character of development thinking and its inconsistencies over time. Its closing argument on critical globalism is analytic as well as programmatic. One of the limitations of discourse analysis (taken up in Chapters 1 and 7) is that it fails to engage the specifics of political economy. Chapter 4 revisits the political economy approach by way of a critique of Samir Amin's work. His thesis in favour of delinking is contrasted to globalization processes, continuing the argument of critical globalism in the previous chapter. Another theme is Amin's political economy approach to 'culture'. Chapter 5 takes up various ways in which 'culture' has been incorporated into development discourse and policy.

While alternative development is a critique of mainstream development, Chapter 6 subjects alternative development claims to a critical treatment, in particular the claim for an alternative development paradigm. Chapter 7 is a critique of post-development arguments and, I plead guilty, a deconstruction of deconstruction. Chapters 4 to 7 address four different 'alternative' or critical approaches in development: prioritizing structures (political economy), prioritizing culture (culture and development), prioritizing social forces (alternative development), and prioritizing discourse (post-development).

A book with just criticisms and goodbyes to paradigms would be too easy and not quite satisfactory; for years this has been the common fare in development studies. Lengthy analyses or critical accounts often conclude with just a brief note on ways forward and I would like to be more constructive and affirmative. Thus, Chapters 8 to 10 consist in the main of programmatic treatments, or reconstructions in the sense of innovative turns and forward options for development. These treatments on balance argue more 'for' than 'against'. Chapter 8 argues for extending the human development approach to social development and for a supply-side approach to social development, including taking on questions such as social capital. Chapter 9 is a philosophical and methodological reflection on development; it takes the arguments concerning Eurocentrism in Chapter 2 to a wider horizon and argues for critical holism as the Tao of development. The closing chapter on futures of development takes the opening arguments on trends in development thinking and policy into the future tense, redefines development in light of the overall discussion, and concludes with reconstructions in development. A précis is as follows.

Approaches	Keywords	Chapters
Development thinking	Overview	1
	Deconstructions	
Discourse analysis	Developmentalism	2
	History of development thinking	3
Political economy	Dependency theory and delinking	4
Culture & development	Cultural turn, anthropology	5
Alternative development	Social forces	6
Post-development	Discourse analysis as ideology	7
Human development	Capacitation	8
	Reconstructions	
Globalization & development	Critical globalism	3
Intercultural development	Cultural difference as catalyst	4
Social development	Supply-side	8
Critical holism	Tao of development	9
Reflexive development	Collective learning, reform platform	10

Any of these approaches – discourse analysis, anthropology, cultural studies, alternative development, political economy, etc. – can be a vantage point from which to probe the complexities of development. Any approach handled with depth and subtlety can be fruitful if it becomes an instrument and avenue of reflexivity. This is the lesson I arrive at in the closing two chapters. Development is too complex to allow partial approaches to have their way – although these lend themselves to technical finesse and managerial intervention, the managerial fiction of knowledge and mastery itself is part of the problem. Combining different angles and approaches yields a holistic assessment of development. Fallibility and open-endedness are necessary features of development thinking and what matters in relation to any of these approaches is reflexivity; what matters is not merely what but how. This also applies to holism itself: hence critical holism, lest holism become an all-purpose way out of the perplexities of development. These critical treatments are not dogmatic closures but contributions to reflexivity. And it applies to reflexivity, lest this become snake oil: reflexivity must be politically enabling.

From the combination of terms in the title – deconstructions/reconstructions – it is obvious that this is not an exercise in deconstruction in the classic sense (cf. Willett 1999: 2-3) for then reconstructions would not belong. Reconstructions are ways ahead, contextual and time bound, forward options. In time they will yield another set of deconstructions and by then other reconstructions will emerge, which is the way of things. Chapter 1 argues that development is struggle. To be precise, development is struggle over the shape of futures, a dramatic and complex struggle.

1

TRENDS IN
DEVELOPMENT THEORY

Development in Question

Globalization and regionalization are overtaking the standard unit of development, the nation or society. The conventional agent of development, the state, is being overtaken by the role of international institutions and market forces. The classic aim of development, modernization or catching up with advanced countries, is in question because modernization is no longer an obvious ambition. Modernity no longer seems so attractive in view of ecological problems, the consequences of technological change and many other problems. Westernization no longer seems attractive in a time of revaluation of local culture and cultural diversity. Several development decades have not measured up to expectations, especially in Africa and parts of Latin America and South Asia. The foundation of development studies – that developing countries form a special case – has been undermined by the politics of structural adjustment and the universalist claims of neoclassical economics.

Doesn't all this mean the end of development? Everything that development used to represent appears to be in question, in crisis. There are various views of what this crisis means. One is that since development is in crisis, let's close the shop and think of something entirely different – 'beyond development'. This is the position associated with post-development thinking. A different reaction is to qualify the crisis, acknowledging the failures of the development record but also its achievements, avoiding simplistic, one-sided assessments. Thus, health care and education have improved even in the poorest countries and in countries where growth has been stagnant. Another reaction is to acknowledge crisis and to argue that crisis is intrinsic to development, that development knowledge is crisis knowledge. From its beginnings in the nineteenth century development thinking was a reaction to the crises of progress, such as the social problems caused by industrialization. Hence questioning, rethinking and crisis are part of development and not external to it. A related view is not merely to acknowledge questioning as part of development but to consider it its spearhead – viewing development thinking as ongoing questioning, critique and probing alternative options. Development then is a field in flux, with rapid change and turnover of alternatives. Precisely because of its crisis character and predicament development is a high-energy field.

This mapping exercise seeks to make major trends in development thinking explicit. Several of these are examined in detail in the subsequent chapters, building up to an inventory of current and future options and directions in the closing chapter. Trends in this discussion refer to long-term and ongoing as well as plausible future directions in the development field. The focus is on development theories, i.e. organized reflections on development, rather than on development *tout court*. Trend spotting is not exactly an intellectually neutral activity and so it needs to be contextualized. Accordingly, this treatment opens with general observations on the character of development thinking and the status of development theory. The argument then turns to the different meanings of 'development' over time, which places the discussion of contemporary trends in a historical context. The next section juxtaposes these different understandings of development to changing patterns of global hegemony. Zeroing in on the contemporary setting, the different stakeholders and institutions in the development field are mapped out. Against this backdrop we turn to development trends over time, first long-term trends in theory and methodology, and next policy changes.

The Status of Development Theory

What is the contribution of development theory to this situation? Theory is the critique, revision and summing up of past knowledge in the form of general propositions, the fusion of diverse views and partial knowledges in general frameworks of explanation. What is referred to as 'development theory' largely belongs to the level of grand theories, broad explanatory frameworks. This is part of its limited character. There is a lot development theory does not talk about. Many actual development problems are addressed by mid-range or micro theories – questions of rural development, industrialization, urbanization, trade policy, etc. Development theory as such concerns the larger explanatory frames. In addition, 'development theory' usually refers to the leading theories and many rival and subsidiary theories do not quite make it to the limelight.

In social science it is now widely assumed that realities are socially constructed. The way people think and talk about social realities affects agendas, policies, laws and the ways laws are interpreted. Just as perception not merely registers but shapes reality, knowledge does not simply reflect but constructs reality. Knowledge is political, shapes perceptions, agendas, policies. If this were not the case then why bother, why research, why hold conferences? Theory is a meeting place of ideology, politics and explanation. Framing, defining the field, the parameters of phenomena is the business of theory.

Theory is a distillation of reflections on practice into conceptual language so as to connect with past knowledge. The relationship between theory and practice is uneven: theory tends to lag behind practice, behind innovations on the ground, and practice tends to lag behind theory (since policy makers and activists lack time for reflection). A careful look at practice can generate new theory, and theory or theoretical praxis can inspire new practice. Theories are contextual. While theories react to other theories and often emphasize differences rather than complementarities, the complexities encountered in reality are such that we usually need several analytics in combination.

Is development theory a matter of social science or of politics? Writers have different views on the degree of autonomy of development theory. Some treat development theory primarily as part of social science and thus emphasize the influence of classical economic and social thought (e.g. Preston 1996, Martinussen 1997). Others implicitly view development theory mainly as ideology – like a ship rocked in a sea of political pressures and shifting tides. They consider political leanings, in a broad sense, as more important in shaping development theory than theoretical considerations (e.g. Frank 1971). The advantage of this view is that it draws attention to the ideological role of development theory – in setting agendas, framing priorities, building coalitions, justifying policies. Its limitation is that it treats development theory as a by-product of political processes and not as an intellectual process as well. Some cynicism in relation to theory is appropriate: how often is a theory in effect a political gesture? What is the politics of theory? Whom does discourse serve? In between these views is a middle position that recognizes the intellectual as well as the political elements in development theory. It doesn't make sense to isolate development theory from political processes and treat it as an ivory-tower intellectual exercise; but neither can one simply reduce it to ideology or political propaganda. This is the contextual approach to development theory in which both political contexts and influences from social science count (as in Corbridge 1995, Leys 1996). This approach of the sociology of development knowledge is adopted here.

For a development theory to be significant, social forces must carry it. To be carried by social forces it must match their worldview and articulate their interests; it must serve an ideological function. However, to serve their interests, it must also make sense and be able to explain things. By the same token, explanation is not a neutral function. There are as many ways of explaining things as there are positions from which to view realities. The explanation that satisfies a peasant is not the same as one that satisfies a landlord, a banker or IMF official.

We can probably define development as the organized intervention in collective affairs according to a standard of improvement. What constitutes improvement and what is appropriate intervention obviously vary according to class, culture, historical context and relations of power. Development theory is the negotiation of these issues. The strength and the weakness of development thinking is its policy-oriented character. This is part of its vitality and inventiveness. It is problem-driven rather than theory-driven. It is worldly, grounded, streetwise, driven by field knowledge, not just book knowledge. In part for the same reasons, development thinking ranks fairly low on the totem pole of social science. As applied social science, development thinking has a derivative status. It has more often been a follower of frameworks developed in other sciences than a trend-setter. It has been a net importer of social science theories and has been influenced by other social sciences more often than it has influenced them. Evolutionism, Marxism, neomarxism, Keynesianism, structural functionalism, neoclassical economics and poststructuralism are among the social science paradigms imported by development theories at different times. A major area in which development theory has influenced social science generally is dependency theory. Studies in dependency theory were widely read outside development studies; they inspired, for instance, world-system theory.

Arguably, development theory is underestimated in social science. The notion that development theory counts for less because it concerns 'merely the South', while major developments in social theory are spearheaded by the West reflects a deep-seated prejudice. It reflects a (neo) colonial division of labour in the production of knowledge according to which theory is generated in the North and data, like raw materials, are produced in the South (Pletsch 1981). In this schema the developed or advanced societies are supposed to be the mirror and guide of less developed societies. This cognitive colonialism is passé on several counts. This kind of unilinear thinking is no longer plausible. Besides, in the wake of global restructuring, development knowledge is increasingly relevant also in the North. The conventional distinction between developing and developed societies is less and less relevant – the 'South' is in the 'North', and vice versa. As part of the decline of welfare economies there is increasing polarization within countries on account of the decline of public support, public services and facilities. In the United States and the UK, there is mention of 'two thirds societies'. Social exclusion nowadays is a problem that is common to North and South, West and East.

Knowledge production in the South has been influential not merely in the past but also under the shadow of western hegemony. A case in point is Gandhi and his influence on the Civil Rights movement (Nederveen Pieterse 1989). Dependency thinking, Maoism, Guevarism, and more recently the Delhi school of development thought (Dallmayr 1996) are other examples. Japanese perspectives on development have been influential in Asia and beyond (e.g. Wade 1996, Iwasaki et al. 1992).

Development is a strange field. Development practice, policy and studies are all flourishing. Universities open new development schools. Yet for quite some time the field has been said to be in crisis, gridlock, impasse, or passé. Part of this crisis is a crisis of ideologies, which reflects a wider paradigm crisis – of neomarxism and dependency theory, as well as Keynesianism and welfare politics. There have been plenty of critical positions but no coherent ideological response to the neoliberal turn. The crisis is further due to changing circumstances including development failures, the growing role of international financial institutions, and conflicts in developing countries.

According to Marx's eleventh thesis on Feuerbach, 'Philosophers have only interpreted the world in various ways. The time has come to change it.' Arguably, the actual power of development is the power of thesis eleven. Nowadays the ambition 'to change the world' meets with cynicism – because of the questionable record of several development decades, doubts over social engineering and rationalist planning as exercises in authoritarianism, and media triviality ('We are the world'). And because of doubts in modernism and its utopian belief that society can be engineered – how about social engineering if we look at Bosnia, Rwanda, Somalia, Sierra Leone, Liberia?

The status of development theory reflects the theory-lag between development studies and social science generally, a 'colonial legacy' in knowledge and a recurring impasse in the development field. The decolonization of knowledge is a matter of ongoing contestation (Apffel-Marglin and Marglin 1996, Nederveen Pieterse and Parekh 1995). As part of accelerated globalization, neoliberal policies impose neoclassical economics on the South, applying Western standards of policy and systems of accounting to align economies and financial and credit regimes. It is appropriate to consider this episode as part of the wider historical relations between North and South. In tandem with changing geopolitical relations, 'development' has been changing its meaning over time.

Meanings of 'Development' Over Time

Over time 'development' has carried very different meanings. The term 'development' in its present sense dates from the postwar era of modern development thinking. In hindsight, earlier practices have been viewed as antecedents of development policy, though the term 'development' was not necessarily used at the time. Thus, Kurt Martin (1991) regards the classic political economists, from Ricardo to Marx, as development thinkers for they addressed similar problems of economic development. The turn of the century latecomers to industrialization in Central and Eastern Europe faced basic development questions, such as the appropriate relationship between agriculture and industry. In central planning, the Soviets found a novel instrument to achieve industrialization. During the Cold War years of rivalry between capitalism and communism, the two competing development strategies were Western development economics and some form of central planning (in Soviet, Chinese or Cuban varieties). In this general context, the core meaning of development was catching up with the advanced industrialized countries.

Cowen and Shenton uncover yet another meaning of development. In nineteenth-century England, 'development', they argue, referred to remedies for the shortcomings and maladies of progress. This involves questions such as population (according to Malthus), job loss (for the Luddites), the social question (according to Marx and others) and urban squalor. In this argument, *progress* and *development* (which are often viewed as a seamless web) are contrasted and development differs from and complements progress. Thus, for Hegel, progress is linear and development curvilinear (Cowen and Shenton 1996: 130). Accordingly, twentieth-century development thinking in Europe and the colonies had already traversed many terrains and positions and was a reaction to nineteenth-century progress and policy failures where industrialization left people uprooted and out of work, and social relations dislocated.

The immediate predecessor of modern development economics was colonial economics. Economics in the European colonies and dependencies had gone through several stages. In brief, an early stage of commerce by chartered companies, followed by plantations and mining. In a later phase, colonialism took on the form of 'trusteeship': the management of colonial economies not merely with a view to their exploitation for metropolitan benefit but allegedly also to develop the economies in the interest of the native population. Development, if the term was used at all, in effect referred mainly to colonial resource management, first to make the colonies cost-effective, and later to build up economic resources with a view to national independence. Industrialization was not part of colonial economics because the comparative advantage of the colonies was held to be the export of raw materials for the industries in the metropolitan countries. Indeed there are many episodes, amply documented, when European or colonial interests destroyed native manufactures (textile manufacturing in India is the classic case) or sabotaged efforts at industrialization in the periphery (Egypt, Turkey, Persia are cases in point; Stavrianos 1981). This is a significant difference between the colonial economies and the latecomers in Central and Eastern Europe.

In modern development thinking and economics, the core meaning of development was economic growth, as in growth theory and Big Push theory. In the course of time mechanization and industrialization became part of this, as in Rostow's *Stages of Growth*. When development thinking broadened to encompass modernization, economic growth was combined with political modernization, i.e. nation building, and social modernization, such as fostering entrepreneurship and 'achievement orientation'. In dependency theory, the core meaning of development likewise was economic growth, under the heading of accumulation. Its distorted form was dependent accumulation, which led to the 'development of underdevelopment', and an intermediate form was 'associated dependent development'. The positive goal was national accumulation (or autocentric development). With the onset of alternative development thinking, new understandings of development came to the fore focused on social and community development. With human development in the mid-1980s came the understanding of development as capacitation, following Amartya Sen's work on capacities and entitlements. In this view the point of development, above all, is that it is enabling. The core definition of development in the Human Development Reports of UNDP is 'the enlargement of people's choices'.

Two radically different perspectives on development came to the fore around the same time. Neoliberalism, in returning to neoclassical economics, eliminates the foundation of development economics: the notion that developing economies represent a 'special case'. According to the neoliberal view, there is no special case. What matters is to 'get the prices right' and let market forces do their work. Development in the sense of government intervention is anathema for it means market distortion. The central objective, economic growth, is to be achieved through structural reform, deregulation, liberalization, privatization – all of which are to roll back government and reduce market-distorting interventions, and in effect annul 'development'. In other words, one of the conventional core meanings of 'development' is retained, i.e. economic growth, while the 'how to' and agency of development switches from state to market. Accordingly, neoliberalism is an anti-development perspective, not in terms of goals but in terms of means. Post-development thinking also puts forth an anti-development position. This is still more radical for it applies not merely to the means (the state is accused of authoritarian engineering) but also to the goals (economic growth is repudiated) and the results (which are deemed a failure or disaster for the majority of the population) (Rahnema and Bawtree 1997; discussed in Chapter 7 below). An overview is in Table 1.1.

Thus, the lineages of development are quite mixed. It includes the application of science and technology to collective organization, but also managing the changes that arise from the application of technology. Development virtually from the outset has included an element of reflexivity. It ranges from infrastructure works (roads, railways, dams, canals, ports) to industrial policy, the

Table 1.1 *Meanings of development over time*

Period	Perspectives	Meanings of development
1870 >	Latecomers	Industrialization, catching-up
1850 >	Colonial economics	Resource management, trusteeship
1940 >	Development economics	Economic (growth) – industrialization
1950 >	Modernization theory	Growth, political & social modernization
1960 >	Dependency theory	Accumulation – national, autocentric
1970 >	Alternative development	Human flourishing
1980 >	Human development	Capacitation, enlargement of people's choices
1980 >	Neoliberalism	Economic growth – structural reform, deregulation, liberalization, privatization
1990 >	Post-development	Authoritarian engineering, disaster

welfare state, new economic policy, colonial economics and Keynesian demand management.

There are several ways of making sense of this shift of meanings of development over time. One is to view this kind of archaeology of development discourse as a deconstruction of development, i.e. as part of a development critique. Another is to treat it as part of historical context: it is quite sensible for development to change meaning in relation to changing circumstances and sensibilities. 'Development' then serves as a mirror of changing economic and social capacities, priorities and choices. A third option is to recombine these different views as dimensions of development, i.e. to fit them all together as part of a development mosaic and thus to reconstruct development as a synthesis of components (e.g. Martinussen 1997: Ch. 3). A limitation of this perspective is that it takes history out of development. If we consider each theory as offering a Gestalt of development, a total picture from a particular angle, then the array of successive and rival theories offers a kaleidoscopic view into the collective mirror. By any account, the different meanings of development relate to changing relations of power and hegemony, which is part of the view in the collective mirror.

Development is Struggle

Besides different meanings of development over time, there are different dimensions to 'development' at any one time. To each development theory there are, implicitly or explicitly, various dimensions or layers: first, the historical context and political circumstances. Each perspective unfolds in a particular historical setting. Understanding development theory in context means understanding it as a reaction to problems, perspectives and arguments at the time. Another dimension is explanation or assumptions about causal relationships. This implies epistemology or rules of what constitutes knowledge. In addition, it involves methodology,

---

❑   *Context* – historical context and political circumstances
❑   *Explanation* – assumptions about causal relationships
❑   *Epistemology* – rules of what constitutes knowledge
❑   *Methodology* – Indicators and research methods
❑   *Representation* – articulating or privileging particular political and class interests
    and cultural preferences
❑   *Imagination* – images, evocations, symbols of development, desire
❑   *Future* – policy, agenda, future project

Figure 1.1   *Dimensions of development theories*

or indicators and research methods. Development thinking also performs a role
of representation, of articulating and privileging particular political and class
interests and cultural preferences. Development theories also reflect images of
improvement or desirable change. A further element is the agenda-setting role of
theory, as a set of policy implications and a future project.

Understanding development theory means being aware of these multiple layers
(Figure 1.1). Accordingly, each development theory can be read on multiple
levels. The 'layers' of development can also be understood in terms of the ongoing
and shifting relations among the following components: Practice→ Research→
Policy→Ideology→Image→Theory→Ideology→Policy→Practice→
Theory→Ideology→Image→Policy…

A central issue is the relationship between knowledge and power. That every
truth is a claim to power and every power is a centre of truth is the point of discourse analysis and part of a postmodern understanding of knowledge. This
involves more or less subtle considerations. For instance, one can argue for a relationship between technological capacities and epistemology and politics. 'Heavy
technology' such as the steam engine then correlates with an epistemology of
determinism and a politics of hierarchy; whereas soft or light technology, such as
touch-button tech, implies much subtler epistemologies and more horizontal relations (Mulgan 1994). Broadly speaking each development theory can be read as
a hegemony or a challenge to hegemony. Explanation is not always the most
important function of theory – agenda setting, mobilization and coalition building are others.

In line with the neocolonial intellectual division of labour in which 'theory' is
generated in the West and data are supplied by the South, grand theories have
typically been fashioned in the West and therefore articulate Western political
interests and follow Western intellectual styles and priorities. Reading development theory then is also reading a history of hegemony and political and intellectual Eurocentrism (Amin 1989, Mehmet 1995, and Chapter 2 below). Notable
exceptions are dependency theory (which was also informed by Marxism, i.e.
originally a Western counterhegemony), alternative development and human
development thinking, which largely originate outside the West.

We can map the main contours of development thinking in different periods
and place them in the context of the pattern of hegemony in international relations

Table 1.2   *Development theories and global hegemony*

Development thinking	Historical context	Hegemony	Explanation
Progress, evolutionism	19th century	British Empire	Colonial anthropology, Social Darwinism
Classical development	1890-1930s	Latecomers, Colonialism	Classical political economy
Modernization	Post-war boom	US hegemony	Growth theory, structural functionalism
Dependency	Decolonization	Third World nationalism, NAM, G77	Neomarxism
Neoliberalism	1980s >	Globalization. Finance and corporate capital	Neoclassical economics, monetarism
Human development	1980s >	Rise of Asian and Pacific Rim, big emerging markets	Capabilities, developmental state

and the structures of explanation prevalent at the time (Table 1.2). Thus, we relate the global relations of power or international hegemony to intellectual patterns of hegemony (in line with Gramscian international relations theory; Cox 1991). The assumption in this schema is that the explanatory frameworks that inform development thinking are shaped by the paradigms that are available in the intellectual market at the time.

The Development Field

Development thinking and policy, then, is a terrain of hegemony and counter-hegemony. In this contestation of interests there are many stakeholders and multiple centres of power and influence. Taking a closer look at the contemporary development field, we can schematically map the main actors and forces as shown in Table 1.3.

To the surface structure of dispersed centres of influence we may add the *infrastructure* of behind-the-scenes forces, i.e. those on whom the overt centres of influence themselves depend or are following. Thus, what matters are not simply the World Bank or the IMF, but their boards of trustees and other significant forces who influence the parameters of policy. For instance, current analysis refers to the 'Treasury-Wall Street-IMF complex' as a successor to the military-industrial complex (Wade and Veneroso 1998). Further, at some remove (because these relations are not always clear-cut and straightforward), we may add the development thinking that would be congenial to these circles and the disciplines that typically inform their angle of vision. The dispersal of stakeholders in development roughly correlates with the disciplinary sprawl of development studies, so this fragmentation may have not only an intellectual basis in the academic division of labour but also an institutional basis.

Table 1.3 *Actors in development field 1990s: Different stakeholders, different development*

Institutional	State	IFIs	UN system	Civil society
Structure	Governments, ministries South & North	IMF, World Bank	UN agencies	INGOs, NGOs
Infrastructure	Bureaucracies, interest groups, parties, factions, citizens	WTO, G7, central, international & development banks, MNCs	UN General Assembly, governments, ILO, WHO, etc.	People. Social movements, trade unions, parties, firms, churches, etc.
Locations	Capitals, etc.	Washington, DC	New York, Geneva, Paris, Nairobi, etc.	Dispersed
Development thinking	Economics (neoclassical to Keynesian) & human development	Neoclassical economics, monetarism, neoliberalism	Human development	Alternative development (& post-development)
Disciplines	Economics, political science	Economics	Economics, political economy, IR, political science	Sociology, anthropology, ecology, gender & cultural studies

This is only a schematic representation. Obvious provisos are that within the infrastructures of power different ideologies may prevail, NGOs need differentiation into various types, etc. From this mapping of the development field several points follow. (1) It is not really possible to generalize about development – the question is, whose development? Different stakeholders have different takes on the meaning of development and how to achieve it. This is not a minor point but a fundamental circumstance. Development intrinsically is a field of multi-level negotiation and struggle among different stakeholders. (2) Schematic as it is, this outline may enable us to fine-tune thinking about the relationship between power and knowledge in development. (3) The field is in flux. Thus, the World Bank has been shifting position repeatedly in view of policy failures and political pressures and trends. (4) New concerns and priorities that are broadly shared by development stakeholders – such as globalization, poverty alleviation, gender awareness, environmental management – prompt new combinations and partnerships that crosscut 'boxes'. (5) Emergencies occur that make for crosscutting alliances and approaches – such as complex emergency, humanitarian action, conflict prevention and post-conflict reconstruction. In this light this kind of map is already overtaken on the ground, which serves as a reminder that the map should not be mistaken for the territory.

Trends in Development Theory

Obviously, the selection and representation of trends are tricky issues. If it is true that development is a mirror of the times then a development trend report is a look in the collective mirror – and there are many angles to take and arguments to fit the occasion. There is no methodology to achieve this in a neat and clean fashion. The format adopted here is a concise profile of trends, by way of introduction to later discussion in the book. Limitations of this kind of discussion are the absence of magnitudes or relative values and the fact that everything is contextual. Certain trends may well be significant but without a quantitative analysis this remains inevitably impressionistic. First we will discuss long-term trends in development theory. Because they are long-term changes (over fifty years or more) they have a certain degree of plausibility but, on the other hand, they are also rather general and of a high level of abstraction. Even so a long-term perspective in a field dominated by short-termism may be welcome. Next we will look at current trends in development thinking and policy.

Arguably, the long-term trends in development theory parallel general shifts in social science. They may be characterized as a gradual shift from nineteenth-century to late twentieth-century epistemologies. In the first place this involves a shift from structuralist perspectives that emphasize the role of macro-structures towards more agency-oriented views. Classical and modern development thinking were fundamentally structuralist: the emphasis was on the large-scale patterning of social realities by structural changes in the economy, the state and the social system. This also applies to critical development thinking of the time, which was informed by Marxism, which in its orthodox forms is basically structuralist. It further applies to the structuralist school associated with Raúl Prebisch, which preceded the emergence of dependency theory in Latin America, and to neomarxism, dependency theory, modes of production analysis, structuralist Althusserian Marxism and the regulation school.

In social science generally this outlook began to change with the growing influence of phenomenology (dating back to nineteenth-century antecedents) and a variety of orientations such as existentialism (and its emphasis on individual responsibility), hermeneutics (involving a more complex epistemology), symbolic interactionism and ethnomethodology (in anthropology), new institutional economics and rational choice, public choice and capability (in economics) and feminism (e.g. standpoint theory). In Marxism, it began to change with the influence of Gramscian Marxism. In different ways, these orientations all imply a shift in emphasis from structuralist toward institutional and agency-oriented views. This can also be described as a change from deterministic to interpretative views (cf. Bauman 1992 on the changing role of the intellectual from legislator to interpreter) and from materialist and reductionist views to multidimensional and holistic views. A different account of this shift is from structuralism to constructivism, i.e. from an account of social realities as determined and patterned by macro-structures, to an account of social realities as being socially constructed. The lineage of constructivism includes phenomenology – as in Schutz (1972) and Berger and Luckmann (1967); and Max Weber – much of Weber's work is constructivist in outlook. A familiar turning point is Giddens' structuration theory (1984). Poststructuralism and postmodernism, taken in a methodological sense, are further expressions of this reorientation (Rosenau 1992).

In development studies, these broad changes involve various implications. One of the consequences of the emphasis on agency is that development thinking becomes spatialized and more local, or regional. Another implication is the concern for differentiation and diversity. Early and modern development thinking were fundamentally generalizing and homogenizing; structuralism is intrinsically essentialist. By contrast, the post-impasse trend in development thinking highlights diversity and differentiation (Schuurman 1993, Booth 1994b). Along with this comes a movement away from grand overall theories and big schema policies. There are no more general recipes, no development policies that are relevant across countries and regions. The singular makes way for the plural generally – not simply development but what kind of development, not simply growth but what kind of growth. Thus, new qualifications proliferate, such as sustainable development, people-friendly growth, pro-poor growth, etc. Such qualifications had always figured in the critical literature; now they enter mainstream discourse. Among the concrete expressions of the agency orientation in development thinking are work on strategic groups, the actor-oriented approach (Long 1994) and the general emphasis on a participatory approach (e.g. Oommen 1998).

The concern with diversity and agency introduces a new kind of tension: what then is the relationship between the local and the global, between the internal and the external, the endogenous and exogenous, between micro- and macro-policies? The shift from structuralism to constructivism and from structure to agency refers to a shift in emphasis and perspective; one does not replace the other but complements it. Structural changes and macro-policies obviously matter, such as structural adjustment lending and the Multilateral Agreement on Investments. What has changed is that these no longer constitute the field but are perceived as only part of the field. Many stakeholders actively negotiate them politically and analytically and feel they can do something about them. The impact of these actors on public debate and policy making can be measured (e.g. Clarke 1998). This is a step towards the democratization of development politics. Constructivism, in this sense, is the methodological expression of a political transformation.

This perspective offers one angle on current trends in development studies. Several trends are linked to these general changes (outlined in Figure 1.2), or follow from it, without being reducible to it. Current trends are discussed further with a view to changes in different spheres. In methodology, what stands out is the trend towards interdisciplinarity and the role of discourse analysis. In general sensibilities, the cultural turn is significant. In development policy, significant themes are intersectoral cooperation, social diversity, human security, gender and environment, and changes in development cooperation and structural reform.

Interdisciplinarity

A significant methodological change is the gradual trend toward interdisciplinarity. Traditionally sectoral theories have dominated development studies. They have been marked by a gap between economic development and social and political development, although in grand theories (such as modernization and dependency theory) these were somehow articulated. A transitional phase has been the shift from disciplinary case studies and policies towards multidisciplinary approaches. Increasingly we now see – although fragmented development economics, politics, etc. also continue as usual – more attention to cross- or transdisciplinary work. Several developments contribute to this: failures in development policies; new

From	To
Macro-structures	Actor-orientation, agency, institutions
Structuralism	Constructivism
Determinism	Interpretative
Homogenizing, generalizing	Differentiating
Singular	Plural
Eurocentrism	Polycentrism

Figure 1.2   *General trends in development theory over time*

problems that require combined approaches; crises and emergencies that prompt new combinations of efforts. Novel disciplinary combinations and themes include, for instance, new institutional economics, sociology of economics, the social economy, development as social process or as public action. Notions such as the embeddedness of economic and market activities in political institutions, social capital, cultural practices and social relations, imply new combinations of disciplinary sensibilities. New methodologies, such as social accounting, require such new combinations. Accordingly, there is a new awareness that development requires a multidimensional, holistic approach (Chapter 9).

Discourse Analysis

The origins of this methodology are in linguistics and literature studies, while it owes its influence to the general impact of poststructuralism. In this regard development studies follows a general trend in social science. The upshot is to treat development as story, as narrative, text. This has generated a wave of deconstructions and critiques of development texts (cf. Chapter 2). According to this literature, the power of development is the power of storytelling – development is a narrative, a myth (Crush 1996a, Rist 1997). By now this has become a standard genre (cf. Grillo and Stirrat 1997).

Discourse analysis in development involves a wide medley of motifs. At a general methodological level, it no doubt represents a gain. In itself, this is not remarkable; it is simply the 'linguistic turn' applied to development studies. It is the awareness that development is not simply theory or policy but in either form is *discourse*. This means a step beyond treating development as ideology, or interest articulation, because it involves meticulous attention to development texts and utterances, not merely as ideology but as epistemology. Thus, it involves sociology of knowledge not only in terms of class interests (as in ideology critique) but also in terms of an inquiry into what makes up an underlying 'common sense'.

An effective use of discourse analysis is as an analytical instrument applied for example to development policy (e.g. Apthorpe and Gasper 1996, Rew 1997). A different application is to argue that since development is discourse it is therefore fictional, untrue, bogus, deceptive. It is a form of Western modernism and scientific distortion that sets illusory goals of material achievement and in its pursuit wreaks havoc upon Third World people. In this mode, discourse analysis turns into anti- or post-development thinking (e.g. Escobar 1992b, Sachs 1992a). In the process, methodology turns into ideology – an instrument of analysis becomes an ideological platform, a political position; politics of knowledge turns into knowledge of politics. There have been similar agnostic moves in Foucault and Derrida's work. In development studies this shift from methodology to ideology likewise involves the admixture of outside elements: an esprit of anti-modernism with romantic overtones (as in Ivan Illich), or post-Gandhian utopianism (as in Nandy 1989). Development as a discourse that is alien to the Third World (Western), authoritarian (state, IMF), engineering (modern), controlling and steamrollering and perverting local culture, grassroots interests and perceptions: this development critique is the newest critical populism.

A slightly different current is to apply discourse analysis in the sense of 'unmasking' development as 'myth' or 'fairy tale' (e.g. Rist 1997); i.e. development is 'only a story', only a narrative, only a grand narrative. In a methodological sense this is a contradictory move: the very point of discourse analysis is that discourse matters, talk and representation matter; representation is a form of power, it constructs social realities. Some analysts seem to want to have it both ways: development is a story *and* it is 'only a story'. This confuses two different methodological dispositions: that of ideology critique (which measures ideology, taken as masked interests or false consciousness, against some yardstick of 'truth') and discourse analysis.

The methodological gain of discourse analysis is to add a level of reflexivity, theoretical refinement and sophistication to development studies, and thus to open the politics of development to a more profound engagement. Its weakness and limitation – in development studies just as in literature criticism and cultural studies – is that it may skirt the actual issues of power. It may divert attention from relations 'on the ground'. In that case, from determinism we risk slipping into *discursivism*, i.e. reading too much into texts, or textualism, and overrating the importance of discourse analysis, as if by rearranging texts one changes power relations. This comes down to an alternative structuralism: from economic and political macro-structures to linguistic and epistemic structures; or, the order of language as a stand-in and code for the order of social relations.

The emergence of new fields of interest also shapes development studies. Gender, ecology, democratization, good governance, empowerment, culture, communication, globalization now figure prominently in development agendas. Ecology involves not just resource economics but novel syntheses such as ecological economics and ecological politics. Gender plays a fundamental role in development practice and discourse. 'Empowerment' and 'participation' are also ubiquitous in development management. Besides more effective public administration, accountability, democracy and citizenship figure prominently. Globalization is also a major vortex of change in the development arena. These fields of interest generate new theoretical and policy angles but so far not necessarily new overall theoretical frameworks.

Several themes are not new in themselves but the emphasis they receive is novel. Or, some themes acquire a new significance over time. Thus, corruption has been a familiar theme in development work but at each turn of the wheel it takes on a different meaning. In the context of modernization it was taken as a residue of premodern, particularist leanings. In the dependency framework corruption was a symptom of dependent development and of the comprador politics of the lumpen bourgeoisie. Kleptocracy, 'crony capitalism' and 'money politics' are variations on this theme. In the context of neoliberalism corruption becomes rent seeking, an ominous sign of state failure and market distortion and 'a hazard to free trade and investment' (Leiken 1996: 55) and the remedy is transparency. From a political angle, corruption is a matter of public accountability and democracy.

Culture and Development

Conventionally development has been a monocultural project. Modernization and Westernization were virtually synonyms. As part of 'nation building' develop-ment was taken as a homogenizing project. In the context of decolonization struggles this began to change: along with the indigenization of politics and administration, indigenous culture and knowledge became an additional topos. Thus, culture was incorporated into development studies but in a subsidiary fashion ('add culture and stir'). The critique of Eurocentrism generated a con-cern with polycentrism, cultural multipolarity (Amin 1989) and pluralism. The UNESCO-sponsored World Decade on Culture and Development also resulted in growing regard for cultural dimensions of development (World Commission on Culture and Development 1996). In the wake of the cultural turn in development culture represents another dimension of development, which is no longer ignored or viewed as just an obstacle, as in orthodox modernization thinking (Chapter 5 below). 'Culture' now figures in several ways. One is the regard for *cultural diversity* – obviously, in an age of ethnicity and religious resurgence this is not an entirely innocent theme. A second and related concern is *cultural capital*, both as a human capacity and a form of human capital, and as a political currency (both in ethnic and religious mobilization and as an asset in economic relations). A step further is to view cultural diversity itself as an engine of economic growth (Griffin 1996).

The Unit of Development

In development thinking from the classics to dependency theory the conventional unit of development was the nation. The key development statistics and measures used by the international institutions are still country statistics. However, while the nation remains the central domain of development it is no longer the only game in town. Gradually development is becoming a multilevel, multiscalar series of efforts, simultaneously taking place at levels lower than the nation, at the national level, and at levels beyond the nation.

Below the national level are community development, local economic develop-ment (LED) and microregional development. Community development, a subsi-diary theme in colonial times and modernization, received a new emphasis with alternative development. Local development in its various forms connects with questions of rural/urban disparities, urban development, regional inequality, new regionalism, ethnic mobilization ('ethnodevelopment'), and new localism with a view to endogenous development and in reaction to globalization. Beyond the nation are questions of macroregional cooperation and global macroeconomic poli-cies. Macroregional cooperation concerns the conventional issues of economies

DEVELOPMENT THEORY

Table 1.4 *Current trends in development theory*

Trend	Conventional & recent views	New themes
Differentiation	Grand theories	Middle-range theories, local knowledge
Reflexivity, self-questioning	(1) Unreflexive use of language, indicators, models; (2) Discourse analysis	Development as social learning, social feedbacks, reflexive development
Interdisciplinarity	Sectoral theories. Gap between economic and social/political development. (Multi) disciplinary case studies, policies	Bridging approaches: embeddedness, new institutional economics, sociology of economics, social capital, social economy, holism
Intersectoral cooperation	State-, market- or society-led development	Intersectoral synergies. Public action
Social diversity	Homogenization, essentialism (1) Betting on the strong;	Balance. Politics of difference Risks of polarization,
Human security	(2) humanitarian assistance, from relief to development	transnational social policy, global social contract
Gender awareness	(1) Gender blind; (2) WID [Women in Development] (add women & stir)	Gender interests, gendering development
Environment	(1) Mastery over nature; (2) sustainable development (add environment & stir)	Green GDP, political ecology
Cultural turn	(1) Westernization; (2) homogenization vs. indigenization (add culture & stir)	(1) Cultural diversity; (2) cultural capital as political currency; (3) as engine of growth
Unit of development	(1) Nation; (2) local	Local, national, regional and world development & multiscalar partnerships

of scale, increase of market size, regional standardization and interfirm cooperation as well as the horizons of the regional Development Banks. Besides country statistics other development statistics are regional, concerning 'Latin America', 'Africa', 'Asia', 'the Caribbean', etc. The region, in other words, is becoming almost as familiar a unit of development as the nation. A third scale of development action is the world: local, national and macroregional decision making interfaces with global macro-policies on the part of international institutions and the UN system.

Hence, development policy is increasingly a matter of decision making dispersed over a wide terrain of actors, institutions and frameworks. Development theorizing, which is habitually centred on the state, needs to accommodate this widening radius. It needs to be renewed by reconceptualizing development as multiscalar public action. Contemporary development policy is incoherent because the different levels of development action – local, microregional, national, macroregional, international, global – are not adequately articulated. Thus a comprehensive, holistic approach to development is not only multidimensional but also multiscalar, such that development efforts at different levels are cumulative and interconnect.

Intersectoral Cooperation

After development thinking has been, more or less successively, state-led (classical political economy, modernization, dependency), market-led (neoliberalism) and society-led (alternative development), it is increasingly understood that development action needs *all* of these in new combinations. New perspectives and problems (such as complex emergencies, humanitarian action) increasingly involve cooperation among government, civic and international organizations, and market forces. Human development, social choice, public action, urban development and LED all involve such intersectoral partnerships. For government at local and national levels, this increasingly involves a coordinating role as facilitator and enabler of intersectoral cooperation.

The theme of development partnership at present serves an ideological role as part of a neoliberal new policy framework which papers over contradictions and the rollback of government (e.g. Hearn 1998). However, the underlying significance is much more profound: just as sectoral approaches and disciplinary boundaries have been losing their relevance, sectoral agendas are now too narrow. The ideological use that is being made of this conjuncture should not obscure the significance of the trend itself.

International development cooperation has been changing in several ways. The emphasis has shifted from projects to programmes and from bilateral to multilateral cooperation. The trend is towards, on the one hand, formal channels (particularly multilateral cooperation through international and regional institutions) and, on the other, informal channels (NGOs) (Bernard et al. 1998). A précis of current trends is in Table 1.4.

These themes are elaborated in the chapters that follow. These changes in development thinking, such as interdisciplinarity and discourse analysis, and in policy, such as the changing unit of development and intersectoral cooperation, do not add up to a single pattern, but they significantly change the Gestalt of development. Their overall significance is taken up in the closing chapter on futures of development.

2

DILEMMAS OF DEVELOPMENT DISCOURSE: THE CRISIS OF DEVELOPMENTALISM AND THE COMPARATIVE METHOD

In the holograms of hegemony panoramas of power subtly fade into theories of history. Evolutionism was an imperial vision, modernization theory bears witness to the American century, and development theory translates into contemporary relations of power. In the discourses of history produced by Western hegemony, knowledge and power are intricately interwoven.

In his analysis of what he calls the post-totalitarian system Václav Havel observes, 'The principle involved here is that the centre of power is identical with the centre of truth' (Havel 1985: 25). This also applies to the centres of power and leading truths in the Western world. The central thesis of developmentalism is that social change occurs according to a pre-established pattern, the logic and direction of which is known. Those who declare themselves furthest advanced along its course claim privileged knowledge of the direction of change. Developmentalism is the truth from the point of view of the centre of power; it is the theorization (or rather, ideologization) of its own path of development, and the comparative method elaborates this perspective.

From Evolutionism to Development

Herodotus' *Histories* are replete with cross-cultural comparisons phrased in terms of correspondences as well as differences (Hodgen 1964: 25). From the outset in the Western tradition, intercultural comparisons interacted with conceptions of history. Aristotle made comparisons not simply between types but within a presumed order of growth and development of types, that is, according to a comparative-developmental perspective. 'When Aristotle compared his own polity to that of the Cyclopes in Homer, and then adduced "barbarous" people living even in his time, he was pointing to a presumed line of development from kinship through the community to the polis. Contemporary barbaric peoples seemed to Aristotle fit evidence of what the Greeks themselves had once been like' (Nisbet 1969: 193).

This is to be read both in the context of Greek development and relative to the Athenian empire of Aristotle's time. In other words, cross-cultural comparisons have never been culturally neutral. Comparison established boundaries of inclusion and exclusion, identifying others in a mirror of similarity and difference, defining alterity as part of the discourse of identity.

Accordingly, the comparative-developmental discourse of nineteenth-century evolutionism conformed to a pattern that had classical antecedents. Victorian anthropology, race science and evolutionism formed part of the discourse of the British Empire. The comparative method served as an adjunct to evolutionism, for instance, in the hands of Herbert Spencer, where it consisted of 'the accumulation of customs and ideas gathered from many places and periods, to substantiate developmental schemes arrived at through speculation' (Mair 1965: 42).

During the nineteenth century, race science served as the nexus between natural history and social history, between biological and social evolutionism. Along with evolutionism it explained and justified European supremacy: identifying the Caucasian, Nordic and in particular the Anglo-Saxon race as superior in its endowments, with Europe leading the way in the trajectory of evolution and exhibiting the most advanced stage in the progress towards human perfectibility. Thus imperial history was translated into natural history.

Nineteenth-century social science was profoundly preoccupied with mapping and conceptualizing Europe's Great Transition, which was variously associated with industrialization, urbanization, capitalism, the Enlightenment. The main types of conceptualization to emerge have been stages theories, dichotomous theories and critical variable theories. Comte's social dynamics, Marx's 'economic law of motion of modern society', Morgan's reflections on the development of kinship systems, Maine's views on the family and property, and Tylor's on culture were *stages theories*. They all share the Enlightenment depiction of social evolution as a succession of stages: primitivism, savagery, barbarism, civilization.

Dichotomous theories conceptualize social change as a bipolar process – from status to contract, from mechanical to organic solidarity (Durkheim), Gemeinschaft to Gesellschaft (Tönnies). Stages theories may be interpreted as dichotomous theories 'spelled out' or extended. A different type of theory conceptualizes social change in terms of a single critical variable, such as differentiation, increase in complexity, or rationalization (Weber).

Central to the general understanding of social change was the biological metaphor of growth. Change, as Nisbet (1969) points out, was regarded as natural, directional, immanent, continuous, necessary, and proceeding from uniform causes. Social evolution was unilinear, its direction the same for societies the world over. Peoples at earlier stages of evolution were viewed as 'contemporary ancestors', a perspective that has been referred to as 'coevalness denied' (Fabian 1983). Evolution sorted history, producing an imperial panorama that dehistoricized non-Western peoples, or rather, which granted them a history only from the perspective of the imperial lighthouse.

From the point of view of the centre, global *space* appeared transformed into a *time* sequence, with Europeans as the only contemporaries, the sole inhabitants of modernity. Empire, then, was a time machine in which one moved backward or forward along the axis of progress. This Eurocentric perspective also served as a manual for imperial management of societies at different evolutionary stages.

Europe defined the world. Like Adam in an earlier script she gave names to phenomena in the genesis of the new world society brought forth in the wake of European expansion and conquest, industrial revolution and advance of the world market. The naming process itself was an extension and function of the process of conquest. In political studies too this had been the standard discursive practice. To a considerable extent political science is a comparative science. From the classical authors onward, from Aristotle to Montesquieu, the comparative method in political studies served as a substitute for experiment. John Stuart Mill reformulated the comparative approach with the methodology of concomitant variables. With the onset of evolutionism the comparative method became an adjunct to evolutionist speculation.

Twentieth-century social science, from the 1930s on, rejected race science and social evolutionism. Two Western world wars undermined the faith in progress. Cyclical theories of history of a pessimistic cast prevailed, in the imagery of rise, decline and fall, as in the work of Oswald Spengler, Pitrim Sorokin, Vilfredo Pareto, Arnold Toynbee. In anthropology, cultural relativism seemed appropriate amidst the social realities of the interbellum. German critical theory contemplated the 'dialectics of Enlightenment'.

After the Second World War, evolution resurfaced. On the one hand, there were attempts to reformulate evolution and on the other, it resurfaced in moderni-zation theory and in the (in several respects interchangeable) discourse of development.

What Victorian anthropology was to the British Empire, modernization theory is to United States hegemony – its justification, rationale and agenda. It arose as the theoretical corollary of American globalism in the context of the Cold War and decolonization. Initially it took shape as a substitute for knowledge; the con-ceptual schemes of modernization served as surrogates for a tradition of inquiry into African and Asian societies which was lacking almost entirely in the United States.

Modernization theory evolved from a marriage of evolutionism and functiona-lism, with modernization conceptualized either as a critical variable or a dichoto-mous theory. Examples of critical variables – which is not the most common form of modernization theory – are rationalization and industrialization. The advan-tages of this conceptualization are that modernization is regarded as an open-ended rather than a goal-directed process and that the defining terms are relatively narrow. On the other hand, 'When defined in relation to a single vari-able which is already identified by its own unique term, the term "modernization" functions not as a theoretical term but simply as a synonym' (Tipps 1973: 205).

An additional option is to interpret modernization in terms of a set of critical variables: rationalization and industrialization. This may be an open-ended per-spective as well, but here the problem is one of boundaries: which variables to include. What about adding to the profile of modernity, market relations, urbani-zation, the nuclear family, individualization, democratization, or for that matter, anomie, alienation, and so forth? Each additional variable would mean defining modernity in terms of another, implied theory, and a combination of variables is but an amalgam of theories.

Most concepts of modernization are of the dichotomous type and follow some version of the tradition–modernity contrast. The modernization scenario laid out in Talcott Parsons' 'pattern variables' is a familiar example: modernization is defined as a movement from particularism to universalism, from ascription to achievement, from functional diffuseness to functional specificity, and from affective roles to affective-neutrality.

In this context the meaning of modernity changed again. When the term arose in sixteenth-century European discourse it served to distinguish between moderns and ancients, with the 'Middle Ages' as the middling term (Jones 1961). By the nineteenth century it had come to mean contemporaneity, and by the twentieth it had acquired a distinctly positive ring and was identified with improvement and efficiency (Williams 1976). In American discourse, on the other hand, modernity is contrasted with 'tradition' (frequently operationalized as 'resistance to change'). Feudalism, which in European discourse would belong to the middle or transitional stage, the precursor to modernity, from the American point of view appears as part of the general morphology of backwardness.

In the European context modernity was originally a Renaissance concept; in the American context however it is an Enlightenment concept. Europe and North America followed different paths of modernization. European societies are layered and composite, including peasant, feudal, monarchical, urban mercantile and industrial identities; more composite and complex than North American society, where industrialization came upon rural settlements (colonies termed 'plantations' in the seventeenth century) which adopted an Enlightenment political structure. Accordingly, European understandings of modernization tend to be more layered and complex than American views. Modernization theory as such is more specifically an American discourse.

Intrinsic to the tradition–modernity dichotomy is the idea that 'tradition' is a residual and diffuse concept, denoting everything 'unmodern', so that the two terms in the dichotomy are not symmetrical, not of equivalent conceptual status. The same applies to the notion of 'non-Western' societies (cf. Huntington 1976). As Frank notes: 'This entire approach to economic development and cultural change attributes a history to the developed countries but denies all history to the underdeveloped ones' (Frank 1969: 40).

In the fine print of modernization theory the evaluation of 'tradition' is usually not so diffuse. Thus, as Edward Said points out, the fictions of modernization theory rhyme well with Orientalism. For instance, with respect to the Islamic world it holds 'that before the advent of the United States, Islam existed in a kind of timeless childhood, shielded from true development by an archaic set of superstitions, prevented by its strange priests and scribes from moving out of the Middle Ages into the modern world. At this point, Orientalism and modernization theory dovetail nicely' (1981: 28). Dichotomous conceptualizations of modernization are teleological – the destination is assumed to be known. They are normative, universalizing 'Western values', and ethnocentric, with the United States (the American way of life) as the epitome of modernity. Modernization theory differs from evolutionism in that modernization is no longer regarded as immanent and inevitable; change is not always progressive. Outside stimuli, help from more advanced societies, may be necessary. Besides, there may be multiple roads towards the goal of modernity – democratic or totalitarian.

Modernization theory competed with communism in a world split by the Cold War. The open door of 'free enterprise' economics and the neomercantilism of centrally planned economies were the two main avenues of modernization. The aim of comparative politics was to assess which way the 'preindustrial countries' would go. All the same, modernization was virtually synonymous with Westernization. In the words of Edward Shils:

> Modern means being Western without the onus of dependence on the West... The image of the Western countries, and the partial incorporation and transformation of that image in the Soviet Union, provide the standards or models in the light of which the elites of the unmodern new states of Asia and Africa seek to reshape their countries. (Shils 1966: 10)

Indeed, politics was by no means of marginal concern in American modernization theory. This understanding of politics was essentially the politics of the American Revolution. Walt Rostow, the author of the classic of modernization theory, *The Stages of Economic Growth* (subtitled *An Anti-Communist Manifesto*), later devoted a study to *Politics and the Stages of Growth*. Even as he equated modernization with economic growth, its motive, Rostow declared was generally non-economic. Indeed, 'The glory of America has been not its relative material wealth but the sense of its transcendent political mission in reconciling liberty and order' (Rostow 1971: 6). Here a pure Enlightenment argument (liberty, order) mingles with Christian metaphors (glory, transcendence, mission).

Political modernization the American way means a programme of eighteenth-century political rationalism with Jeffersonian icing. This programme can be summed up in the following political principles: the legitimacy of the state is derived not from supernatural but from secular sanctions inhering in the people; the continual widening of citizenship, or incorporation into a consensual moral order, ultimately including all adults; and the growing scope and reach of the power of state agencies (Eisenstadt 1966).

Modernization meant the adoption of 'Western' political institutions. How this worked out in the 'unmodern' countries depended on the character of 'traditional' institutions and the manner of 'Westernization'. This was the thrust of comparative politics (e.g. Almond 1964). In reality this programme was not that of 'the West' but only that of the American and French Revolutions, updated in American discourse such that the United States emerges as the culmination of 'the West'.

Generally, definitions of political modernization have been careful not to conflate modernization and democratization. Political modernization theories, whether following functionalist or market models, define democracy as formal democracy, in effect the exercise of citizenship rights by the propertied class. It is significant that the key American theories of political modernization make democracy contingent upon economic growth – read: the formation of a propertied class. This is middle-class democracy. It is the theory and practice of the White revolution bitterly resisting the Red revolution, the bourgeois revolution of the rights of the propertied classes resisting the proletarian revolution of the dispossessed: for the latter is regarded not as the fulfilment and completion of the former but as its negation. Accordingly, modernization is essentially social engineering from above and an operation of political containment rather than democratization. American modernization projects such as community development and the Green Revolution exemplify this character of White revolution.[1]

Stages theories of political modernization could accommodate any form of authoritarianism as a 'necessary' stage towards transcendence – provided they were not communist. Hence the crucial distinction between authoritarian and totalitarian political systems. Modernization theory has been emphatic in distancing itself from Marxism, the main source of bourgeois angst. Time and again modernization has been defined as a way of class compromise and not class struggle. In the European context, this cleavage reproduced the nineteenth-century dispute between right and left Hegelians.

The deepest disputes in Western social science have not been between developmentalism and an alternative but between strands of developmentalist thought. Developmentalism thus comes in multiple varieties, liberal and radical, with Marxism as the quintessential radical evolutionism. Marx formulated developmentalism in a nutshell in the preface to the first edition of *Capital*: 'The country that is more developed industrially only shows, to the less developed, the image of its own future.' Marxist stages theory (primitive communism, slavery, feudalism, capitalism, socialism) and the 'iron necessity' with which social changes ensue according to historical materialist determinism exemplify unilinear evolutionism.

These features of classical Marxism have been abandoned in Western Marxism. Gramsci utterly rejected the thesis that there exist objective laws of historical development similar in kind to natural laws, and the belief in a predetermined teleology. Gramsci's historicism and his concern with the 'ethico-political realm' and the spiritual and moral character of hegemony broadened the terrain conceptually and politically. Still, Gramsci's thought follows the format of radical modernization theory, conceived more broadly and less mechanically. Lenin's interest in Taylorism is paralleled by Gramsci's fondness of Fordism and his views on futurism and Americanism. Gramsci did not share the reservations regarding technology and the *Kulturkritik* of German critical theory. The concept of 'passive revolution', which Gramsci used to characterize the Risorgimento, may also be read as a notion of modernization and, in effect, a concept of White revolution.[2]

In Marxist perspectives, modernization is equivalent to capitalist development and the role of the state is to facilitate this process. In postcolonial society, according to Alavi (1973), the state mediates the competing interests of the three propertied classes – the metropolitan bourgeoisie, the indigenous bourgeoisie, and the landed classes.

With the waning of United States hegemony, the war in Vietnam, the upheavals of 1968 and the end of the post-war boom, and in the context of social theory, the mounting criticism of functionalism and Parsonian sociology, modernization theory lost appeal. In general discourse the keyword became 'development', which was generally short for economic development. Thus from a broad, sociological and ethnocentric concept of modernization the discourse shifted to a narrow, economic and ethnocentric concept.

Underwritten by the international community, encoded in the Development Decades of the United Nations, the discourse of development appears more neutral than previous formulations of social change. Development is primarily economic development and as such measurable. It is basic to the discourse of international institutions such as the IMF, World Bank, development banks and combines of donor countries. Development theory reflects a mixture of discourses, primarily neoclassical economics with affinities to modernization theory and evolutionism. If modernization theory is steeped in eighteenth-century political rationalism, development is steeped in nineteenth-century economic rationalism, oscillating between neoliberal and neomercantilist perspectives, between the self-regulating market and state intervention. The categories used in the UN system of highly developed, developed, less developed and least developed countries structurally resemble the stages of evolutionism; they replicate similar underlying developmental assumptions in a 'modern', 'affectively neutral' language. The terminology of centre and periphery – derived from nineteenth-century political geography – replicates the centrist logic of the diffusionist school of evolutionism.

'Development' tends to be short for the Western development model. The perspective remains linear, teleological, ethnocentric. On the other hand, development theory is nowhere nearly as 'optimistic' as previous developmentalist perspectives and the nineteenth-century faith in perfectibility and progress. The faith in Progress applied principally to the metropolitan, imperial world. Now neo-Malthusian notions – overpopulation, 'basket cases', lost continents, triage, lifeboat ethics – cloud the horizon of development.

The state in development discourse is attributed a role as conductor and conduit of development, the executive agency of development policy. Initially boundless optimism prevailed: following a concept of state capitalism, the state was the prime mover of development. Increasingly this has turned into scepticism about to the capacities of Third World states for social engineering. In the West this is paralleled in generalized doubts concerning state capacities and the possibility of social engineering (Migdal 1988). In the 1980s the notion of the state as obstacle prevailed (Doornbos 1989). Market-led development corresponds to the latest neoliberal creed. The twentieth-century seesaw between liberalism and state intervention parallels the zigzags of nineteenth-century discourse and practice in economic theory and policy.

Dependency theory criticized development thinking for being ahistorical, for concealing historical relationships and denying the relationship between development and underdevelopment, in other words, for denying the role of imperialist exploitation in European modernization, as if modernization occurred independently of the stream of world history. Summed up in the words of Frank (1969: 46): 'If the now underdeveloped were really to follow the stages of growth of the now developed ones, they would have to find still other peoples to exploit into underdevelopment, as the now developed countries did before them.'

Dependency theory accounts for the limited capacities of Third World states with the concept of the dependent state. The role of the state in this perspective is to facilitate world market access into society. 'The state in the periphery has the function again to remove economically as far as possible the political border between the world market and the national economic area that this same state brings into existence' (Tilman Evers quoted in Frank 1981: 234). Thus, in effect, the interests of the metropolitan bourgeoisie are viewed as being preponderant over indigenous interests.

Dependency theory and other critiques of development thinking generated reflections and strategies of 'alternative development'. Whether we are talking about development alternatives or alternatives to development is one of the questions that present themselves (e.g. Kothari 1988, Apter 1987, Chapter 7 below).

What these pairs of perspectives – modernization theory and Marxism, development thinking and dependency theory – have in common is economism, centrism, and teleology. Economism because economic growth is the centrepiece of social change, teleology in that the common assumption is goal-oriented development, centrism because development (or underdevelopment, according to the dependency view) is led from where it is furthest advanced – the metropolitan world. As such they are variations on a theme. This testifies to the strength and complexity of developmentalism as a paradigm. Part of this strength is that developmentalism is a layered, composite discourse that combines several discourses: liberal and radical, secular and religious.

Development as Redemption

What sets Western universalism apart from other, non-Western universalisms, according to Rajni Kothari (1988: 192), is its secular character. Generally developmentalism is cast, according to its self-definition and the way it is perceived, as a rationalization process, the advance of enlightenment. As such it carries the appeal of secular utopianism. However, this secularism is not simply to be taken for granted. Indeed developmentalism is also regarded as a secularized version of the Christian perspective: 'throughout its history the idea [of progress] has been closely linked with, has depended upon, religion or upon intellectual constructs derived from religion' (Nisbet 1980: 352).

Developmentalism conforms to a Christian format and logic in viewing history as a salvific process. Thus it merges Christian and Enlightenment discourses so that the momentum of faith corresponds with the logic of reason – reason and rationalization operating toward the fulfilment of the expectations of faith. Providence recast as Progress. Predestination reformulated as determinism. The basic scenario of the scripture, Paradise–Fall–Redemption, comes replicated in evolutionary schemes. Primeval simplicity and innocence (the good savage or the pastoral past), followed by the fall from grace (corruption, decay, capitalism, urbanism – varying according to the discourse), which is in turn to be followed by a redeeming change (modernity, technology or revolution). This transmutation and secularization of scriptural utopianism had begun to take place in the seventeenth and eighteenth centuries, while some of the first steps were taken in the context of the Reformation. A recent explicit fusion of scientific and Christian futurisms, of biology and faith, is the work of the palaeontologist Teilhard de Chardin (1955).

As European states emancipated from clerical authority while taking over the church bureaucracy, likewise in social philosophy emancipation from the dogmas of faith took place both through emulation of biblical scenarios and promises, and by their substitution and transcendence by different methods and symbols, as in Robespierre's altar of Reason and Comte's Civilization in the role of the Supreme Being. Developmentalism arose from a rejection of religious explanations and clerical claims while following parallel cognitive patterns.

In the age of empire, India took the place of Eden and the Hebrews for the English and the Germans, and Egypt for the French. Sanskrit was regarded as the *fons et origo* of everything, or alternatively Egypt appeared as the source of all civilization (Said 1985: 137). The horizon broadened but the lens was unchanged.

Enlightenment discourse followed the same star as Judaeo-Christianity; while the manner of redemption was different. David Livingstone passionately believed that what was missing in the African interior was the light of the gospel. In his footsteps, Henry Morton Stanley called out in the heart of the Congo jungle that there should be light – except that he meant electricity.

Hence the Western ambivalence *vis-à-vis* non-Western cultures – primitivism betokens purity, reminiscent of paradise, development brings corruption and decay, while redemption lies only in the completion of development, the full achievement of modernity. The latter, also for Western societies, can be achieved only through further technological development. Hence the missionary zeal frequently associated with modernization and development, comparable to earlier missionary passions of conversion, improvement and reform. Developmentalism and its master plan is not merely a matter of reason and logic, it is also, at heart, the performance of a religious duty, the quest of a utopian rendezvous, the pursuit of a messianic course. That this passion has been secularized does make a difference; although the attitude toward reason and science tends to be as totalizing as in the previous overtly religious outlook.

This convergence of discourses is one explanation of the inner strength of the developmentalist paradigm, but not the only one. There are yet other reasons why it is difficult to think outside of this conceptual frame, some of which may be found in the context of language.

Spatial metaphors are deeply embedded both in everyday English language and in the language of social theory. An inquiry into the semantics of social theory by Anne Salmond (1982) shows, first, that knowledge is a landscape, i.e. knowledge has spatial existence; secondly, that intellectual activity is a journey. Related notions, that knowledge is territory and argument is war, are the basis of the accusation of intellectual 'imperialism' in theoretical texts. Understanding as 'seeing' and explanations as light sources ('illuminating') are related to the notion of intellectual activity as a journey. That theoretical systems are buildings is a metaphor related to structuralist discourse. Spatial distinctions of high and low, and of levels, further structure discourse. Notions of intellectual advancement and the progress of science follow likewise.

So the general conception of knowledge and social theory itself tends to be structured in terms of spatial or organic metaphors and of (linear) motion in space. Knowledge itself 'develops'. Developmentalism 'grows' out of these semantics of space/time.

The Crisis of Developmentalism

The crisis of developmentalism as a paradigm manifests itself as a crisis of modernism in the West and a crisis of development in the South. The awareness of ecological limits to growth is a significant part of the crisis of modernism. New social movements in the West enunciate the end of linear progress (Melucci 1988: 254). Modernity is viewed increasingly as a theory and practice that is more exclusive than inclusive. The charmed circle of achievement and success, which is glamorized in media and advertisements, exacts a high toll and excludes and marginalizes many. There are other writings on the wall. The United States, the postwar epitome of modernity, claims the largest underclass of any Western country and a growing number of homeless people. In terms of infrastructure and economic investment it is itself in need of rebuilding. Japan, a newcomer in the annals of developmentalism, boasts high productivity but does not set an example the way previous centres of developmentalism did. It does not serve as a cultural role model; instead it largely follows in Western footsteps. East Asian 'tiger' economies, the newest arrivals to modernity, do not serve as examples either in terms of democracy or ecological management.

In the South, the crisis of development takes multiple forms. Failures of development policies correlate with a profound impasse in development thinking. The rhetorical character of developmentalism stands exposed in several ways. Development discourse in its ahistorical and apolitical character is incapable of coming to terms with the realities of world power and global interests, as is evidenced in the question of Third World debt. The metropolitan logic in development thinking is enshrined in the conditionalities of the IMF. Resistance to development in the South is also an affirmation of autonomy and an expression of cultural resistance to Western ethnocentrism.

The critique of development is associated with a critique of science. As Maurice Bazin (1987) observes: 'Third World peoples were first made to believe in God, now they have to believe in science... first comes Salvation, then Progress; first through spiritual confessors, then through presidents' science advisers'. Shiv Visvanathan (1988: 285) remarks: 'What we are witnessing today is a civil rights movement against development-as-terrorism, based on the recognition that the modern state committed to science has become the prime anti-ecological force in the world.' The critique of science also has a Western tradition (e.g. Aronowitz 1989; Chapter 9 below).

Universalizing from Western experiences developmentalism created an ahistorical model of change which created a 'Third World' that was but an historical construct and constructed 'the West', which had no basis in historical reality either. The actual modernization paths of Western countries diverged among themselves (e.g. early, late industrializers) and deviated from the ideology of 'development'. Different countries applied diverse combinations of mercantilism and free trade, varying according to periods and contexts. Thus, to characterize the bias of developmentalism, ethnocentrism would not even be a correct term, for the divergence among Western countries is much larger than the ideology of modernity and development suggests. Even among Western countries a concept such as democracy does not carry the same meaning.

Development is also a neocolonial discourse – 'Where colonialism left off, development took over' (Kothari 1988: 143). As such its premises began to come apart even as its policies were still being formulated. The comparative-developmental paradigm could not withstand the momentum of decolonization. The assumption that the Western concepts of the nation, state, civil society and representative government are universal increasingly proved invalid, as political developments in Africa and Asia showed. The crisis of Orientalism, diagnosed by Anouar Abdel-Malek (1963) and examined by Edward Said (1985), is a case in point. Universalism is an adjunct of hegemony and as hegemony shrinks so does truth.

Options

The comparative method in social science has followed the tracks laid by developmentalism and, accordingly, the crisis of developmentalism is also a crisis of the comparative method. In comparative politics this has given rise, according to Bertrand Badie (1989), to a threefold crisis of universalism, of explanation, and of the relationship between history and comparative political analysis. A crisis of universalism because, since the end of the 1970s, the transcultural nature of concepts derived from Western discourse is increasingly in doubt. A crisis of explanation because the assumption of a unitary, transcultural logic is not tenable: comparative analysis, therefore, cannot be causal; it can only be interpretative. The prioritization of economic development in development and modernization thinking assumes that economic factors are equally important everywhere and that the relationship between economics and politics is perceived similarly everywhere.

Accordingly, the present direction in political studies tends to be away from grand theory and a general model of history towards more modest aims. Badie, in a drastic departure from developmentalism and the comparative method, advocates the reconstruction of political science as a cultural science. This means the return of anthropology to political science. Semiotics would be accorded an important place in political studies, in order to compare different meaning systems of social actors; linguistics, to examine the social history of political vocabularies; and history, to problematize the historical autonomy of the unit of analysis. This approach, according to Badie, cannot be of the same theoretical status as the classical comparative approach. The limitation of the cultural analysis approach is that it can produce description and interpretation but not explanation. To address this, in part, recourse is sought to Weberian sociology of action that would be interpretative and would address action in terms of its meaning to the actors themselves.

Another shift in the direction toward cultural specificity is the plea for the indigenization of sociological theory. This follows from the critique of universalism and seeks to be a remedy for intellectual dependence and imperialism in social science.[3]

Scepticism also speaks out of the words of Partha Chatterjee with regard to the future of Third World nationalism: 'A historical discourse, unfortunately, can only struggle with its own terms. Its evolution will be determined by history itself' (Chatterjee 1986: 162). Here also the assumption is the absence of a general model of history, the absence of a universal discourse.

The general current in comparative studies, however, particularly in historical studies, continues to follow different methodological options. Theda Skocpol defends the approach of comparative historical analysis, a method for examining large historical questions by comparing different societies. Causal associations are tested by comparing positive cases (in terms of the hypothesis tested), and positive with negative cases, which are otherwise similar in relevant respects. This approach would be 'generalisable across cases and historically sensitive' and 'an ideal strategy for mediating between theory and history'. This method is followed in Barrington Moore's work and in her own comparative study of social revolutions (Skocpol 1979: 35–40, 1984; Moore 1969).

A similar intermediary position of methodological caution and theoretical aspiration is found in the work of Charles Tilly (1984). In its rejection of grand theory this is a partial criticism of universalism but it does not exclude the possibility of universal explanatory hypotheses. It matters whether one's comparisons tend to be mainly within a single zone of world society (as in the case of Tilly's work, which is concerned with European politics) or whether the comparisons are not merely across cultures but across cultural zones, notably North–South (as in the case of Badie and the advocates of indigenization of social science): in the latter case greater methodological caution is warranted.

This array of options raises a number of questions. While the crisis of developmentalism and the comparative method is beyond repair, a complete U-turn toward 'methodological individualism' and cultural specificity may be an overreaction. There are limiting conditions to cultural specificity to the extent that societies the world over are exposed to and part of a 'globalizing' momentum – the inroads made by the world market, the role of industrial and postindustrial technologies, the homogenizing influence of the interstate system, the galaxy of international bodies and conventions, the influence of crosscultural media communications, and the increase in human mobility (migration and tourism). When globalizing tendencies are advancing and barriers are being broken down, is it the time for a retreat into theoretical provincialism?

In world-system theory, globalism itself is made the single overarching dynamic. The argument of globalism is taken to the point where nation states are not units of development; only the world system develops. Here the problem of comparative analysis does not and cannot arise: as a single system without an exit the world by definition is governed by a single logic. Thematizing the economic logic of world market extension, world-system theory treats culture as an epiphenomenon (Robertson and Lechner 1985). What is not acknowledged in world-system theory, however, is that economism itself is a cultural precept.

So neither universalism nor relativism, globalism nor provincialism provides adequate answers. This relates to a number of further questions. When we discard evolutionism, should we also discard evolution? When we reject developmentalism, should we also drop development? The discourse of Western hegemony belongs to the past and is epistemologically and politically untenable. Yet, the other extreme, relativism, would leave us without a common human discourse. If five hundred years of Western expansion and hegemony have also, even if in adverse and perverse ways, contributed to the unification of the world and humanity, relativism would make it impossible for us to harvest whatever fruits there are to this globalizing momentum. If universalism in contemporary social theory is a veil of Western ethnocentrism, does it mean there are no universals at all? Does it mean that everything resolves into cultural specifics and perspectives without the possibility of a common human discourse? Or rather, does it mean that the question of what is universal is to be posed anew, not in Eurocentric but in polycentric ways?

From Bipolarity to Polycentrism

> It's not a matter of emancipating truth from every system of power (which would be a chimera, for truth is already power) but of detaching the power of truth from the forms of social, economic and cultural hegemony within which it presently operates. (Foucault 1980: 133)

> You do not stand in one place to watch a masquerade. (An Igbo saying, quoted in Clifford 1988: 189)

I come back to the observation of Václav Havel quoted earlier: the identity of the centre of power and the centre of truth. In terms of the balance of power, the world of colonialism was a world of multipolar competition among the Western powers, that is, a multipolar competition among countries that were part of the same civilizational framework. This began to change when Japan joined the circle of powers in the early 1900s and again with the onset of the Bolshevik revolution. With Yalta and the Cold War the world of bipolar competition took shape, with two centres of power and two centres of truth. Both discourses have been developmentalist in outlook, although they subscribe to different varieties of modernization – 'forging ahead' (or 'muddling through') and 'catching up'.

For a while, in the aftermath of the Gulf war, it seemed as if we moved from a bipolar world to a unipolar world of United States hegemony revisited. It is clear however that the United States is nowhere near its previous position of leadership, economically and financially, although it may retain a position of military and political hegemony. The larger transition we are experiencing at present is from the bipolar world of superpower rivalry, of capitalism and communism, to a world of multipolar competition again, except this time the centres of power, or potential centres of power, belong to multiple civilizational frameworks. These centres of power need not be identified here – some can readily be imagined. In some spheres of international affairs, geopolitics and the world economy, polycentrism is operative already. Trilateralism may be regarded as a stage of polycentrism. The transition we are in now concerns its further unfolding in political discourse and culture.

This relates to what we might term, with Manoranjan Mohanty (1989), in analogy with the terms of trade, the question of the 'changing terms of discourse'.

Previously, the main counterdiscourse to Western hegemony was Marxism, another Western and developmentalist discourse from the same civilizational family. Now cross-civilizational questions may become more important.

Indian thinkers have been leading the way in the critique of modernity (e.g. Desai 1971). Another line of approach has been to separate modernization from Westernization. There are examples of this in the Arab world (e.g. Abdel-Malek 1980/1983). Alternative conceptualizations of modernization have been formulated in Japan (Kishimoto 1963). This line of reasoning is presently being followed in China as well (Li Lulu 1989). A related approach is a dialogue of paradigms of rationality among different cultures (Park 1985, Kang 1985).

With bipolarity, ideological, military, political and economic cleavages accumulated to create clear and distinct lines of demarcation. Polycentrism cannot be expected to unfold in this fashion. This also accounts for the peculiar, uncertain and fuzzy character of the period we are in. Structurally, culturally and ideologically, the momentum of globalization – the impact of Western hegemony, the world market, and technologies of production and communication – shapes the emerging centres of power. Nationalism does not have an ideological autonomy comparable to communism.

The transition from bipolarity to polycentrism affects the terms of discourse in contradictory ways. On the one hand, the field of debate is opened wide, the focal point is no longer confined to the bipolar confrontation of capitalism and Marxism. On the other hand, the transition is taking place in the context of globalization: it's a question of cultural multipolarization in conjunction with globalization. So might both tendencies be meaningful and complementary – globalism and localism, increase in scale and segmentation?

The Deconstruction of the West

Rapid developments of the recent past – in particular the opening of Eastern Europe – have stimulated attempts to revive modernization theory, in the form of neomodernization analysis (Tiryakian 1991). It is difficult to read this other than as an expression of Western triumphalism. Samir Amin in an analysis of Eurocentrism restates the familiar terms of the *fin-de-siècle* dilemma: 'socialist universalism or Eurocentric capitalist barbarism' (Amin 1989: 152). Both perspectives remain well within the developmentalist paradigm. At another pole of the debate, Rajni Kothari (1988: 216) perceives a rather different dilemma: 'If "development" itself has become a problem, and has sowed the seeds of discontent and ethnic conflict, a corrective to development can only come from other worldviews, other visions.'

In the West, as mentioned before, the paradigm of modernity is increasingly contested. It appears hazardous in view of ecological limits to growth and limits to well-being. It is questioned by new social movements that challenge the notion of a universal historical master plan (e.g. Melucci 1989: 188-9). The Enlightenment promise and programme appear questionable in view of tragedies of the twentieth century, the Shoah, Hiroshima, and Gulag. Epistemologically, modernism and its simple positivism no longer stand up to contemporary standards of the critique of knowledge. Out of the implosion of linear, futurist discourses postmodernism has emerged. Initially a movement in art, architecture and literature, postmodernism stresses ambiguity, indeterminacy, irreverence and deconstruction. It indicates historical and semantic instability. As a social philosophy it may be regarded as the cultural expression of the postindustrial or information society.

So far the debate between modernism and postmodernism has been conducted mainly within a Western framework (Nederveen Pieterse 1989: Ch. 3), even though it is quite germane to the development debate. The relevance of postmodernism to the South is being explored (Slater 1992, Lee 1994, Giri 1998). However, to the extent that the South is regarded as still being in the throes of modernization, as either preindustrial or industrializing, postmodernist perspectives tend to be dismissive of the South. Postmodernism instead of exploding developmentalism merely recapitulates it (as it is implicitly premised upon a sequence of preindustrial, industrial, postindustrial stages) upon a different plane.

Postmodernism is a Western deconstruction of Western modernism and to address the problem of developmentalism more is required. What matters most and comes across least in many analyses of development discourse is the complexity and 'holism' of Western developmentalism. Developmentalism is not merely a policy of economic and social change, or a philosophy of history. It reflects the ethos of Western culture and is intimately intertwined with Western history and culture. Ultimately the problem of developmentalism cannot be settled in terms of political economy, nor in terms of social philosophy, the critique of ideas or unpacking discourse; it requires a profound historical and cultural review of the Western project. This task we might term the deconstruction of the West (stretching a fashionable term).

The deconstruction of the West is about returning the West to world history. This follows from the logic of decolonization. It also follows from the crisis of the Western development model, not least in the West itself. This may yield a basis for reopening the debate on rationality and values. Here I will only indicate briefly what directions the deconstruction of the West might take.

The deconstruction of the West can be taken as a historical as well as a conceptual project. Taken as a historical project the key question is: To what extent is what we call 'Western civilization' actually a universal human heritage, which comes to us, for historical and geographical reasons, in the guise of a Western synthesis? In this context certain forms of being 'anti-Western' are as irrelevant as, for instance, being anti-algebra, which in the first place is not Western but Arabic in origin, and in the second place does not make sense. In a conceptual sense this translates into the question of what, in 'Western' contributions, is particularist and what is universal, what is culture-specific and what is general or generalizable.

Martin Bernal's (1987) *Black Athena: Afroasiatic roots of classical civilization: the fabrication of Ancient Greece 1785-1985* and the research programme indicated in its title is part of what needs to be done. The 'separate history' of the West goes back a long way, but, more significantly, it has also been retrospectively invented, and continues to be invented. In fabricating their past to suit their imperial frames, Western elites have obfuscated Western history and, in the process, world history.

The analysis of Western discourses is important, but a wider cultural confrontation is also required: the analysis of cognitive patterns underlying discourse, of Western iconography and art, of Western popular culture (cf. Nederveen Pieterse 1994). Here we approach the point of reversal: the erstwhile model examined as a problem. Part of the project of the deconstruction of the West is anthropology in reverse: the analysis of the West in terms formerly reserved for history's backwaters; the analysis of Western fetishism, not as a fad but as an act of therapy. This is where the significance emerges of Gandhi and other non-Western critics of the West who cared enough and carried cultural weight enough to vocalize their critiques.

These inquiries pave the way for a more specific project: the deconstruction of 'development'. This again can be taken in several modes. It can be taken in the sense of the deconstruction of development discourse. This approach has been adopted in this chapter in a historical-interpretative fashion. It may be taken also in a stricter sense, of deconstructing development discourse in Foucauldian fashion (Escobar 1985, DuBois 1991) or in the fashion of Derrida (e.g. Johnston 1991).

In addition, the deconstruction of development can apply to development policies and take the form of the disaggregation of policy formulations, e.g. between those which are (a) inevitable, (b) necessary, (c) desirable or acceptable under certain specified conditions, and (d) nonsensical and reflecting Western biases and ethnocentrism. Accordingly, the deconstruction of development is the prerequisite for its reconstruction. This cannot be a single reconstruction but should be polycentric reconstructions, given varying itineraries and circumstances in different countries.

It is obvious that carrying out this agenda would require filling in many blank spots and that this would both settle and raise a number of problems. But it also means changing the terms of the debate. The predominance of developmentalism structures the debate in terms of either 'Westernization' and modernization, or 'anti-development' positions, while other registers remain beyond earshot. The deconstruction of the West is a poser. It is a way to reopen the discussion that has so far been conducted in the terms of a universalist logic. The middle way between universalism and relativism is pluralism.

Notes

1 Henry Kissinger 1970 among others elaborated on the concept of White Revolution.

2 E.g., 'a process of modernization presided over by the established élites, who used the "revolutionary" changes to maintain their supremacy' (Femia 1981: 48).

3 For articles devoted to universalism and indigenization see Akiwowo 1988 and 1999; cf. Ake 1979.

3

THE DEVELOPMENT
OF DEVELOPMENT THEORY:
TOWARDS CRITICAL
GLOBALISM

The prevalent note in development thinking nowadays is saying goodbye to paradigms. Many articles open by saying goodbye to modernization and dependency, while insisting that no new paradigm will be proposed. The objections to these paradigms are familiar enough and there's no need to restate them here. Still this is not just a time of 'waiting for a text'. Several new departures in development thinking parallel general tendencies in social theory, such as the problematization of modernity, poststructuralism and postmodernism. Development discourse is examined in Foucauldian terms of power/knowledge (Sachs 1992a, Marglin and Marglin 1990, DuBois 1991, Escobar 1985), deconstructed (Johnston 1991), subjected to archaeological excavation (Sachs 1999), or juxtaposed to explorations of the postmodern (Schuurman 1993, Slater 1992). These contributions expand on the critiques of Eurocentrism, Orientalism, and occidental cultural homogenization in postcolonial and cultural studies. No doubt the debates on modernity and postmodernity carry major implications for development theory for they are concerned with redefining 'development' writ large.

These contributions are limited by their preoccupation with discourse. While deepening our critical insight they do not offer alternatives. At the same time that postmodern interrogations provide the basis for a new critique of modernization theory, modernity as a theme is making a comeback, but now in the plural – as late or advanced modernity, modernity 'reworked', neomodernization theory, or new modernity. The latter involves the notion of 'risk society' and the argument of a 'new modernity' in which all societies, developed and less developed, are exposed to a globalization of ecological and other risks (Beck 1992).

A recurring feature of many discussions is that development theory is being attributed more coherence and consistency than it possesses. Thus in being criticized as the 'religion of the West' (Rist 1997) or as the 'myth of development' (Tucker 1999), developmentalism is homogenized and discussed as if it were cut from a single cloth. The deconstruction of development texts is not the same as unpacking development theory, disaggregating its lineages, dimensions and projects.

The very notion of *development* is increasingly being bracketed. The questioning comes from various directions: from deconstructions of development discourse but also from the momentum of globalization on account of which the special status of developing economies – the original rationale of the development argument – is gradually being eroded. In this context, structural adjustment represents a radical break with the development tradition, less because of its neoliberal thrust than, more importantly, because of the implicit argument that *all* societies must adjust to global economic imperatives. The implication is that either development is gradually fading out as an outdated perspective belonging to a bygone era of economic apartheid, or it is broadened to apply to all societies, as a global logic. If this were the case it would be logical to assume that the content and meaning of development would be changing too.

These various notions – deconstruction of development, structural adjustment, globalization, global risk – seem to point in a similar direction: the demise of 'development' and its gradually emerging reconstruction as *world development*. A related question is the relationship between endogenous and exogenous dynamics in development: this too, on different grounds, may point toward a reconceptualization of development as a global problematic.

This chapter seeks to develop three arguments. First, it argues that development thinking has not been the single paradigm for which it has often been taken, but that all along it has been a heterogeneous set of approaches that has been not only variable over time but highly diverse at any given time. Secondly, it zeroes in on one particular unresolved dilemma in several forms of development thinking: the disparity and tension between endogenous and exogenous dynamics in development. Thirdly, it explores the current tendency to rethink development as a process that is not reserved to 'developing countries' but that all societies are developing, as part of a global process. Thus it juxtaposes development discourse and globalization. I argue that globalization should neither be blocked out or ignored, in the name of delinking, import substitution or neomercantilism, nor unconditionally embraced. The term I propose for this in-between position is critical globalism.

The first part of this chapter takes the form of development discourse analysis. The second part continues this analysis with metatheoretical reflections. The strength of discourse analysis is to make subjectivities transparent, which may offer grounds to renegotiate subjectivities; but it is limited in that it does not *per se* engage objective dynamics. So in the third part the mode of argument changes as well. The closing argument on development and globalization seeks to gather the insights gained from analysing development discourse and to combine these with changes in objective circumstances so as to arrive at critical policy orientations.

Notions of Change

There is a tendency among users as well as critics of development theory to attribute to it a certain coherence and consistency, with the exception of one or another favourite cleavage. This easily produces a dichotomous view of development theory, as in Marxism versus neoclassical economics, mainstream versus counterpoint, etc. Development theories promote the façade of consistency as part of their single-minded future-building project. Critics contribute to it by following the logic of binary opposition. It may be fruitful instead to view development theory *in the plural*, not as the unfolding of a grand paradigm, neatly bifurcating in contesting models, but as a hybrid made up of uneven elements, of borrowings and incursions from alien sources, and improvisations spurred by crises. In a word, to consider the inconsistencies of what goes under the heading of development theory.

Robert Nisbet is widely regarded, including by critics of many claims of developmentalism, as an authoritative source on the history of Western notions of change, while he is also a spectacular representative of the tendency to 'homogenize' developmental thinking. In *Social Change and History* he maintains that 'For twenty-five hundred years a single metaphoric conception of change has dominated Western thought' (1969: 211). The theory of social development, in his view, derives from the ancient metaphor of growth. With the Greeks this took on the form of *cycles* of change; in the Christian version formulated by Augustine it was modified to an *epic* form, which was still cyclical but without recurrence; and by the seventeenth century it was again modified to produce the modern idea of linear progress. In the eighteenth century this set of assumptions engendered the idea of 'natural history', and in the nineteenth century, the theory of social evolution that was common to Hegel, Saint-Simon, Comte, Marx, Spencer, Morgan and Tylor. This theory, according to Nisbet, regarded change as natural, immanent, or proceeding from forces within the entity, continuous, directional, necessary, corresponding to differentiation in society, typically moving from the homogeneous to the heterogeneous, and finally, as proceeding from uniform causes.

Nisbet concedes that in twentieth-century social science there was a revolt against evolutionism, replacing unilinear evolutionism with multilinear evolution, but he maintains that even the critics reproduced the underlying metaphor of growth: 'although they were denouncing the schemes of social evolution, they were accepting at full value the concepts of change that underlay the theory of social evolution' (1969: 225). That is, the belief in origins, immanence, continuity, uniform causes, etc. is reproduced in twentieth-century conceptions of social change. This bold thesis raises several questions: is this representation plausible, or does it in itself reflect a belief in origins and continuity?

A different way of reading the development of development theory may be genealogy in the Nietzschean sense. Nietzsche, as Foucault reminds us, was opposed to the search for 'origins': 'because it is an attempt to capture the exact essence of things, their purest possibilities, and their carefully protected identities; because this search assumes the existence of immobile forms that precede the external world of accident and succession'. However, Foucault continues, 'if the genealogist ... listens to history' he finds behind things 'not a timeless and essential secret, but the secret that they have no essence or that their essence was fabricated in a piecemeal fashion from alien forms' (Foucault 1984: 78). An example of the preoccupation with origins is Hegel: 'The principle of development involves also the existence of a latent germ of being – a capacity or potentiality striving to realize itself. This formal conception finds actual existence in spirit; which has the history of the world for its theatre, its possession, and the sphere of its realization' (quoted in Nisbet 1969: 159).

For Nietzsche this would be an example of the 'Egyptianism' of philosophers, the obstinate 'placing of conclusions at the beginning' (in Foucault 1984: 90). History is replaced by metaphysics, by Neoplatonic essences beyond time. Let's contrast this with Nietzsche (1976: 470): 'By searching out origins, one becomes a crab. The historian looks backward; eventually he also *believes* backward.'

Nisbet's history of the idea of development as a continuous outgrowth of the Greek metaphor of growth exhibits not only the preoccupation with origins and continuity but also an essentialism of ideas. It lays claim to a grand cohesiveness of Western thought, uniting the pagan and Christian, classical and modern notions in a single weave. It sets the West apart from the rest of the world, while it tacitly removes the main lines of cleavage within Western thought, those separating ancients and moderns, religious and secular elites, elites and dissidents (such as Nietzsche's *esprits libres*). An exercise in high humanism, it produces an elite representation of Western notions of change, with the classics duly towering above subsequent thinkers as the true ancestors of Western thought.

What faithful conformism to begin with the Greeks, the proverbial 'cradle of Western civilization'. Why not consider the divergencies *among* Greek notions of change? For example among the Peripatetics, the followers of Aristotle, who along with the Neoplatonists adhered to a cyclical notion of time, whereas the Stoics moved away from this, and historians such as Herodotus and Thucydides broke altogether with the doctrine of recurrence.

In his essay on Chinese 'Attitudes toward time and change as compared with Europe' Joseph Needham groups non-Christian Greek thought together with Indian thought and the Hindu and Buddhist notion of the endless repetition of the wheel of existence. Needham refers to 'the intense history-consciousness of Christendom' and contrasts linear Judaeo-Christian time to cyclical Indo-Hellenic time. With regard to China he concludes: 'Strange as it may seem to those who still think in terms of the "timeless Orient", the culture of China was, on the whole, more of the Iranic, Judaeo-Christian than of the Indo-Hellenic types' (Needham 1981: 131). This gives us a rather different view of the distribution of civilizational perceptions of change, and a totally different map of world history from Nisbet's. The grounds for the singularity of the West as a special case, a deviation from the 'general human pattern', are eliminated.

Why not highlight, rather than continuity and uniformity, the discontinuities and divergencies in Western notions of change? Western views, of course, have also been an amalgam, as we can see, for instance, in the *mélange* of Christian views in Augustine's time and later in the return to cyclical thinking in Nietzsche ('ewige Wiederkehr' or eternal recurrence), Spengler and Toynbee (Needham 1981: 128). A re-examination of Western notions of development may reveal a far more heterogeneous history, replete with moments of improvisation, dissonance, discontinuity. Leaving aside that Nisbet simplified the notions of change of Greeks and Christians – which to an extent he nuanced in a later work (1980) – let's turn to the moderns.

Nisbet rightly mentions that the nineteenth-century theories of social development applied to different entities – to reason for Turgot and Condorcet, to knowledge and civilization for Comte, to freedom for Hegel, to democracy for

Toqueville, to the forces of production for Marx, to social institutions for Spencer, to kinship, property and civil government for Morgan, to legal institutions for Maine, to culture and religion for Tylor. Nisbet insists: 'it was the *entity* ... for which natural development in time was claimed. It was *not* the sum total of geographical areas on earth' (1969: 167). But this is not the whole story of the theory of social evolution. Evolutionist stages theories, such as that of Victorian anthropology – primitivism, savagery, barbarism, civilization – were also taken to apply to human cultures, which were identified with societies (cf. Stocking 1987). Theorists of social evolution regularly applied their views to geographical areas – Hegel on Africa, Marx on Asia are familiar examples.

Nisbet's focus is on development conceived as natural and endogenous to the entity or society, but another dimension to nineteenth-century developmental thought which is glossed over in his account is development arising from exogenous influences and conditions – from diffusion, international influences, or what we would now call globalization. Marx's theory is both: 'the new grows in the womb of the old' refers to endogenous, organic growth; while his statements on capitalism as a 'permanently revolutionizing force', on its progressive effects on the 'rural idiocy' of the countryside, and of colonialism on 'stagnant' societies refer to external dynamics.

Nisbet is sensitive to Western ethnocentrism: 'No one can miss the fact that in every instance – there is no exception – the direction of change found by the evolutionist was toward the specific set of qualities possessed by Western Europe alone' (1969: 169-70). But, just as geography is missing, the imperial setting is absent from his account. In fact it has been argued that imperialism is marked by 'the primacy of the geographical', for it is after all 'an act of geographical violence' (Said 1993: 225). While this is a particularly narrow reading of imperialism that overlooks its political economy (which may well transcend geographical, territorial boundaries), the element of geography should not be ignored.

Nisbet's argument of continuity overlooks the actual shifts in Western developmental thinking, it papers over the dynamics over time of European views. Briefly, seventeenth- and eighteenth-century views tended to be ambivalent as to Europe's status in the world and looked up to non-European models such as China, Turkey, Persia, the noble savages of America, the Pacific and Africa. Only in nineteenth-century theories of social evolution did the European will to power prevail; they took a single-focused form which provided greater consistency, particularly during the second half of the century, than before or after.[1]

If Nisbet's representation is fundamentally flawed, how can we account for the fact that his kind of view has found such wide acceptance? A related question is to what extent we can recognize the same implicit model of endogenous, organic growth in contemporary development theory.

Development Theories in the Plural

If we consider twentieth-century development thinking and its theoretical lineages, does Nisbet's metaphor of growth hold? Is the tenor one of continuity and consistency or one of disparity and improvisation? The term 'development theory' suggests a coherence that in fact is hard to find. What we do find is a plethora of competing and successive currents, schools, paradigms, models and approaches, several of which claim to exclude one another. For a start, development theory refers to two terrains which have tended to converge only at certain junctures: development sociology and development economics. Further more or less obvious distinctions run between theory and ideology, policy and practice.

Development sociology has been by and large the critical successor to the nineteenth-century theories of social development. Development economics, on the other hand, owes its origin to a deviation from late nineteenth-century economic orthodoxy. Kurt Martin (1991) has made the interesting argument that development economics resuscitates and revisits the basic findings of classical political economy, of Smith, Ricardo and Marx, who were development economists in that their basic problematic was the transition from agrarian to industrial society. Neoclassical economics came into being only after 1870, as a theory of fully industrialized economies (FitzGerald 1991).

'Development' if understood as the problematic of the transition from agriculture to industry has been revisited and reinvented several times over; it has been a question facing several generations of late developers. It was the question facing Central, Eastern and Southern European economies during the early twentieth century: hence the involvement of Central Europeans in the early stages of modern development theory. Hence Alex Nove's claim that development theory was 'born in Russia in the twenties' (Martin 1991: 28). Accordingly, several modern development theories replicate earlier findings.

The formative period of 'modern' development economic theory was the 1940s and 1950s. The colonial economies were the *terrain* of development theory but the problematic was that of the *transition* or, in a word, industrialization. Thus, while 'colonial economics' was transformed into 'development economics', it borrowed from the existing theories of transition, either from classical political economy or from other 'late developers'.

So the theory of unequal exchange was originally advanced in 1929 as an argument for protecting industry in agrarian countries (Martin 1991: 38). At the time, unequal exchange was viewed as a feature of centre–periphery trade. In his 1928 analysis of European capitalism Werner Sombart applied this terminology to Great Britain as the dominant centre and Central, Eastern and Southern Europe as exploited and dominated peripheries. In fact the terminology of centre and periphery derives from an older, late nineteenth-century discourse of German political geography, in which the term *Randlage* was used for periphery. For geographers such as Friedrich Ratzel this discourse carried definite political, nationalist overtones, as part of the rivalry between Germany and Britain. Via Dietrich Haushofer it entered the discourse of geopolitics of National Socialism and informed the urge for *Lebensraum* (Nederveen Pieterse 1989: Ch. 1). Accordingly, the centre–periphery argument served nationalism in both offensive (national expansionism) and defensive (protectionism) modes. In the 1960s it was reutilized as a cornerstone of dependency theory. In Arghiri Emanuel's contribution to dependency theory, unequal trade came to describe the dualism of the world economy between North and South.

The premise of modern (i.e. postwar) development economics was that it was a separate branch of economics, different from economics in the industrialized countries and from neoclassical equilibrium theory. State intervention and planning, along with accumulation and growth, were part of its 'founding discourse', which showed general affinities with Keynesianism. Foreign assistance, accompanied by the idea of mutual benefit, was another feature of the original discourse. In this respect it diverged from both neoclassical economics and Marxism.

In relation to international trade, again radically different theoretical outlooks prevailed. On the one hand were liberalism and the tradition of the Manchester School, following the Smithean premise that free trade and the international division of labour based on comparative advantage would eventually benefit all countries. On the other was neomercantilism, arguing, in the footsteps of Alexander Hamilton and Friedrich List, that infant industries require tariff protection. Mainstream economic theory from the 1870s onward promoted the free trade argument, while the neomercantilist policies which sheltered the late developers (the American Republic, later followed by Germany, France, Russia) were relegated to the margins, as deviations from the norm, to be reclaimed later as part of neomarxist theory. At that stage the theory of unequal exchange served as an argument for tariff protection in less developed countries.

From the outset development thinking has been marked by an uneven and contradictory patchwork with divergent paradigms operating in different terrains and sectors: in industrialized economies, neoclassical economics coexisted with industrial policy; in trade, liberalism in theory coexisted with neomercantilism in practice; in finance, versions of monetarism prevailed. Each of these divergent perspectives and policy orientations made its imprint on developing economies, all of them simultaneously in different sectors, although usually articulated under the umbrella of an overarching development rhetoric. Which development posture prevailed reflected the historical bloc of class alignments that held the upper hand.

As a concept 'development' papers over the different interests involved in economic, social and political change. 'Development' suggests the possibility of a package formula in which all these interests come to some form of crystallization and convergence. As such it displays an intrinsically positivist bias. Obviously, social and economic change is always a field of contestation among different stakeholders. Each of these will construct a story – of the past, present and future – to validate its claims. A political economy of development theory (as a subset of the general sociology of knowledge) might not have too much difficulty in identifying the shifting 'historical blocs' that have set the agenda of development ideology at different points in time,[2] except, of course, that at no time it has been a single or uncontested agenda.

New trades and manufactures (Manchester School) contested the political economy of monopoly enterprise (mercantilism, old colonial system). The political economy of competition capital and manufacturing was contested by finance capital (monetarism). All along, the political economies of capital in their different articulations have been contested by the political economies of labour (trade unionism, syndicalism, Marxism, socialism). The claims of national firms and agricultural interests (protection) have been contested by internationally oriented enterprise (free trade). These various sets of contradictions have been played out through contestations between alignments of interests favouring either state intervention or market forces. Like masks in a puppet show, both 'state' and 'market' have themselves signified complex fields of forces and interests. 'State' and 'market' have been on either side of these contesting forces. The state has been the meeting place where a political and social contract between the diverging interests was fashioned.

Accordingly, development thinking implicitly carries two sets of meanings: an actual diversity of interests and perspectives, and a hegemony, i.e. an inherently unstable settlement of these differences resulting in a development posture. The hegemonic effect occurs both at national and at international levels (Cox 1991). In a sense, there are as many ideologies of development as there are players in the field, but some players are more equal than others.

In the 1960s what consensus existed in development economics was destroyed 'so that it is no longer possible to talk of a mainstream of development economics' (Martin 1991: 55). In the 1970s the Chicago version of monetarism became dominant. Monetarism is not to be equated with neoclassical equilibrium theory: it is 'little more than a revival of nineteenth century bankers' principles of "sound money" – currency convertibility, stable parity, fiscal thrift, low wages and minimal government influence in business' (FitzGerald 1991: 15).

The ensuing wave of generalized neoliberalism rejects the 'limitations of the special case' and argues that poor countries are poor mainly because of mismanagement. Put in another way: the compartments which hitherto separated development economics from the mainstream economics which prevailed in industrialized economies, international trade and finance, fell away, so that development economics is being integrated into general economics. Whether or not there is a ground for a separate theory of development is presently one of the key debates (Martin 1991: 55; Hettne 1995). The logic of structural adjustment programmes follows from the demise of separate development economics.

These shifts of alignment make for a second deep rupture in the overall history of 'development'. The career of development has typically been one of state intervention. Now in many parts of the world we witness the marginalization of the state and a new ascendancy of market forces. A feature of this process is the renewed predominance of finance capital since the 1970s and the cycle of debt expansion and debt crisis, which turned the IMF and World Bank into leading arbiters of development policy, with the banking orthodoxy of sound money, or monetarism, being recycled as the newest beacon on the development horizon. Robert Kuttner notes that under these circumstances what public sovereignty remains 'has been entrusted to perhaps the most conservative and market-oriented of all public institutions – central banks ... the triad of central bankers, IMF, and World Bank has been so thoroughly creditor-oriented that it might as well have been the House of Rothschild or the House of Morgan' (1991: 260-1). In the alignment of the late twentieth century, as in the late nineteenth century, finance capital predominates as the cement of the historic bloc of interests that frames 'development'.

Along with the discourse the models shifted – no more United States and American Dream, no more China, Cuba, Tanzania, Nicaragua either, but the accumulation models of the NICs of East Asia. It spelled the 'end of the Third World' (Harris 1986) and of Third Worldism. In the process another contradiction emerges, another instance of development double-speak, for indeed the East Asian experience is not a model of unfettered market-led development but, on the contrary, the model of the developmental state (Johnson 1982, White 1988). In other words, current development ideologies are another highly diverse and deeply divided range of discourses.

These divergencies can be observed on the level of development theory, which is increasingly diversifying (Booth 1994b); development ideology, where neoliberalism appears to have passed its peak; and development policy, which is inspired as much by ad hocism and pragmatism as it is driven by ideological posturing and on-the-spot manoeuvring. Here from time to time I use development thinking as a middling term, indicating the mixed character of development speak – an uneven *mélange* of theoretical precepts, ideological subscriptions and political preferences.

One line of thinking holds that the dividing line between development successes and failures in terms of growth does not run between models or theories, but that what matters most is not the 'model' but how it is implemented. For instance, what matters is not whether or not a state intervenes but what kind of state intervenes and in what political culture. Several Asian countries have sought to implement NIC strategies with strong doses of state intervention and this has generated high growth rates in several East and Southeast Asian countries; in Thailand, Malaysia and to some extent Indonesia. The formula however has not worked in the Philippines and Sri Lanka. To explain this variation factors have been brought in such as economic and political history, political culture, political institutions (Litonjua 1994) and ethnic politics and 'crony capitalism'.

It might be difficult to oppose privatization in general if privatization can also serve as a barrier against corrupt politicians. This however does not settle the underlying problem of accountability: on the contrary, for market forces are likely to be still less accountable than state bureaucracies. The question, then, is not one of state versus market, but rather points towards democratization and democratic reforms of state structures, such as decentralization, which can make the state more accountable.

These insights have instilled a sobering awareness. Matters are not simply decided on the basis of models. Policy implementation is affected by factors such as political culture, historical itineraries, and location in the regional and international environment. This also affects the behaviour of the World Bank, which in the actual implementation of its policies is more concerned with negotiation than with simply imposing its economic model (Mosley et al. 1991). In the process we are referred back to what development economists call 'non-economic factors'.

Modernization Revisited

In development sociology the leading paradigm has been modernization. Modernization theory took shape in the 1950s in the US and bears an American stamp – if we recall that Dahrendorf called the US the country of *angewandte Aufklärung*, the applied Enlightenment. At the time the US entered its era of globalism, a 'can do' attitude characterized its approach, as in the functionalist modernization advanced by Hoselitz: 'You subtract the ideal typical features or indices of underdevelopment from those of development, and the remainder is your development program' (Frank in Worsley 1984: 18).

Most forms of evolutionism conceived of development as being natural and endogenous, whereas modernization theory makes room for exogenous influences. Modernization theory is usually referred to as a paradigm, but upon closer consideration turns out to be host to a wide variety of projects, some presumably along the lines of *endogenous change*, viz. social differentiation, rationalization, the spread of universalism, achievement and specificity; while it has also been associated with projects of *exogenous change*: the spread of market relations or capitalism, industrialization through technological diffusion, Westernization, nation-building (nationalism as a derivative discourse), state formation (as in postcolonial inheritor states). If occasionally this diversity within modernization is recognized, still the importance of exogenous influences is considered minor and secondary.

> I do not view 'modernization' as a single, unified, integrated theory in any strict sense of 'theory'. It was an overarching perspective concerned with comparative issues of national development, which treated development as multidimensional and multicausal along various axes (economic, political, cultural), and which gave primacy to endogenous rather than exogenous factors. (Tiryakian 1992: 78)

This may be the steepest contradiction within modernization theory: between modernization as an endogenous and an exogenous dynamic. It may also be the most significant contradiction in development thinking generally: the hiatus between development as an endogenous process and as externally induced change, under the aegis of imperialism, capitalism, globalism.

The theory of dualism, developed in the 1940s and 1950s by Boeke, Lewis and Kuznets, accommodates this contradiction with the idea of a traditional and modern sector. In effect the traditional sector represents endogenous growth and the modern sector the interaction with outside forces, in terms of production techniques, trade, values and aid. The diffusion approach was institutionalized in the 'geography of modernization', focusing on transportation and on core urban areas as the vehicles for the 'mobilization of the periphery' (Brookfield 1975: 110-16). Phrased in another way, there is a hiatus between development theory as a national project and as an international or global dynamic. From the outset the main development theories, both economic and sociological, have been a national, or more accurately, a state project. Neomercantilism, 'socialism in one country', Keynesianism, self-reliance all represent state projects. By contrast, the market-oriented approaches of neoclassical economics *and* neoliberalism have been equally comfortable in national and international domains.

This may give us a clue to the impasses of development theories. The major turns in development have been shaped by supranational dynamics entirely outside the scope of standard development theory: the breakdown of the Bretton Woods system, the emergence of OPEC, the gradual shift from the Atlantic to the

Pacific era, the shift to flexible production. Time and again crisis has been a greater teacher than theory: the energy crisis, the debt crisis, the ecological crisis, the crisis of currency instability – and each crisis concerns supranational dynamics.

Neomarxism, dependency theory, world-system theory follow the external model: capitalism flows in, travels from the centre to the periphery, 'external areas' are incorporated into the world system. Their positive programmes, however, at any rate in the case of dependency theory, defend development as a national logic. Cardoso and his notion of 'dependent development' represented a more sophisticated position that did take into account external influences. The difference between Bill Warren and most dependency thinkers was that Warren followed a transnational and diffusionist approach to accumulation and development, whereas the *dependentistas* operated within nationalitarian logic. Likewise, the key concepts of critical and alternative development thinking implicitly echo and revisit endogenous development as the norm: the self-reliance, autocentric development and delinking advocated in some forms of dependency theory, historicist views on modernization, polycentrism, indigenization, and 'another development'.

The *unit* of development, however, is not a given or a constant. The boundaries between what is internal and external are by no means fixed. Development discourse and its implicit assumption of the 'country', 'society', 'economy' as the developing unit papers over this issue and assumes much greater nationwide cohesiveness and thus state control than is realistic. This relates to the familiar question of the reach and strength of the state (Migdal 1988). The assumption itself has been questioned on several grounds. The by now classic argument of world-system theory maintains that it is not the society that is the developing unit but the 'world system' (i.e. the unit integrated by an international division of labour of goods necessary for reproduction). Michael Mann (1986) contends that the very term 'society' is misleading and proposes instead 'social networks' that sprawl across borders. Crossborder enterprises such as the *maquiladores* at the Mexican–US border have also drawn attention. The unit of development is shifting further in light of the growing concern with regions and localities as the sites of development, which finds expression in the regionalist turn (Amin and Thrift 1993) and the 'new localism' (Goetz and Clarke 1993).

The nation state is caught in a dialectic of subnationalism and supranationalism. Still, the weakening of the state is by no means a straightforward process. 'One of the paradoxes of the late twentieth century is that the tendency of the state to intervene in economic affairs has increased – political rhetoric notwithstanding – at a time when the effectiveness of its interventions has declined' (Griffin and Khan 1992: 64). There is no question as to the central and enduring importance of the state. In the words of Robert Kuttner: 'until world government arrives the nation state is the necessary locus of social contracts between market and society' (1991: 9). Unfettered markets increase inequality and in the age of information economies, which puts a premium on human resource development, inequality is an economic liability. Generally, then, current arguments go far beyond the ideological dispute of state versus market; the real issue is the kind of role that the state is to play. Martin Carnoy (1993: 91) contends: 'The role of the nation-state in creating an innovation society is thus absolutely crucial to the well-being of its citizens in the information age.'

The debates in development economics are closer to policy than those in development sociology. The policy options in most countries remain narrow: internationalization or globalization meaning liberalization; state-led internationalization with restrictions and regional cooperation; and alternative or 'another' development.[3]

Critical Globalism

The argument of this chapter is that an essentialist notion of development, of good, natural, endogenous development bedevils development thinking. What else is the notion of 'stunted development' (Marx on Ireland), 'stagnation' (Marx on India), underdevelopment (dependency theory), 'maldevelopment' (Amin 1990c) but the deviation from a norm of good, that is natural development? This might explain the appeal of Nisbet's kind of approach for it asserts an organic model of development as the norm. Even modernization thinking, which is highly diffusionist in policy, remains endogenist in theory. One reason for this is that as such it can be assimilated in the general strain of 'organic development'. In addition to the trend toward discursive consonance and consistency there are political reasons why endogenism is appealing.

The politics of development, from the earliest 'late developer' to the latest, has in the main been state politics. Endogenous development, which is intrinsic to the developing entity, is by definition controllable by the state. The career of modern development theory is synchronic with the career of decolonization and to a considerable extent it has served as a state doctrine of new nations. If endogenism is a powerful political tool, it is also a prism through which exogenous influences can be negotiated, a screen behind which contradictions can, in the name of the 'national interest', be concealed. In the age of globalization, however, endogenism backfires and a new settlement is required.

The weakness of the endogenous outlook on development is its single and narrow focus. In turning one's back to and seeking shelter from international turbulence one may in fact make development more vulnerable to it. Accordingly, what is needed is to rethink development as a regional, transnational, global project, such that the international domain is not left to the strong players and their 'might is right' alone; in a word, to theorize world development. Hettne (1990: 34) contends 'that the crisis in development theory is a reflection of the disparity between the growing irrelevance of a "nation-state" approach and the prematurity of a "world" approach'.

Part of the problem of development thinking is the hiatus between development economics and development sociology. Or, phrased otherwise, its lack of comprehensiveness: *market*-oriented approaches marginalize the state; *state*-oriented approaches marginalize market forces; both marginalize society; *civil society*-oriented approaches marginalize the state and often the market as well, and international forces remain largely untheorized. Market-oriented globalism (neoliberalism, monetarism, structural adjustment, export-led growth) clashes with state-oriented endogenism or indigenization (delinking, import substitution), leaving social forces (grassroots, NGOs, informal sector) in no man's land.

Critical globalism means theorizing the entire field of forces in a way that takes into account not just market forces but also interstate relations, international agencies and civil society in its domestic as well as transnational manifestations (cf. Scholte 1993, Nederveen Pieterse 1989). This is an argument for interdisciplinarity in development studies. Secondly it means a critical position *vis-à-vis* globalization, avoiding the clichés of globo speak.

This brings us to the question of the relationship between globalization and development. If delinking is no longer a viable option (Chapter 4 below), neither is globalization *tout court* an attractive avenue. It might be argued that globalization is the successor paradigm to dependency, except that it is not a paradigm but a shorthand description of a set of processes. What is relevant is an underlying shift in attitude: if from the point of view of dependency theory, exogenous influences have been viewed with suspicion, from the point of view of globalism, they are celebrated.

There is a wide spectrum of positions. Extreme globalization thinkers such as Ohmae (1992) celebrate globalization and present it as global destiny; a destiny that very much resembles a worldwide duty free store. Neomarxists denounce the 'tyranny of globalism'. In making this case Petras and Brill (1985) in effect reassert the primacy of endogenous dynamics. But, even if market globalism is the issue, the alternative is not to retreat to statism or endogenism.[4]

The problems with this position are several. First, globalization is narrowed down to globalism, which in turn is identified with market internationalism. Globalization then is no more than a trendy word for advanced capitalism. It is neoliberalism masquerading as global momentum. Obviously this captures only one face of current globalizations. The second limitation is historical shallowness. Globalization is not a new dynamic – it would be so only and typically from the point of view of the endogenist reading of history. Arguably globalization has been a long-term process and what distinguishes contemporary globalization is that it is an accelerated globalization (cf. Nederveen Pieterse 1995). The third aspect that is overlooked in this position is that globalization does not come alone but in a package. Speed is not all that distinguishes contemporary globalization. Globalization presently is much more than merely intensified economic internationalization because it comes together and is interwoven with the growth of the information economy and the onset of flexible production systems (e.g. Castells 1993).

Cardoso (1993) brings various elements, old and new, together. There is a note of frustration that has not changed: 'the South is in double jeopardy – seemingly able neither to integrate itself, pursuing its own best interests, nor to avoid "being integrated" as servants of the rich economies' (1993: 156). And there is a recognition of change. Globalization, according to Cardoso, necessitates the 'redefinition of dependency'. In this context two points are emphasized: the South has lost its great comparative advantage, the abundance of land, mineral resources and cheap labour, for these are no longer of vital importance to the globalized economy. The second major change is that economic development now affects all of society, for the democratization of society and state are now necessary conditions for organizational and technological innovation. The bottom line is that only one choice remains: 'either the South (or a portion of it) enters the democratic-technological-scientific race, invests heavily in R&D, and endures the "information economy" metamorphosis, or it becomes unimportant, unexploited, and unexploitable' (1993: 156).

Obviously not all developing countries are able to connect with the new global economic dynamics. Castells observes the emergence (or consolidation) of a Fourth World: 'Within the framework of the new informational economy, a significant part of the world population is shifting from a structural position of exploitation to a structural position of irrelevance' (1993: 37). Cardoso concurs: 'They will not even be considered worth the trouble of exploitation, they will become inconsequential, of no interest to the developing globalized economy' (1993: 156). This is hardly a new theme. Decades ago a similar point was made about the lack of interest of multinational corporations in investing in peripheral countries; but because of structural changes in the world economy it has taken on new gravity and a new, rough edge.

'Globalism' means either fostering or managing globalization. Critical globalism refers to the critical engagement with globalization processes, neither blocking them out nor celebrating them. As a general policy framework for developing countries it refers to a cautious and forward-looking engagement with globalization processes, weighing the ramifications of different types of capital flow, financial transactions and technological transformations. If Samir Amin proposed selective delinking, critical globalism might be summarized as selective globalization. The keynote of globalization is that the nation state can no longer be taken for granted as the unit of development; crossborder transactions and micro- or macro-regionalization may well become major avenues of development. As a global agenda, critical globalism means posing the central question of global inequality in its new manifestations. As a research agenda, it entails, among other things, the identification of the social forces that carry different transnational processes and examining the varying conceptualizations of the global environment and the globalizing momentum; an analysis of global babble and whose interests are being served.

The overall situation raises a number of questions, on one of which I want to focus. What, under the circumstances, is the meaning of world development? Because of the combined changes of globalization, informatization and flexibilization there is a new relevance to the notion that 'all societies are developing'. This is not just a pleasant sounding cliché but a reality confirmed by the transformations and transitions taking place everywhere, on macro as well micro levels. The entire world is 'in transition'.

One way to read the current dispensation is that the gap between semi-peripheral countries, at least the most advanced among them, and core countries is narrowing, while the gap between peripheral countries and the others is widening. There is a new meaning to Trotsky's law of combined and uneven development. The scope of economic innovation combined with the operation of the 'law of the retarding lead' (or the dialectics of progress) places new investors in technology, infrastructure and human resource development in several respects in virtually the same position as the conventionally industrialized countries. If we compare the profiles of economic renewal and industrialization strategies in the United States (e.g. Reich 1983, Kuttner 1991) with those of South Korea, or for that matter Brazil, there is considerable overlap. Thus, the 1986 industrial technology White Paper of the Korea Industrial Technology Association mentions as development targets for the 1990s, the realization of advanced industrial society and the establishment of knowledge-intensive industries; as regards technology strategies, the continuous supply of high-quality brain power and R&D for future-oriented projects and advanced high-technology development; and as regards leading industrial sectors, information industry, advanced materials, bio-engineering and systems engineering (Lim 1995: 2). This is the convergence thesis of industrial societies revisited, but on different grounds and combined with new patterns of disjuncture.

At the same time, the unit of development is no longer what it used to be. The conceptualization of the unit of development that was relevant politically and economically under the previous dispensation changes under the sign of globalization. The unit is no longer simply national (to the extent that this endogenist political fiction was relevant at all) but increasingly regional, local. Thus, the Frostbelt of traditional industries in the United States has been decaying while Silicon Valleys are prospering. Within countries there are growing regional disparities. The stilted arrangement of core – semiperiphery – periphery, all along an echo of geopolitics translated into economic geography, is even less adequate than it used to be.

In these circumstances the notion of world development takes on different meanings. One window is the growing awareness of global risk, involving ecological hazards but also phenomena such as currency instability. Accelerated globalization heightens the need for global governance. The fact that world development takes place at different speeds and makes for a world of 'variable geometry' (to borrow the term used for the European Union) itself calls for global engagement and management. For marginalized countries and regions do find niches in the interstices of the maelstrom of globalization – through labour migration, crime networks, drug trafficking, political and cultural defiance. Religious and ethnonationalist resurgence in a globalized world of instant communication, portable technological capabilities and two-way migration flows has become a neighbourhood affair.

Another window is the role of the state in relation to economic development in the context of globalization: this may well be a greater role but especially a different role, considering that the state is no longer the same: it has been internationalized. A further window is that, because of the new disjunctures, there is a new relevance to the project of international reformism. Represented at various junctures by the New International Economic Order project, the Brandt, Brundtland and South Commission Reports, supported by the 'middle powers', the Non Aligned Movement and G77, this remains one of the key dimensions of reorienting development. International reformism is host to many projects, for instance the formation of an international public sector or the project 'towards an international social welfare state' (Pronk 1990, 2000, Deacon et al. 1998). Global democratization is a vital part of this agenda. This involves the democratization of international institutions, the reform of the United Nations and the restructuring of the Bretton Woods institutions. Griffin and Khan (1992) see three possible scenarios in which global governance may develop. One, the gradual withdrawal of the United States from international governance. Two, de facto international governance by entities such as the G7, bypassing established institutions and constituting a global plutocracy. Three, a consensus in favour of the reform of existing institutions or the creation of new ones, strengthening the multilateral approach to international governance. They favour the latter option and advocate better structures of global governance, including the reform and strengthening of the UN system, bringing the Bretton Woods institutions under UN supervision and introducing forms of international taxation. Even though political conjunctures have not been favourable to fashioning a global reform coalition, this remains a crucial agenda for development reconceived as world development. There are subjective dimensions to these concerns as well. In international relations the concern with cooperation, rather than conflict, has been termed an 'institutionalist' approach. In this context, institutions are understood as 'recognized patterns of practice around which expectations converge' (Oran Young in Keohane 1984: 8).

It is not obvious how this relates to the grassroots, small-scale, small is beautiful approach of 'alternative development'. The weakness of the alternative development approach as it stands is that the role of the state is neglected while the local/global nexus is undertheorized. One of the questions that looms in the background is whether social movements and NGOs should serve as buffers against globalization, providing shelter from the storm, shielding local culture, local identity, or whether their role should be to help connect regions and communities to the globalized economy. This is not a time for easy answers. But it bears pointing out that NGOs, especially international NGOs, are part of globalization – viewed multidimensionally. If this is the premise, then for NGOs to block globalization *tout court* would be one hand doing what the other doesn't know. As NGOs are part of a globalizing ethos, what they do and can do is negotiate the kind of globalization they are willing to be part of. They can use their influence to make and shape the case for social development, not just as a matter of tinkering in the margins but as representing the cutting edge of contemporary development. (Social development is here used in the substantive sense; cf. Chapter 8.) What NGOs have stood for, that 'development is for people', now figures higher on the agenda than ever. A case can be made (developed in Chapter 8) that the lessons of East Asia and the combined package of globalization/informatization/flexibilization converge on some of the same points that NGOs have all along been pleading for: human resource development, social infrastructure, social institution building. In East Asia this has generally been done by development states while NGOs flourish in a democratic climate. NGOs can play key roles in the development of social institution building which, according to the new institutional economics, is part of the crux of development success or failure.

The question whether the role of NGOs should be to connect with or disconnect from globalization is a non-issue. The position of specific NGOs in globalization processes depends on their place in the spectrum of types of NGOs. International advocacy NGOs can contribute to shaping national and international opinion climates in favour of democratic global governance. Part of this horizon is collective action operating across national and zone boundaries, as part of transnational civil society. Global democratization requires several intermediate steps conceptually and strategically, but that is not the subject here (cf. Nederveen Pieterse 2000a).

The outpouring of books in Western sociology concerned with problematizing modernity (e.g. Toulmin 1990, Bauman 1992, Beck 1992) inspired by poststructuralism and globalization, carries a potential for the renewal of development thinking and a new critique of modernization theory, especially if taken in combination with non-Western studies interrogating modernity.[5] Development thinking needs to leave totalizing paradigms behind and to choose for diversified approaches, building on the critical resources that are available. This requires recognizing the heterogeneous, multivocal character of development theories. Doing so ties in with the current premise in development research of no longer homogenizing the 'Third World' and seeking general theories and explanations, but focusing instead on the diversity of development circumstances.[6] When globalization and diversity are combined, as in 'glocalization', globalization can be conceptualized as changing patterns of diversification.

Notes

1 This is discussed at greater length in Nederveen Pieterse 1989: Ch. 15 and Nederveen Pieterse 1994.

2 This relationship between interests and development discourse is suggested for development ideology, not for development theory, which has greater autonomy.

3 On alternative development see Chapter 6 and on 'alternatives to development' see Chapter 7 below.

4 Cf. Hettne (1990: 244): 'there have been two kinds of bias in development theory: endogenism and exogenism. Both approaches are, if carried to their extremes, equally misleading. The obvious remedy is to transcend the dichotomy and find a synthesis.'

5 The historicist approach to modernization and the notion of multiple paths of modernization are well established in China, Japan and India (Singh 1989). In a broad way this parallels the theme of polycentrism, as against Eurocentrism (Amin 1989). Of some relevance also is the older tradition of comparative political studies (e.g. Macridis and Brown 1964). Cf. Chapter 2 above.

6 One option is to work with typologies. The regulation school offers neostructuralist typologies based on regimes of accumulation and modes of regulation; Mann (1986) focuses on different forms of organizational power; Mouzelis (1988) is concerned with modes of domination. These typologies differ from the bloc approach (North–South), from the continental or regional approach (Europe, Asia, etc.), as well as from the determinist, base–superstructure categories used in neomarxist (mode of production), dependency and world-system theories (core, semiperiphery, periphery), for they are neither geographical nor economistic.

4
DELINKING OR GLOBALIZATION?

To those who are familiar with his earlier work, Samir Amin's new books are not really new; they provide elaborations and further arguments in support of his theses rather than breaking new ground. But they offer an opportunity to reconsider the arguments of one of the most outspoken dependency theorists and a way to measure what has changed since the time that Samir Amin, along with Andre Gunder Frank and Immanuel Wallerstein, seemed to represent some of the most exciting and challenging work in international political economy. Revisiting these positions is an opportunity to gauge how part of this familiar family of perspectives and analytics of development Marxism is withstanding the time test of plausibility.

The focus of this chapter is Amin's argument of delinking – the keynote of his thinking as well as his most distinctive contribution to alternative development thinking. Delinking or autocentric development, as the positive part of his dependency argument, remains a significant policy orientation – at minimum, as the counterpoint to and polar opposite of what is now termed globalization and globalism. The proposition of delinking, advanced in earlier works, is taken up in all the three books considered here, frontally in *Delinking* (DL: Amin 1990a), updated in *Maldevelopment* (MD: Amin 1990c), and in relation to cultural politics in *Eurocentrism* (EC: Amin 1989).

Amin cannot be accused of optimism. He objects to other forward development approaches such as the 'global Keynesianism' of the New International Economic Order proposals and the Brandt and Brundtland Reports, because the assumption that autocentric development would not be in conflict with worldwide interdependence is 'based on a naive illusion as to the laws governing existing world capitalism' (MD, 60). Nor does he share the optimism about NICs and likewise he rejects the category 'semiperiphery' proposed by the adherents of world-system theory: 'the NICs are not semi-peripheries on the way to catching up but in every sense the real peripheries of tomorrow' (DL, xi). He notes that NICs are the most indebted of all Third World countries and predicts: 'The real periphery of tomorrow will be the NICs of Asia and America ... while the African "fourth world" will no longer represent the "typical periphery", but the last remnants of the periphery of yesterday en route for destruction' (MD, 65).

Structural adjustment in his view is just another instalment of the liberal doctrine and the liberal utopia, which is doomed to failure because it ignores the fundamental factor of unequal development as the reality of capitalism. This reality is 'recolonization, sweetened by charity' (DL, xi). The choice facing Third World countries therefore is 'adjustment or delinking' (MD, 70). In brief, delinking is the refusal to submit to the demands of the worldwide law of value, or the supposed 'rationality' of the system of world prices that embody the demands of repro-duction of world capital. It, therefore, presupposes the society's capacity to define an alternative range of criteria of rationality of internal economic options, in short a 'law of value of national application'. (MD, 70-1)

The social forces that are to carry this programme are a 'popular alliance' forged by 'the revolutionary intelligentsia' made up of organic intellectuals. In political terms, delinking is a national and popular project. Amin envisages 'national popu-lar states' along the lines of people's democracies on the model of Maoist China (MD, 189). This project belongs to the 'second wave of national liberation': while 'the first wave of national liberation is spent', 'the forces entrusted with the second wave – with its national and popular content – have not yet been assem-bled around an adequate alternative plan. We are passing through a trough in the wave, shown by this disarray and intellectual and political surrender.' (MD, 73)

Several obstacles on the way fall under the heading of 'the cultural aspect', which is taken up in all three works. The closing chapter of *Delinking* is devoted to the question, 'Is there a political economy of fundamentalism?', in which he contrasts fundamentalism and rationalism as two irreconcilable approaches. In *Maldevelopment*, the discussion of 'the cultural dimension of development' com-prises ethnicity (essentially, according to Amin, a matter of ruling class competi-tion) and the Nahda (the movement for 'reawakening' in the Arab world from the late nineteenth century). In *Eurocentrism*, Amin engages the 'cultural constraints' on the path towards delinking at a fundamental level as part of a wide-ranging historical exposition. *Eurocentrism* may be the most interesting of these books because it seems to be a novel departure in Amin's work: a political economist venturing into culture, the traditional stepchild of Marxism.

Amin seeks to steer clear of culturalism ('a tendency to treat cultural charac-teristics as transhistorical constants', EC, 6) as well as 'vulgar Marxism'. He takes issue both with Westernization ('superficial', leads to 'compradorization') and cultural nationalisms ('feed fundamentalism', MD, 72). Amin makes a num-ber of interesting, at times penetrating, observations on cultural history. The opposition Orient/Occident in his view is not tenable:

> The opposition Greece = the West/Egypt, Mesopotamia, Persia = the East is itself a later artificial construct of Eurocentrism … the geographic unities constituting Europe, Africa, and Asia have no importance on the level of the history of civilization, even if Eurocentrism in its reading of the past has projected onto the past the modern North–South line of demarcation passing through the Mediterranean. (EC, 24)

Amin draws attention to the legacy of Hellenism that permeates both Christianity and Islam and that has been inappropriately annexed to Europe. This approach parallels Martin Bernal's *Black Athena*. In an interesting aside he observes that Hellenism 'was inspired by Buddhist thought, encountered in Afghanistan' (EC, 65).

Amin questions two erroneous axioms in Western thought: 'The first is that internal factors peculiar to each society are decisive for their comparative evolu-tion. The second is that the Western model of developed capitalism can be generalized to the entire planet' (EC, 109). Besides, of course, there is a funda-mental tension between these assumptions. Interesting, furthermore, are Amin's discussion of early Islamic metaphysics and later the Nahda.

It follows from his critique of culturalism that Amin is disposed to acknowledge the plasticity of culture. He rejects, therefore, 'the sharp, cutting judgements that have been made about Christianity, Islam, Hinduism, Buddhism, Confucianism, Taoism, and animism, claims that certain religious conceptions were "openings" to progress and others obstacles' (EC, 84). Instead he recognizes the flexibility and 'plasticity of religions': 'religions are transhistorical, for they can readily outlast the social conditions of their birth' (EC, 84). Thus, Islam 'has proven itself as flexible as its rival twin, Christianity; an Islamic "bourgeois revolution" is both necessary and possible, even though the concrete circumstances of the region's contemporary history have not allowed it so far' (EC, 65). It is consistent with this general view that Amin rejects Weber's Protestant Ethic argument:

> My thesis is not Weber's, but the thesis of a Weber 'stood on his feet' ... Weber considers capitalism to be the product of Protestantism. I am suggesting quite the opposite: that society, transformed by the nascent capitalist relationships of production, was forced to call the tributary ideological construct, the construct of medieval scholasticism, into question. (EC, 86)

In other words, capitalism generated Protestantism. These critiques of culturalism are pertinent particularly at a time of the revival of culturalist arguments, such as the notion of the Confucian Ethic, the rhetoric against 'Islamic fundamentalism' and Samuel Huntington's 'Clash of Civilizations'. But several questions arise. Does Amin also manage to stay clear of 'vulgar Marxism'? How does Amin's rejection of Islamic fundamentalism differ from the mainstream Western position?

Amin's analysis is based on a schema in which modes of production correlate with cultural and ideological patterns, in brief, as follows:

Mode of production	Culture
Communal	Ideology of nature
Tributary	Religion, metaphysics
Capitalism	Economism

The notion of a tribute-paying mode of production, ranging from the empires of antiquity to feudalism, was first advanced in *Unequal Development* (Amin 1976). Within each mode, central and peripheral variations are recognized, in line with Amin's insistence on the fundamental nature of centre–periphery relations. Thus, Confucianism in China was the ideology of a fully developed tributary mode of production, while Japan was a peripheral society in relation to China and Shintoism a proportionally underdeveloped version of a tributary ideology.

Even though Amin warns against the aspiration to formulate 'general laws' and thence the slippery slope of a cosmogony *à la* Engels (EC, 30), it is difficult to see how his own schema escapes this fate because likewise it relies on general laws. Although Amin is circumspect in some of his formulations, his analysis nevertheless consistently follows the base–superstructure schema, squarely within historical materialism. In his words, 'The religious revolution takes place on its own terms' (EC, 87), i.e. Protestantism develops on its own – in the trail of and conditioned by capitalist development. The problem with the reflection theory of culture (culture reflecting material conditions) is that it becomes impossible to conceptualize 'cultural contradictions', for instance those observed by Daniel Bell (1978). This kind of base–superstructure logic we no longer find in current international political economy, at any rate not in Harvey, Jameson or Cox. But then, they do not take on grandiose historical analyses, on the basis of scant sources.

Eurocentrism, then, is not a novel departure theoretically; in fact, Amin restates and elaborates on what he wrote on the relation between modes of production and culture in works dating back to the 1970s.[1] Amin's approach, as a circumspect reformulation of historical materialism, is generally steeped in nineteenth-century epistemology, and accordingly his reading of history is itself deeply Eurocentric. The categories of barbarism for the communal mode and civilization for the tributary mode (EC, 15-16) come right out of the textbook of Eurocentrism. Amin's repeated recourse to the 'Socialism or Barbarism' rhetoric again reinvokes the evolutionist framework. Correlations between production systems and culture were first formulated in the French and Scottish Enlighten-ment and later entered Victorian anthropology and the analytics of Marx and Engels. Here they are recycled as instruments of historical analysis, without a sense of the historical character of the categories themselves.

A Eurocentric bias also comes across in some of the fine print of his history. Amin's reading of the Renaissance as the birth of Eurocentrism recycles another Eurocentric cliché: 'Things begin to change with the Renaissance because a new consciousness forms in the European mind' (EC, 75). According to Amin, we now say that this was due to the emergence of capitalism, but, he points out, 'At the time, Europeans attributed their superiority to other things: to their "Europeanness", their Christian faith, or their rediscovered Greek ancestry ... Eurocentrism in its entirety had already developed' (EC, 75).

This is an odd argument. First, it is an endogenist perspective on changes taking place in Europe, as if these were not conditioned by developments outside Europe. Secondly, why focus on the Renaissance – why not on the Crusades, as the first episode of Christendom trying to break out of the encirclement by the worlds of Islam and Byzantium? Thirdly, *which* Renaissance? The fourteenth and fifteenth centuries, the standard favourite from the Enlightenment to the present, or the twelfth-century Renaissance – that stood on the shoulders of the Islamic eleventh-century cultural awakening?[2]

That 'Eurocentrism in its entirety had already developed' by the fifteenth century is an unhistorical claim. Eurocentrism, in Amin's view, 'implies a theory of world history and, departing from it, a global political project' (EC, 75). For one thing, 'Europeanness' (rather than *christianitas*) does not come into the picture until the eighteenth century: the emergence of a 'European' consciousness dates from *circa* 1700 (e.g. Lively 1981). Why make such odd and unnecessary claims? This matches his criticism of Edward Said, according to whom Orientalism had its beginnings in the Middle Ages – and hence does not correlate with the epoch of capitalism. Since Amin rebukes Said for not acknowledging the differences between medieval Orientalism and the nineteenth-century version, he opens him-self to the same criticism by not acknowledging the differences between Renais-sance Eurocentrism and the nineteenth-century version. As a consequence he constructs Eurocentrism as a static and monolithic concept.

Amin takes on 'Islamic fundamentalism' as one of the culturalist constraints on the path towards delinking and because in the Islamic world it is itself an alternative project of delinking. Amin rightly criticizes the general clamour about Islamism in the West: 'There is an element of hypocrisy on the part of the West in lamenting current Islamic fundamentalism when it has fought in every way possible against the progressive alternative' (MD, 109). Yet the foundation of his own critique is the cliché dichotomous view of fundamentalism versus rationalism: 'Rationalism and fundamentalism constitute two states of mind irreducible to one another, incapable of integration' (DL, 184). This dichomotizing view is an instance of Marxist allegiance to Enlightenment thinking at a time when this is left behind as too simplistic in most other quarters. The tension between science and religion, rationality and the irrational is now perceived as far more problematic than in the age of Voltaire and Diderot. A more complex frame of analysis would enable us to see the modern and rational features (in a context of limited political options and vocabularies) of the Islamist turn, an approach which is now common to all but the most parochial Western accounts (e.g. Esposito 1992).

Amin's predictions are consistent with his analysis: in a book first published in 1985 he predicts that the socialist countries (USSR, China and others) will seek 'to retain control of their external relations' rather than submit to the exigencies of capitalist expansion and predicts catastrophe as a result of these developments in ten years' time (DL, xi).

All these features – evolutionism, Renaissance worship, dichotomy rationalism and irrationality, predictions of catastrophe – belong to a familiar profile: it may not be enough to be a neomarxist to be free from the rendezvous with nineteenth-century epistemology. Neomarxism does not mean reconstructed Marxism. Amin devotes an unremarkable chapter to the Eurocentric lineage of Marxism in which he observes that 'Marxism was formed both out of and against the Enlightenment' (EC, 119). Marx shared the excessive optimism prevalent in the nineteenth century, but actually existing capitalism has not homogenized but polarized the planet, and hence Amin's analytic medicine is, predictably: unequal development and centre–periphery contradictions. This step from Marxism to neomarxism leaves all the other questions about the Eurocentric lineages of Marxism unsettled – thus, how can one repudiate Eurocentrism and yet continue to talk of barbarism and civilization as if we are still in the nineteenth century? Why, for all its powerful analytics, does Marxism keep being delivered in packages of pig iron?

Unequal development becomes the answer to all questions. It is Amin's amulet and talisman against liberalism as well as classical Marxism, the backbone and central tenet of his perspective. As a general view this is problematic in several respects. First, Amin presents unequal development not only as the basic law of capitalist development but in his view also the tributary mode is marked by centre–periphery relations (the Islamic world and Europe, China and Japan). In fact, the relationship between feudal China and Japan is presented as proof of the general validity of the centre–periphery principle, for this 'has produced the same "miracle" witnessed in the Mediterranean region: the rapid maturation of capitalist development in the periphery of the system' (EC, 64). Thus, peripheries in the tributary mode have a head start in capitalist development. This sounds like Trotsky's law of combined and uneven development fine-tuned by means of his argument of the advantage of backwardness. If this were valid as a general law we would expect the Mongol Empire to have had a head start in capitalist development. Second, if in Amin's view there is a dialectical relationship *between* the tributary and capitalist modes, then it follows that a dialectics *within* the capitalist mode would be equally plausible. There is no acknowledgement however in Amin's work of such dynamics within capitalist relations. Quite the contrary, hammering on centre–periphery contradictions and rejecting the notion of semiperiphery, Amin does not show any awareness of historical movements of rise and decline within capitalism: centres declining to peripheries, peripheries ascending to core status – even though this is a well-developed line of analysis (e.g. Friedman 1982). In line with the principle of perpetual polarization, peripheries ever remain peripheries: 'all the regions that were integrated in the world capitalist system with peripheral status have remained like that to the present ... New England, Canada, Australia and New Zealand were never peripheral formations; by contrast, Latin America, the Caribbean, Africa and Asia – with the exception of Japan – were and have remained so' (MD, 169).

Third, 'centre' and 'periphery' are adopted as unproblematic categories across history, as transhistorical coordinates – as if these nodal points themselves are not historical constructs, which cannot simply be extrapolated backward or forward in time. Thus, in the context of post-Fordism and flexible accumulation, centre and periphery carry quite different meanings than in the context of Fordism and, in turn, during the accumulation regimes of competitive and monopoly capitalism. These notions themselves need to be rethought and reworked, as part of a historical economic geography, or what Foucault called a 'history of space'. Moreover, there have been episodes of peripheries playing a central role (e.g. OPEC provoking the 1973 energy crisis). In fact, it may be necessary to mix and combine these polarities, as in the 'pericentric' theory of imperialism.[3] Furthermore, in the context of the coexistence and articulation of modes of accumulation within the same space, spaces are layered in fulfilling multiple configurations – central in some relations, peripheral in others.

Amin rejects culturalism because of the tendency to treat cultural forms as transhistorical constants, but historical materialism is not exposed to the same scrutiny: its coordinates are unreflexively presented as transhistorical constants. Unequal development, centre and periphery are used as analytical tools as if they are constants from feudal times through the stages of capitalist development. Apparently Amin views unequal development as a transhistorical law of evolution. Thus stretched over time, the argument becomes proportionally thin and it becomes imperative to take into account countertendencies, which are absent in Amin's account, except for the instances mentioned. The result is a one-dimensional and one-sided representation of history. With respect to capitalist development, the overall result is a monolithic view in which polarization is recognized as the only dynamic. Amin's ignoring the dialectics within capitalist development is the corollary of and rationale for posing an alternative external to 'the system'. This is precisely the point of delinking.

The original form of delinking (decoupling, dissociation) was *mercantilism*, a strategy of states in the early stages of industrialization: close the borders to foreign products to protect infant industries. This was an option mainly for larger countries, such as China and India, that had the potential to effect an industrial transition on their own. At present levels of technology, industrialization without foreign investment has become unrealistic: the cost and quality differential between domestic and imported end products has become too great. Besides, this was a matter of delinking for relinking, 'reculer pour mieux sauter', re-entering the world market once a certain level of competitive ability had been achieved. Presently, on the basis of backward technology, relinking would hardly be possible. The second form of delinking was disengagement from capitalism as part of the *transition to socialism*. This strategy of neomercantilist closure and 'socialism in one country' was not voluntary but imposed from without. A subsidiary plot in this scenario was a strategy of weakening world capitalism from without: 'In time, if enough peripheral societies are closed, the capitalist world system will shrink, and ... this shrinkage will reduce prosperity in the core' (Chirot 1977: 169). If this might still have been believable in the 1970s (in combination with capitalist crisis), it is no longer now. The third form of delinking has been part of *national liberation* and anti-imperialist in content. With the wave of decolonization past and non-alignment at its lowest ebb, this is no longer on the cards. All along delinking has also been a statist project, premised on a strong and hard state capable of imposing tight controls and political repression. Now, with higher levels of communication and mobility, even if this kind of state-controlled closure were considered desirable, the scope for this option has considerably narrowed if not vanished.

The politics of delinking is the litmus test of Amin's perspective. But this case is not as obvious as it appears because his views have been changing over the years. In the early 1980s Amin defined delinking as semi-autarky (Amin 1982: 225). Now Amin repeatedly points out: 'De-linking is neither commercial autarky, nor chauvinist culturalist nationalism' (MD, 231). In every definition and discussion, Amin presents delinking as a national project that is to be based on a national and popular alliance. One wonders how, in the age of postnationalism, this is to materialize. Yet in another formulation, delinking parallels *polycentrism*. Polycentrism (originally inspired by Togliatti) has been an ambiguous turn in Amin's thought. Does it supersede unequal development and centre–periphery relations? Doesn't it reproduce 'centrism' and centre–periphery relations on other, regional or internal, levels? Earlier, in 1982, Amin cautioned against 'regional subimperialisms' and 'mini-hegemonisms' in Latin America, the Middle East, Africa and Southeast Asia. Now a section heading puts it in these terms: 'The genuine long-term option: transnationalization or a polycentric world and broad autocentric regions' (MD, 228). If delinking is now in effect redefined as an autonomous form of regionalization, how then is this to be carried off by a national and popular alliance? How does this mesh with delinking as a 'law of value of national application'? Are nationalism/populism not superseded by regionalization?

Amin's current formulations of delinking are so broad and opaque that delinking can mean almost everything to everyone, to the point that his prescriptions become self-contradictory. Delinking can mean, presumably, a popular anti-Western, anti-capitalist posture – yet Amin precisely wants to save 'the universalism begun by capitalism' 'at the level of a popular, cultural and ideological universalism' (MD, 231). Delinking can mean self-reliant development: as such it is meaningless because self-reliance has long been a universally endorsed development cliché. Or, delinking can mean regionalization – which is also an increasingly widely endorsed, though difficult to implement, policy orientation. The problem is that the centrepiece of delinking – autocentric accumulation – is a loose screw because the *unit* that is to be autocentric, the nation or the region, is not defined, or rather its definition can shift according to circumstance. Elsewhere, with respect to Southern Africa, Amin speaks of delinking as a regional scenario (Amin et al. 1987), but in subsequent statements on the future of South Africa he continues to view delinking as a national agenda (Amin 1992). It is not possible on the basis of Amin's formulations to distinguish delinking as a strategy of national or regional self-reliance.

On an empirical level too I believe Amin's general argument is belied by ongoing developments, more clearly now than ten or fifteen years ago: the deepening of globalization; the overall development of NICs; and the development of regional associations and trade agreements across centre–periphery boundaries (NAFTA, ASEAN, APEC, SAARC, EU, EFTA).

In a world in which countries in the South vie for preferential trade access to markets in the North and for foreign investment, technology and finance, delinking is not the most obvious policy option. Actual delinking is presently the shortest way to the Albania effect: isolation from foreign trade, technology, finance, communications, and precisely the obverse of the universalism that Amin advocates. It may be true that a number of African countries are in the process of being virtually cut off from global connections – Amin calls this 'passive delinking' (MD, 65; DL, xi). The record of voluntary delinking gives us, besides Albania, Sekou Touré's Guinea, Pol Pot's Cambodia, Yemen and Burma, while North Korea and Iraq are rather instances of involuntary delinking. Delinking has also meant linking up with socialist bloc countries – since 1989 this option has no longer been open. Due to the deepening of globalization, the overall balance has shifted to the disadvantage of the strategy of closure.[4] More than ever, delinking has become a cul-de-sac.

It is not surprising that at present the only ideologies of delinking that remain are neither industrialization strategies nor part of a transition to socialism. Radical Islamism is civilizational in emphasis – its economic foundation is oil revenues and as such it is a distributionist mode of rentier development; a posture rather than a strategy. Green projects, also endorsed by some indigenous peoples, envisage delinking along the lines of a 'small is beautiful' 'no growth' scenarios (discussed by Amin in MD, 165-73). Delinking has further been upheld by small Maoist currents, e.g. in the Philippines and the Senderistas in Peru, where the emphasis is anti-imperialist and low on economic strategy; or in Nepal.

At the present juncture, regional integration may increasingly become one of the major (alternative) development strategies – the buffer against globalization, or more precisely, a way to negotiate globalization (e.g. Gray 1993, Oman 1993), taking into account, of course, that there are different modes of regionalization. Now that national delinking is no longer a viable option, Amin is reformulating delinking in such a way that it is a form of regionalization. None of the current forms of regional cooperation in the South (e.g. the Maghrib Union, Mercosur,

Central American cooperation), however, subscribe to regional delinking or 'collective self-reliance'. Rather the objective is, through pooling resources and sovereignty, to achieve economies of scale and scope, to attract more foreign investment by increasing market size, and to arrive at a stronger bargaining position *vis-à-vis* external forces. Regional integration, then, is itself a function and subsidiary mode of globalization, and not a counter to globalization.

The problem with Amin's position is that delinking offers a rhetoric of autonomy in combination with, apparently, a multipurpose politics. It is, therefore, a posture rather than an analytic or a distinct policy. The most pernicious problem with the delinking posture is that it is a posture of retreat, of turning one's back on the big bad world – in a world in which strength is generated through engagement with realities, no matter how unpleasant, and dialogue with opponents. 'In this world, the only thing worse than being part of the evolving economic hierarchy is being excluded from it' (Henwood 1993: 8).

Amin's perspective on development is narrower even than world-system theory. World-system theory at least acknowledges dynamics and dialectics within capitalist development; the notion of semiperiphery is part of that. Frank and Wallerstein never agreed with Amin's delinking strategy. In their view delinking had been neither successful nor voluntary. At the same time, world-system theory also theorizes capitalism as a closed system and shows the same tendency of seeking an alternative external to it, as in the concept of 'antisystemic movements'. Conversely Amin views social movements as *part* of the system (MD, 111). In other words, among the rejectionists of capitalism there are marked differences as to just where to find the exit from capitalism.

Amin's politics is statist. For Amin the state is 'the means to national protection and assertion, the instrument of what we have called "de-linking"' (MD, 181). This places Amin squarely within the original tradition of national liberation. That he opposes neoliberalism is clear enough, but he does not seem to follow the subsequent developments – the development of an argument encompassing a state regulatory role along with other public agencies and NGOs. The greatest weakness of this body of work, ultimately, is that it is theoretically unreflexive, reproducing an unreconstructed neomarxism without adequately reflecting on its own principles of analysis.

There are underlying problems with this outlook, which are not confined to Samir Amin. One is the tendency towards stereotyped thinking about capitalism in terms of general laws of motion of capital written on stone tablets. While the greatest contribution of Marxism has been its powerful analytics in showing the varieties of capitalism, the greatest weakness of Marxism has been to underestimate the varieties of capitalist development.[5]

Notes

1 In particular Amin 1980, Chs. 2-4.

2 Episodes discussed in Nederveen Pieterse 1989, Ch. 5.

3 The pericentric theory of imperialism is discussed in Nederveen Pieterse 1989, Ch. 1.

4 Compare the balance sheet drawn by Chirot on 'The issue of closure' (1977: 203-8).

5 The varieties of capitalism and their interactions are taken up in Chapter 10 below. The present discussion does not address Samir Amin's later works (such as 1997 and 1999).

5

THE CULTURAL TURN
IN DEVELOPMENT:
QUESTIONS OF POWER

After the cultural turn has upset most social sciences, it finally comes to economics and to the bundle of practices called development. Why is culture being introduced into development discourse? Western ethnocentrism as the *implicit* culture of developmentalism is no longer adequate in the age of 'polycentrism in a context of high interaction', or globalization. In relation to global concerns such as ecological questions the West is no longer a privileged interlocutor. The old paradigm of modernization/Westernization is no longer valid not just on account of polycentrism but also in view of the questioning of modernity and the advent of the postmodern. Questioning Western itineraries is now no longer an anti-imperialist preoccupation but a matter of soul-searching in the West. The waning of the great Cold War ideologies has shifted the goalposts and ethnic and religious movements emerge in their stead. Hence 'culture' has been taking on a novel prominence.

How is culture 'put into' development discourse? The current reproblematizations do not start from a blank slate but recycle and rework established discourses. The articulation of culture and development is both a renegade notion at odds with established practices and a new brick in the wall of clichés. Culture comes into development studies at a time of retreat from structural and macro approaches in development theory in favour of micro and actor-oriented approaches (e.g. Long and Villarreal 1993). If agency is prioritized over structure (such as the state, the national economy), the cultural worlds and maps of meaning of actors become a vital variable. The move away from structures to actors may be described, in part, as an informalization of development, and in that context, culture tends to be viewed as, so to speak, the structure of the informal. The crucial weakness of culture and development discourse, at any rate policy-oriented discourse, is that it misses the point that culture is an *arena* of *struggle*. Culture tends to be treated as if it is or conforms to a structure, on the analogy of the state or nation – existing out there, as an ambience one can step in and out of, a resource to be tapped, as national culture or, given the fragmentation of nations and retreat of states, as local culture. This chapter first discusses national culture, then local culture. National culture is worth considering also for the sake of raising the question whether the present preoccupation with local culture risks repeating the same mistakes as were made by the talk of national culture earlier. The key questions are questions of power: how is the relation between culture and power conceptualized in these different discourses? The final section returns to culture and development discourse, under the heading: 'Add culture and stir'.

National Culture

The discourse of national culture carries instrumentalist overtones: culture as a device in nation building. Following the tracks of decolonization and Third World nationalism, anti-colonialism involved a cultural argument all along. Thus Amilcar Cabral argued in 'National liberation and culture':

> A nation which frees itself from foreign rule will be only culturally free if ... it recaptures the commanding heights of its own culture, which receives sustenance from the living reality of its environment and equally rejects the harmful influences which any kind of subjection to foreign cultures involves. Thus one sees that if imperialist domination necessarily practices cultural oppression, national liberation is necessarily an act of culture. (Cited in Miller 1990: 46)

The liberation movement, according to Cabral, must bring about 'a convergence' toward 'a single national culture', which itself is a step toward 'a universal culture' (ibid.). Fanon, likewise, devoted a chapter to 'national culture' in *The Wretched of the Earth* (1967). Here he outlined three phases in the cultural development of colonized peoples: (1) assimilation of the culture of the colonizer, (2) recollection of original cultural resources, but removed from the masses, and (3) combat, revolution and the formation of a national culture in which the artist 'rejoins the people'. Recent discussions of the role of cultural struggle in South Africa, Palestine and Northern Ireland show similar politicized discourses. In South Africa it prompted the slogan of 'cultural weapons' as Inkatha's response to the ANC's 'culture as a weapon'.

In postcolonial countries, calls for 'cultural protectionism' are not uncommon. In an African context, this is advanced as part of a wider programme: 'The New African Cultural Order would consist of researching and safeguarding the African personality and culture. This is a task for every one of us, but it must be stimulated and coordinated by conscientious, capable and responsible African politicians' (Gbotokuma 1992: 28).

In the Philippines, Renato Constantino criticizes the 'new cultured Filipinos' as 'a breed apart from the mass of Filipinos', 'a class without roots – adopted children of a foreign culture'. 'In the end, it is the people and their culture that will endure. National culture will be developed by and will emerge from the real people' (1985: 48-9).

There are several strands in this discourse: the identification of cultural identity with the nation; the subsumption of culture under a political agenda; the nomination of politicians as custodians of culture; a culture talk derived from other discourses – from politics of struggle, or from economics Soviet style, in the 'commanding heights'. Culture is denied autonomy and encapsulated within the political discourse of 'anti-colonialism equals nationalism'. The same options that pertain to the postcolonial nation are extended to culture. Dependency theory – which serves by and large as the political economy of Third World nationalism – is stretched to apply to culture: protectionism, dissociation, endogenous development are prescribed for national culture as they have been for the national economy. What ensues is cultural dependency theory.

The national culture argument also structures the wider terrain. As Tomlinson notes: 'a majority of the discourses of cultural imperialism, and certainly those with the most prominence – the UNESCO discourse, that thematized by the term "Americanisation", much of the talk of media imperialism – treat the issue as one of domination of national culture by international culture' (1991: 73). UNESCO's institutional discourse follows the same nationalitarian tracks: '*National culture* is the mould into which, by the very nature of UNESCO as an inter-national body, cultural identity tends to be squeezed' (ibid.: 72). Another current in UNESCO discourse is towards pluralism, and in this context cultural identity is discussed in terms of 'people' rather than 'nations'. However,

> The UNESCO discourse cannot negotiate this complexity with any coherence. In its recommendations on the issue of cultural domination it urges member states to: 'strengthen national languages with a view to affirming cultural identity and helping it to recover its natural role which is that of expressing the different aspects of activity and life and thereby furthering national development.' (ibid.)

References to 'cultural democracy' are not sufficiently clear to settle these issues. When virtually all the world's societies are multicultural in composition equating cultural identity with national identity is a fallacy, as is obvious, for instance, in the case of language as a centrepiece of cultural identity.

With respect to cultural imperialism the 'national' formulation breaks down, as Tomlinson points out, in two ways: 'not only may there be difficulty in identifying a unified national cultural identity in the "invaded" country, but the same might be said of the putative "invader". What, then, is the "American way" that threatens global hegemony?' (1991: 74).

'National culture' discourse displays a particular logic. In postcolonial countries, at least in the new nations among them, there has been a replication of the process of nation building in the West. In France, as the saying goes, it took two hundred years to create 'Frenchmen'. In late nineteenth-century Europe, nation building was in its most intense phase – by means of public education, the mass production of monuments and the large-scale invention of traditions (Hobsbawm and Ranger 1983). It concerns, in effect, a process of state building through nation building. In postcolonial countries the erection of prestige architecture has the function of creating markers for national consciousness and identity, in the process inviting genuflection before the nation's leadership (Schudson 1994). This has also been a profoundly gendered process: the state (masculine) protects (nurtures, guides) national culture (feminine); nationalism has been a profoundly masculinist discourse. The relationship between feminism and nationalism, West and South, has been fraught with ambivalence (e.g. Kandiyoti 1991, Enloe 1990).

In Western countries the project of nation building involved intense strife because it intervened in the existing cultural division of labour along lines of region, religion, language, class, gender. The *Kulturkampf* in Germany is a case in point. What ensued was not cultural homogeneity but rather particular state-managed settlements. Dutch pillarization, in force from 1917 into the 1960s, is a well-known instance. The construction of national identity, then, is a matter of cultural struggle – usually conducted along lines of language, religion or region. The contemporary terminology for this kind of conflict is ethnicity.

National culture can serve as a first-rate excuse domestically and internationally. Thus, culture has been working overtime in Japan:

> when 'culture' is used to explain Japan, statements such as 'we do this because it is our culture' (i.e. 'we do this because we do this') are not perceived as tautology but are believed to give a valid reason for accepting all manner of practices whose political nature has been lost sight of. Culture thus becomes an excuse for systematic exploitation, for legal abuses, for racketeering and for other forms of uncontrolled exercise of power. In the international realm, culture is made an excuse for not living up to agreements and responsibilities, and for not taking action in the face of pressure from trading partners. (Wolferen 1990: 322)

When several years ago the Dutch minister of foreign affairs protested against the execution of political prisoners in Indonesia after they had been imprisoned for many years, his Indonesian counterpart pointed out that this was in character with Indonesian culture.

Accordingly, the subsumption of cultural identity under national identity is not an innocent move. Endorsing the myth of national culture and cultural unity, it glosses over the dark side of nationalism. The politics of nation building involves the marginalization of aliens, suppression of minorities and of indigenous peoples – a process sometimes captured under the heading of internal colonialism. While on the one hand national monuments are erected, on the other hand, outside the glare of the spotlights, aliens are expropriated, minorities constructed and refugees created. The harvest of this policy is the contemporary wave of ethnic mobilization for in virtually all cases of ethnogenesis, ethnopolitics and movements for regional autonomy or secession, the main catalyst is the imposition of monocultural control by the state. National culture serves as a code for state culture.

Local Culture

National culture as the corollary of nation building has been part of modernization discourse. Current culture and development discourse is primarily concerned with local culture. In the terms of a recent discussion: 'The first cultural dimension of development is the local level' (Kottak 1985: 46); national culture is next in the line of priorities, followed by the culture of the planners.

Privileging local culture is interpellated with several arguments. In the strong version of this perspective the local is mentioned in one breath with the grassroots, indigenous, informal, micro. In some culture and development arguments (e.g. Verhelst 1990) these are represented as the last frontier of cultural authenticity. The tendency is to view local culture in terms of prelapsarian purity and unity, homogenizing the local community as the last stand of *Gemeinschaft*, in a manner reminiscent of the way ethnographers used to speak about 'their' villages, or their cultures, as cultural wholes or configurations. The local as a privileged site may imply an argument about how culture develops: organically, from below and within, by way of 'roots', according to a horticultural anthropology.

Since this is the terrain of the return of anthropology, it is worth taking into account that 'Anthropological "culture" is not what it used to be' (Clifford 1992: 101). Clifford elucidates: 'Anthropologists, as Geertz has written, don't study villages, they study *in* villages. And increasingly, I might add, they don't study in villages either, but rather in hospitals, labs, urban neighborhoods, tourist hotels, the Getty Center' (1992: 98).

In many postcolonial countries, the state and nation have been to a significant extent a terrain constructed by colonial administrations – this is the irony of Cabral, Fanon and others, that the trophy gained in the victory over colonialism, was colonialism's legacy. Secondly, it is the terrain of the postcolonial state – and as such the arena of multicultural strife. Local culture, likewise, is not an uncontaminated space but a field criss-crossed by traces of migrants, travellers, traders, missionaries, colonizers, anthropologists. This awareness is part of the ongoing reorientation in ethnography: 'In much traditional ethnography … the ethnographer has localized what is actually a regional/national/global nexus, relegating to the margins a "culture's" external relations and displacements' (Clifford 1992: 100). Or, in the words of Gupta and Ferguson (1992), conventional anthropology allowed 'the power of topography to conceal successfully the topography of power'. According to James Boon: 'What has come to be called Balinese culture is a multiply authored invention, a historical formation, an enactment, a political construct, a shifting paradox, an ongoing translation, an emblem, a trademark, a non-consensual negotiation of contrastive identity, and more' (1990: ix, cited in Clifford 1992: 100).

Accordingly, to situate the local is to view it in its multiple external connections, and next, to regard its performative, dramatic, contrastive character – the local as a *project* enacted in relation to the regional, national, global. Or, the local as strategy, device, ruse. Its 'truth', then, is as much without as within: in the construction and negotiation of external boundaries. In a comparable fashion, the dynamics of ethnicity may be best approached not from within, by stepping into the intricacies of ethnic identification (and then trying to get out), but from without – in terms of postnationalism, retreat of the state, ideological erosion, world market fluctuations, the dialectics of globalization and localization (Nederveen Pieterse 1996).

One option is to take stock of the traces of travellers and the role of strangers (e.g. Shack and Skinner 1979). Conventional wisdom has it that underneath a veneer of modernity lurks perennial African 'tribalism' – in line with an essentialist view of tribe as primordial group attachment; until it is found that the tribes have been in large measure colonial and missionary constructs (e.g. Vail 1989). Then, there is the anecdote

about a prominent member of an East African tribe, a professional philosopher, who had an interest in reviving traditional practices. As it turned out, the old ways and customs had been discarded and forgotten even by the elders of his tribe. The main repository of knowledge about the past was located in ethnographies published in Europe and the United States. He realized he needed an anthropologist as a consultant. He had no difficulty finding someone to take the job. (Shweder 1993: 284)

This is by no means without precedent. *Négritude, Africanité* and Afrocentrism borrowed extensively from European or American ethnography: Marcus Garvey and Aimé Césaire derived their images of Africa from the German ethnographer Leo Frobenius; Senghor borrowed from Lévy Brühl; Melville Herskovitz' work went into the making of African-American 'roots' thinking. Azania, the authentic African name for South Africa, was plucked from a novel by Evelyn Waugh. Ethnographers have generously fed this current, for instance Maquet's book on *Africanity* (1972) or, in a church context, Placide Tempels' work on *Bantu Philosophy* (see the critique of Hountondji 1991). The return of anthropology, then, may also invite the return of anthropological myth. In the words of Roger Keesing (1987: 168): 'We anthropologists have a disciplinary vested interest in portraying other people's culturally constructed worlds as radically different from our own. We are dealers in exotica.'

Of course, recourse to 'tradition' is also tenuous for other reasons. Thus, according to Kaarsholm, in an African context, what is at issue is 'a variety of often conflicting frameworks and discourses – African political, cultural and ethnic traditions, colonial and anti-colonial traditions, traditions of government, the traditions of nationalism and of modern political and cultural institutions. They are all full of contradictions within themselves and do not represent unambiguous positions *vis-à-vis* development' (1991: 4).

Like national culture, local culture is a terrain of power with its own patterns of stratification, uneven distribution of cultural knowledge and boundaries separating insiders and outsiders – hierarchical or exclusionary politics in fine print. The dark side of local culture is local ethnocentrism or, in other words, ethnic fundamentalism. Certainly, local maps of meaning are of vital importance, but so is the awareness that 'Cultures are webs of mystification as well as signification' (Keesing 1987: 161). Gender is part of local constructions.

> Consider a New Guinea culture that consigns women to lifelong jural minority under male control, defines their essential nature as polluting and polluted, extracts their labor in lifelong drudgery for the service of men, excludes them from ritual and political life, all as ordained in the eternal nature of the cosmos and the rules of the ancestors ... it is a smallish group of 'experts' in any generation who – at least for myth, ritual, and other realms of religion – play the major part in creating and changing the culture. The rules of the ancestors and gods seem in such cases to be quite literally man-made. (Keesing 1987: 166)

No wonder that amidst the upsurge of ethnic mobilization women find themselves in a position of 'double jeopardy': under pressure from majority racism and minority sexism at the same time (e.g. Wallace 1992).

As Van Nieuwenhuijze remarked, Westerners did not just venture out on a civilizing mission but also in search of the Golden Fleece (1983: 26). In the epoch of Third Worldism, of Che Guevara and 'one, two, three Vietnams', Third World nationalism represented this golden fleece – national culture as the frontier of honour against imperialism, multinational capitalism and CocaColonization. In the age of globalization, local culture represents the treasure trove of the Golden Fleece – perhaps the world's last. The world's indigenous peoples are the last custodians of paradises lost to late capitalism, ecological devastation, McDonaldization and Disneyfication. With ecological pressures mounting worldwide, this ethos is gaining ground as if queuing up for the last exit.

In each case, the national and the local serve as a frontier – against imperialism, capitalism, consumerism, developmentalism. The border of national culture, guarded by the postcolonial state and by dependency theory, did not hold. Culture and development discourse in its strong form pleads for an alternative development based on local culture. In the process it attempts to erect boundaries – in a time of boundary crossing. It welcomes crossing disciplinary boundaries in order to strengthen the case for erecting cultural boundaries. As such it reflects a politics of nostalgia.

Culture/Power

How is power theorized in these discourses? Two very distinct theories of power are at work. The national culture perspective tends to follow a deductivist approach in which culture is viewed as derived from macrosocial powers. Thus, according to García Canclini, 'To analyse culture was equivalent to describing the manoeuvres of dominant forces', an approach that has been guilty of 'over-estimating the impact of the dominant on popular consciousness' (1992: 21).

In contrast, the local culture perspective follows an inductivist approach: 'the inductivists are those who confront the study of the popular by beginning with certain properties which they suppose to be intrinsic to the subordinate classes, or with their genius, or with a creativity that other sectors of the population have lost, or with oppositional power as the basis of their resistance' (García Canclini 1992: 20).

The inductivist approach has been influenced by anthropological culturalism and by populism. Its weaknesses are that it explains cultural difference but not inequality, decontextualizes the local, and tends to equate 'popular culture' with 'tradition'. As different strands in this perspective García Canclini identifies the biologico-telluric approach, which relies on 'innate forces' in people/nature relationships (as in *Blut und Boden*, blood and soil); and a statist version which holds that the state gives expression to popular values, a view that leads us back to the national culture perspective (1992: 27-30).

Most relevant to culture and development discourse is yet another strand. In Latin America, 'Given the crisis in the political apparatuses and the ideological models, a belief in the "natural purity" of the people as the sole recourse is re-emerging amongst "movements of the base", "alternatives" and groups emanating from the populist parties' (1992: 31). It is this kind of perspective that informs the strong version of the local culture view along with much of the grassroots-oriented alternative development approach, at times homogenizing the subaltern, at other times ascribing a romantic role to grassroots intellectuals (e.g. Escobar 1992b).

Anthropological holism as an ethnographic rhetoric and hermeneutic strategy – one of the sources of inspiration of culture and development – is under attack for underestimating the unevenness of power and the role of elites within indigenous communities (Thornton 1988, Keesing 1987).

Too often power is viewed only as state power, or power exercised with sovereignty, whereas it is more appropriate to view power as a social relation diffused throughout all spaces. However, it is true that differences in scope matter and that the power of a household head differs from that of the head of a multinational corporation. Another limitation is the tendency to think of power in terms of simple schemas, reducing the field of hegemony to a polarized contest between dominant and subaltern forces. Hegemony however may be better thought of as an ongoing jostle, ever in motion and requiring continuous effort. While the situation of polarization between dominators and dominated is out of the ordinary, it rules political discourse as if it were routine and everyday. What *is* everyday are the little tactics of survival and subtle acts of subversion (Scott 1985, 1991). But even in polarized situations – such as the condition of *indigenes* in most of Latin America – it is important to monitor the actual transactions taking place and to probe into the nodal points of interaction. Patterns of exchange between classes and politics of patronage, collective and personal, may be a more valid perspective than the schema of resistance and politics of struggle.

One method to engage this perspective is, as García Canclini points out, to examine consumption patterns in popular strata – without shifting to the rhetoric of consumerism (1992: 41-4). Commodity chains and exchange relations may reveal interclass exchange patterns and at the same time situate the local level in its wider networks (cf. Appadurai 1986).

Add Culture and Stir

Culture has been part of development thinking all along, though not explicitly so. In the 1960s instilling achievement orientation was a development strategy geared to building entrepreneurial spirit, deriving from the American free enterprise culture of entrepreneurialism and the idea that attitudes matter. Economic growth strategies have been based on the culture of economism. Structural adjustment programmes reflect a culture of economic globalism. These positions reflect different inflections of the ethnocentrism of Western developmentalism (Chapter 2 above).

Culture and development (C&D) discourse is a significant improvement on this pattern of implicit cultural bias. Recognizing development practices as culturally biased and specific introduces an element of cultural reflexivity. Of course this forms part of a much broader tide of intercultural awareness. By and large the implication is to reconnect development with anthropology – reconnect to the extent that in colonial times a nexus between efforts at economic development and anthropological research sometimes did exist. Presently this takes the form of an emerging field of development anthropology (Huizer 1993, Rew 1993), notably in the UK, and *Entwicklungsethnologie* or development ethnology (as in the new journal of that name) in Germany, as a supplement to development sociology. *Entwicklungsethnologie* is concerned not only with the analysis of local settings but with 'the comprehension of the project itself as a problem of intercultural exchange and an arena of competing interests' (Antweiler 1993: 40).

The concepts and methodological approaches of C&D incorporate conventional anthropological methods such as participant observation, tailored to the development culture of projects, along with a participatory or action component: Participatory Action Research, Rapid Rural Appraisal, Goal Oriented Project Planning, and beneficiary assessment of projects (Salmen 1987). These may or may not be combined with a critical attitude to development and a general context of 'emancipatory knowledge'.

While the cultural turn in development is a welcome turn, C&D also involves a number of problems and raises questions. C&D policy discourse leans towards simplifications and towards 'add culture and stir', or the failure to reproblematize development. General C&D discourse may be more sophisticated but limited in turn by tendencies toward the reification of culture and the reification of modernity. Another problem is turning towards applied anthropology at a time when anthropology is in crisis.

Development policy discourse is where the cultural turn in development may be making its greatest impact. Here C&D serves as a logical follow-up to the earlier notion that development in order to be effective must be participatory (itself a successor to the previous top-down 'mobilization' for development discourse). Sometimes this C&D policy talk is so superficial however that it is not only bogus and absurd but also meaningless. Thus the Dutch development cooperation policy document *A World of Difference* (Ministry of Foreign Affairs 1991) asserts that 'culture must be the basis of sustainable development', and development must be 'embedded in culture'.

Obviously *any* development strategy is 'based on culture', if only because it is not possible to operate outside culture; that is, as long as we adopt the anthropological understanding of culture as all learned and shared behaviour and ideas. Viewing culture with a big C is another option – as in using popular theatre to popularize family planning or AIDS containment; but this is clearly too narrow a view. The normative statement that development must be 'embedded in culture' glosses over the character of development as a cultural performance in itself: implicitly the reference is to the culture of 'others', of the 'developing' entity, and in an opaque sort of way it is a statement about development as an engagement with cultural difference.

In development, culture is discussed primarily in relation to economic rather than political or social development, which reflects the order of priorities in development culture. Other discussions focus on culture in relation to development projects (e.g. Crehan 1991). Discussions focused on politics often take the form of arguments in favour of decentralization and local government (e.g. Mhlaba 1991). Generally, however, C&D policy discourse tends to be a depoliticizing vision because by inserting culture it takes the politics out of development, while taking the politics out of culture by assuming established cultural boundaries. C&D runs the risk of adding culture to the development repertoire like an additional coating or a local Vaseline, without necessarily changing the development agenda itself.

Add culture and stir, or the failure to reproblematize development is a prominent feature of C&D policy. The case for C&D is generally made in instrumental terms, as a means to explain project failure and improve on the success rate of projects. The *Economist* publishes a steady stream of advertisements for anthropologists to join regional development banks. This is practical from the point of view of the development machinery, questionable from the point of view of the ethics of anthropology, and business as usual for the recipients of development politics on the ground. This parallels the practice of 'business anthropology' or the use of anthropological insights and methods to facilitate doing business across cultures.

The point of C&D is, of course, to rethink and reproblematize development and the intercultural relations that are implicitly negotiated in development from the point of view of anthropology and cultural critique. For this to work out what is required is a further development of C&D theory; it may be argued that the failure to reproblematize development is a function of the reification of modernity. The beginnings of culture and development discourse include Talcott Parsons' pattern variables, for affective neutrality, universalism, etc. are themselves cultural traits. The tendency toward the reification of modernity or underestimating the complexity of modernity follows from the habit of dichotomous thinking, which is as deeply entrenched among the critics of developmentalism as among its adherents. Simplistic schemas – tradition/modernity, premodern/modern, South/North – implicitly cloud over theory. Modernity may be better conceived in the plural, as modernities, and in the context of processes of 'reworking modernity' (Pred and Watts 1992 and below).

A manifestation of the cul-de-sac of C&D theory is the current of anti-development thinking (Chapter 7). Obviously, the rejectionist position is not the best platform for redefining development; it may, in effect, give free rein to business as usual. The Foucauldian approach of discourse analysis is long on history and short on future, strong on critique and weak on construction. It has room only for a reactive position of resistance rather than a pro-active perspective of imagining and developing alternatives. This is a limitation of the Foucauldian approach in relation to development discourse as it is in relation to other terrains.

On the other hand, in practice the agenda of C&D in many ways parallels that of alternative development (Friedmann 1992; Chapter 6 below). A singular difference is the priority given to culture and, accordingly, the key issue is how culture is conceptualized. The tendency toward the reification of culture is part of a tradition that is deeply entrenched within and outside anthropology of identifying culture with territorial units. National culture and local culture are obvious examples of this outlook. In C&D, practices are considered to be 'embedded' in a matrix of meaning and the tendency is to view this matrix as belonging to a social group and, secondly, to localize this group.

One of the ramifications of the local culture argument is *ethnodevelopment*, for which Stavenhagen (1986) made a case that has been taken up by Hettne (1990) and others. While this notion is understandable in its original context of internal colonialism, it is problematic in that it potentially parallels apartheid and 'separate development'. Taking the *ethnos* (people) as a starting point for development does not settle matters because it ignores the fundamental character of development as an intercultural transaction: ethnodevelopment means narrowing development to its endogenous dimension. In addition, ethnic culture is no more homogeneous than national culture for ethnic groups are crosscut by multiple differences along lines of gender, class, place, religion, ideology.

The Dutch development policy document *A World of Difference* avoids the national culture fallacy by identifying communities as the bearers of culture, within a general orientation of pluralism and fostering cultural difference. The latter is a welcome qualification in view of the limitations of the concept of community (e.g. Young 1991).

The counterargument to the territorial reification of culture is that culture cannot be localized because it is not in itself a spatially bounded category. If culture is territorialized, as in national culture or local culture, the boundaries are, ultimately, political frontiers that require political analysis. Culture is intrinsically *translocal* because human learning is. At minimum, then, what is required is to differentiate between open and closed concepts of culture, between translocal and territorial notions of culture (discussed in Nederveen Pieterse 1995).

One can also think in terms of historical layers of culture and intersecting circles of cultural influence. For instance, in Pakistan traces of a deep historical layer of the Indus Valley Mohenjodaro culture mix with the intersecting spheres of influence of Central Asian, Arab and South Asian cultures, all leaving their imprint in language, technology and identity (Junejo and Bughio 1988). In addition, the distinct regional cultures of Baluchistan, Sind, the Punjab and others are overlaid by, on the one hand, Islamic culture and, on the other, rural/urban and gender differences across the regions. Within urban culture we can further distinguish various occupational circles such as the cultures of the military, the bureaucracy, traders and so on. Somehow perched on top of this is 'national culture' (Jalibi 1984). In such a context, what is the statement that 'development must be based on culture' supposed to mean?

An interesting way of thinking about this is to examine how cultural diversity and exchange have influenced 'development' (which is taken up by Griffin 1996 and World Commission 1996). Another way of thinking about this is in terms of cultural mixing and hybridity. From the point of view of any given place, cultures are hybrid: their wholeness consists in their being situationally relevant, strategic sets of borrowed improvisations (Nederveen Pieterse 1995). The localization of culture can be questioned from the point of view not only of history but also of geography and the question of 'place'. What comes to mind is Deleuze and Guattari's argument of deterritorialization and Harvey's work on the relationship between space and place: 'from space to place and back again' (1993). Doreen Massey argues for a 'global sense of place': 'a sense of place which is extraverted, which includes a consciousness of its links with the wider world, which integrates in a positive way the global and the local' (Massey 1993: 66). Rethinking the meaning of boundaries in the age of cultural translation is a keynote in Bhabha's work (1994).

Several of these issues translate into a wider question: the issue is not simply to bring anthropology back into development, but what kind of anthropology – conventional anthropology or reflexive anthropology? C&D connects development and anthropology at a time when anthropology itself is in crisis. Part of this is the crisis of representation in anthropology and of the authority of the ethnographic text. In response, Marcus and Fischer (1986) propose 'the repatriation of anthropology as cultural critique'. This means in effect the merger of anthropology and cultural studies. The limitation of C&D is that in leaning towards applied anthropology it tends to ignore poststructuralist anthropology and its critical innovations, and in looking south to postcolonial countries it ignores the work done in cultural studies in post-imperial countries as well as in the South.

Cultural studies involve different outlooks and concepts. For instance, as a concept *popular culture* is a notion more challenging and fruitful than local culture (or than national culture) because its hybrid character – mixing high and low culture, local and global cultural flows – is implied from the outset (e.g. Rowe and Schelling 1991). By using concepts such as these several of the unnecessary dichotomies which burden and constrain C&D can be overcome and reworked on a more subtle and more productive level of analysis and ultimately policy.

An element that tends to be relegated to the background in C&D literature is the engagement with capitalism – as if the shift toward a cultural definition of problems is also a shift away from a political economy perspective. This is short-sighted because it glosses over the character of 'development' as a stand-in for and an attempt to manage and steer the spread of capitalist relations, and because it ignores a wide body of literature on the cultural dynamics of global capitalism and uneven development (e.g. Pred and Watts 1992, Taussig 1980).

The cultural turn in development is not without its ironies. The tables are being turned, as is altogether appropriate in a post-imperial and postcolonial world in the throes of globalization.

> Over the last few years, at various meetings of men and women and representatives of majority and minority groups from First and Third World countries, I have found that the indigenous 'voice' of the Third World is most likely to be voiced by a Westerner, while the voice of Western theory often comes straight out of Africa or Japan. The effect of all that intellectual place switching is to induce a sense of metaphysical jet lag across genders, cultures, and continents and to open up a conversation about the full range of interpretive possibilities for thinking about the significance of 'difference'. (Shweder 1993: 282)

Development is a cultural practice and in this respect development as a category is no different from culture in that they are both elusive concepts. Defining them is as difficult as, to use a Spanish proverb, putting pants on an octopus. Development thinking if considered carefully is a series of improvisations and borrowings, zigzagging through time, itself a hybrid project intellectually and politically, and not quite the consistent edifice that both its adherents and opponents tend to consider it. The transformations denoted as 'development' change along with the tides and currents of conventional wisdom (Chapter 3).

Development is intrinsically an intercultural transaction. At the cusp of millennium, culture is the major marker of *difference*. It assumes the role religion performed in the Middle Ages, biology ('race') along with time (evolution) in the eighteenth and nineteenth centuries, and ideology in the first part of the twentieth century (cf. Robertson 1992: 98–9). As such, culture has come to mean 'otherness'. Taken in this sense, the statement that culture is to be the basis of development, reads: the other (others, otherness) is to be the basis of development. Development politics, then, is a politics of difference, navigating and negotiating multicultural cohabitation locally and globally. The differences at stake are multiple and of diverse kinds, not just between developed and developing zones and countries, but also within them and crosscutting the difference between developing/developed.

Conventional developmentalism could be viewed as a form of 'symbolic violence': 'the violence which is exercised upon a social agent with his or her complicity' (Bourdieu and Wacquant 1992: 167). Understanding development as a politics of difference is a step toward making development practice self-conscious with regard to its political and cultural bias, a step toward a practice of reflexive development.

C&D may offer relief from development steeped in Eurocentrism, occidental narcissism or trilateralist arrogance, but the remedy against the chauvinism of 'great traditions' is not to adopt the inverse missionary position and the chauvinism of 'little traditions'. C&D is not simply a matter of including culture but also of inter-rogating culture as a terrain of power, culture as ideology. Anti-ethnocentrism, as David Crocker (1991) points out, may ultimately be based on another partial, par-ticularist perspective. This is a question that is not settled in C&D. The alterna-tive advocated by Richard Rorty (1991) is 'anti anti-ethnocentrism', or returning towards the historical tradition of one's own group as the basis for moral judge-ment. This is the position of what he terms postmodernist bourgeois liberalism. This tradition however can be interpreted in many ways; in the case of the United States it is read differently by Allan Bloom and Noam Chomsky, and on the basis of the tradition there is no way of deciding among these readings, precisely because the tradition is heterogeneous and mixed. What is needed is to find a sense of balance that does not yield to futures mapped from above nor to nostal-gia for the rear exit, a new sense of balance between universalism and localism.

6

MY PARADIGM OR YOURS?
VARIATIONS ON
ALTERNATIVE DEVELOPMENT

> Human nature being what it is, while everyone likes to be a social engineer, few like to be the objects of social engineering. (Ashis Nandy, 1989: 271)

This chapter is an inquiry into critical currents in development thinking. The objective is to go beyond the fraternity of rhetorical consensus in criticizing mainstream development and to hold the claims and aspirations of these critical positions themselves against the light. The focus is not only on the critical but also on the affirmative part of these positions. This exercise is not meant as a critique for critique's sake; the question is what these positions tell us analytically and where they lead us in terms of policy and action.

My views on alternative development have been changing over the years. Initially my impression was that alternative development presents a loose profile of critical sensibilities and alternative practices that leaves so many areas open that its claim to present an alternative model or paradigm to mainstream development thinking is exaggerated and misplaced. Further delving and reading enthusiastic accounts (such as Korten 1990, Max-Neef 1991, Rahman 1993, Carmen 1996) persuades me that there is a profound and principled challenge to mainstream developmentalism. Possibly this can take the form of an alternative development paradigm, but closer reflection on this position and its ramifications causes me to question this. I wonder not only how such an alternative development paradigm should be conceived, in terms of analytics and politics, but also whether thinking in terms of paradigms is appropriate at all.

Rather than pursue a single line of argument I have decided to keep these changing positions and moments of reflection in this chapter. Doing so enables me to look at alternative development from more angles and probe further than if I were just presenting a single case. Others may have experienced a similar process of questioning. The structure of the chapter, then, roughly follows the logic of these three positions: (1) alternative development as a loose profile; (2) alternative development as a paradigm; (3) a post-paradigmatic way of thinking about alternative development. Each of these is a different way of constructing alternative development and the relationship to mainstream development. Each of these has its chemistry, reasoning and limitations. During this stroll past alternative development positions my own views shift from critical to supportive to revisionist. Advancing three arguments allows me to say more than if I would just present one; nevertheless the third position is the one I arrive at by travelling through the others.

The argument runs as follows. Alternative development has been concerned with introducing alternative practices and redefining the goals of development. This has been successful in the sense that key elements of both have been adopted in mainstream development. Even if not consistently practised it is now generally accepted that development efforts are more successful if the community participates. NGOs now play key roles on the ground and in development cooperation. This success reflects not simply the strength of NGOs and grassroots politics but also the 1980s rollback of the state, the advance of market forces and the breakdown of regulation. All the same, the goals of development have been generally redefined. It is now widely accepted that development is not simply a matter of GDP growth and human development is a more appropriate goal and measure of development. This also means that alternative development has become less distinct from conventional development discourse and practice since alternatives have been absorbed in mainstream development. In the context of alternative development several pertinent positions and methodologies have been developed – views on the agency, methods and objectives of development. However, alternative development has failed to develop a clear perspective on micro–macro relations, an alternative macro approach, and a coherent theoretical position, although it is often claimed that there is an alternative development paradigm. But is the concept of paradigm appropriate to contemporary social science? Besides, is formulating the relationship between alternative development and mainstream development as a paradigm break substantively tenable and politically sensible?

These reflections on alternative development are followed by queries on mainstream development, which is increasingly caught on the horns of a dilemma between the aims of human and social development and the constraints of structural adjustment and global monetarism represented by the international financial institutions. Presently, unlike the 1970s, the big hiatus no longer runs between mainstream and alternative development, but between human and alternative development on the one hand, and the Washington consensus of structural reform on the other (see Chapters 8 and 10 below).

Alternative Development

To start with there are different ways of conceiving what alternative development is about and what its role is. Alternative development can be viewed as a roving critique of mainstream development, shifting in position as mainstream development shifts, as a series of alternative proposals and methodologies that are loosely interconnected; or it can be viewed as an alternative development paradigm, implying a definite theoretical break with mainstream development. It can be viewed as concerned with local development, with alternative practices on the ground, or as an overall challenge to the mainstream, and part of a global alternative. In many discussions this question of the status and scope of alternative development remains unsettled.

An elementary distinction, following Sheth (1987), runs between structuralist and normative approaches to development alternatives. This involves two basic differences. Structuralist approaches, such as dependency theory and the Keynesian reformism of the new international economic order, emphasize structural macroeconomic change – just as mainstream modernization thinking does – whereas alternative development emphasizes agency, in the sense of people's capacity to effect social change. The second difference is that dependency critiques of mainstream development do not usually question development *per se* but only *dependent* development (or underdevelopment).

A basic question is whether alternative development is an alternative way of achieving development, sharing the same goals as mainstream development but using different means, participatory and people-centred. It would seem this way if we consider the enormous increase of development funds being channelled or rechannelled through NGOs during the past two decades (which now exceed the total annual disbursements through the IMF and World Bank). This suggests ample peaceful coexistence between mainstream and alternative development. Yet the usual claim is that alternative development refers to an alternative *model* of development. Let us consider how this claim runs.

In the 1970s dissatisfaction with mainstream development crystallized into an alternative, people-centred approach to development. According to the 1975 report of the Dag Hammarskjöld Foundation 'What now? Another Development', development should be 'geared to the satisfaction of needs', 'endogenous and self-reliant' and 'in harmony with the environment'. Whether this was meant to be an alternative practice of development apart from the mainstream or whether it was also to change mainstream development was not quite settled. This approach has been carried further under the heading of alternative development. Over the years alternative development has been reinforced by and associated with virtually any form of criticism of mainstream developmentalism, such as anti-capitalism, Green thinking, feminism, ecofeminism, democratization, new social movements, Buddhist economics, cultural critiques, and poststructuralist analysis of development discourse.

'Alternative' generally refers to three spheres – agents, methods and objectives or values of development. According to Nerfin (1977), alternative development is the terrain of 'Third System' or citizen politics, the importance of which is apparent in view of the failed development efforts of government (the prince or first system) and economic power (the merchant or second system). Often this seems to be the key point: alternative development is development *from below*. In this context, 'below' refers both to 'community' and to NGOs. In several respects alternative development revisits Community Development of the 1950s and 1960s. Community Development goes back to American social work, which via British colonialism entered colonial development, and in the 1950s supplemented modernization efforts (Carmen 1996: 46-7). This genealogy accounts for the ambiguity of some of the key terms in alternative development, such as 'participation'.

Alternative development is frequently identified with development-by-NGOs (e.g. Drabek 1987). But given the wide variety of NGOs and NGO practices, the equation 'alternative development is what NGOs do' would obviously be inadequate. NGO ideology is organization-led and too limited to account for alternative development. Alternative development involves further distinguishing elements with respect to development methodology (participatory, endogenous, self-reliant) and objectives (geared to basic needs). But is saying that development must be undertaken from within and geared to basic needs an adequate way of redefining development, or is it only a polemical position? The alternative referred to is alternative in relation to state and market, but not necessarily in relation to the general discourse of developmentalism. It would be difficult to maintain that alternative development has evolved a theory, although among others Hettne (1990) has tried to make such a case, arguing that it represents a counterpoint to mainstream development.[1]

Thus Friberg and Hettne (1985: 207) argue that 'Opposed and dialectically related to the predominant paradigm, there has been a Green Counterpoint'. They relate this historically to the 'populist tradition', including narodnism (i.e. populism in Russia), criticisms of the division of labour, the 'return to Gemeinschaft', as well as 'Third World populism', Gandhi, Maoism and Buddhist economics. Their premise is a radical questioning of development: 'it is the development process itself which engenders most of our problems.... If we have been floating along the stream of evolution, we are now starting to doubt whether it will carry us to the promised land. Instead we hear the roaring from the approaching waterfall. Almost all the traditional indicators of development have changed their emotional loading from plus to minus' (Friberg and Hettne 1985: 215).

A critique of capitalism is part of this perspective: 'The capitalist economy is in fact a parasite upon the non-capitalist economy', capitalism is a form of 'shifting cultivation' (233-4). They anticipate the 'possibility of a slow decline over the coming 500 years without any particular dramatic events as the turning point' (234). They envision a post-capitalist world, to which there are two different roads: the Red road of continued modernization toward a socialist world order, and the Green road of demodernization, informed by the values of cultural identity, self-reliance, social justice and ecological balance (234-5). The 'global Green movement', in their view, derives strength from three different sources: traditionalists in the peripheries, marginalized people at the middle level, and postmaterialists in affluent societies at the centres. Nations founded upon ancient nations or civilizations such as China, Iran, Egypt, Vietnam and also Mexico, Turkey, Japan and India can be 'seen as the main sources, actual or potential, of alternatives to the Western model of development' (238).

This has been quoted extensively because it shows how quickly sensibilities date, or at any rate their articulation, and because it brightly illustrates features that run through various forms of alternative development thinking.

❏ The tendency to represent alternative development as a counterpoint that unites all dissident social forces critical of development, which in turn reflects an underlying desire to forge a grand coalition of opposition forces.
❏ The tendency to equate development with modernization and alternative development with demodernization, premised on the 'incompatibility between modernization and human development' (Friberg and Hettne 1985: 235).
❏ The tendency to view and represent alternative development as an alternative *external* to the mainstream, a counter-utopia carried by different social actors

in the interstices of the mainstream and in countries supposedly outside the thrust of Western developmentalism; in other words, an enclave or 'liberated zone' approach to alternative development.

❑ The alignment of all forms of criticism of mainstream development together as if they form a cohesive alternative, but all good things together do not necessarily make a great thing. Friberg and Hettne (1985: 220) mention 'possible priority conflicts between the subgoals of development' but maintain that they form a coherent whole.

This particular formulation of alternative development is clearly dated and marked by the 1980s upsurge of Green movements. It very much resembles the post-development perspective that took shape in the 1990s (Chapter 7 below). In later formulations Hettne (1990, 1992) abandoned the demodernization/anti-development perspective. Some of the weaknesses of this kind of position (anticipating the discussion of post-development) are the following:

❑ 'Mainstream development' is simplified as a single, homogeneous thrust toward modernization and its diversity, complexity and adaptability are underestimated.

❑ While the theoretical claim is for a dialectical relationship between mainstream and alternatives, the actual argument takes the form of a simple dualistic opposition and the dialectics, the ways in which mainstream and alternatives shape and influence one another, slip out of view.

❑ In order to maximize the opposition between mainstream and alternative, the appeal of the mainstream to various constituencies is underestimated.

Several of these features resemble and replay the narrative of anti-capitalist opposition. The tendency to transpose forms of struggle opposing early industrial capitalism to late capitalism indicates a failure of oppositional imagination. It recycles a struggle scenario under different circumstances and envisions no path but that of rejectionism. This might be one of the problems of alternative development: postconventional ideas and approaches are straitjacketed in conventional political imaginaries. In the process alternative development is loaded with aspirations beyond its scope. Subsequent claims for alternative development by Hettne and others have been more modest, while this kind of grandstanding has now taken the form of post-development. Broadly speaking, then, the development terrain seems to be marked out into three overall positions: mainstream development (which, I will argue later, is by no means a coherent position), alternative development (which itself involves a range of perspectives), and post-development.

At this point, a hostile criticism would be that inflated to 'alternative development' this approach is pretentious because it suggests more than it can deliver, unclear because the difference between what is alternative and what is not is not clarified, and fuzzy to the point of hypocrisy because it sustains the overall rhetoric of development while suggesting the ability to generate something really different within its general aura. Alternative development has been fashionable because it coincided with a crisis in development thinking, and because it matched general doubts about the role of the state, both among neoliberals and from the point of view of human rights. The 'alternative' discourse was a way of being progressive without being overly radical and without endorsing a clear ideology; it could be embraced by progressives and conservatives who both had axes to grind with the role of states. It was a safe, low-risk way of being progressive and its structural obscurity ensured broad endorsement. It was a postmodern way of being post-ideological. It was everyone's way out except that of the last bureaucrat.

Hettne (1990) presents 'Another Development' as a combination of basic needs, self-reliance, sustainable and endogenous development. Attractive as this *mélange* looks it also presents a problem. All good things put together do not necessarily add up to a paradigm. Part of this is the problem of articulation (cf. Laclau and Mouffe 1985). To the extent that each of these discourses has its own logic and autonomy, there is no guarantee that they will blend well together. Their actual course depends on their articulation with other discourses, which may turn out to be progressive or conservative. There is no preordained outcome to the politics of hegemony. At best this gives us an unstable articulation, which is too weak a basis to constitute an 'alternative model'. Ethnodevelopment may clash with ecodevelopment, or may take an ethnonationalist turn. Self-reliance may require economies of scale, which clash with ethnodevelopment. Feminism may clash with indigenous culture, and so on. Running the risk of flippancy, one might say that the kind of world in which alternative development works is a world that does not need it. Thus, while pertinent as an orientation, it is too unstable and narrow to serve as a 'model'.

Hettne seeks to establish a sharp boundary between mainstream development and alternative development but fails to do so. Hettne's schematic representation of mainstream development theory versus counterpoint theory overrates the coherence and consistency of 'development'. Besides, if alternative development is defined as a counterpoint to mainstream development, it is reduced to a reactive position: if mainstream development shifts, so would alternative development. Furthermore, the alternative components mentioned by Hettne are now no longer distinctive: basic needs, participation, sustainability have long been adopted in mainstream development.[2]

The problem is that there is no clear line of demarcation between mainstream and alternative: alternatives are coopted and yesterday's alternatives are today's institutions. The difference between mainstream and alternative, then, is a conjunctural difference, not a difference in principle, although it tends to be presented as if it is. In itself 'alternative' has no more meaning than 'new' in advertising. With Nandy (1989) we might term this the problem of the 'standardization of dissent'. In this sense alternative development replicates 'the value of the new', which is a pathos intrinsic to modernity (Vattimo 1988). As such, alternative development partakes of the momentum of modernity and the everlasting hope that the future will redeem the present.

So far, then, it would be difficult to claim that alternative development represents a paradigm break in development, for it lacks sufficient theoretical cohesion. Alternative development reflects certain normative orientations, follows disparate theoretical strands, is in flux, not fully developed, and its status remains unclear. Part of the polemics of development and situated on its cutting edge, it's made up as one goes along and remains intrinsically controversial and unsettled. Understandings of alternative development vary widely: whichever aspect of mainstream development the spotlight is on, alternative development is held up as its counterpoint. If mainstream development is viewed, as it has been through most of the career of modern developmentalism, as state-led, then alternative development is associated with the informal sector, social movements and NGOs. If on the other hand mainstream development is viewed under the sign of liberalization, as has been the case since the 1980s wave of neoliberalism, then the alternative becomes ... the state. Thus, under the heading of *Alternative Development Strategies in sub-Saharan Africa*, Stewart, Lall and Wangwe (1993) argue for import-substitution industrialization and state protection for industry, a strategy which, in other times and contexts, was itself part of mainstream development repertoires.

This variability is intrinsic to alternative development to the extent that alternative development is by definition reactive, contrapuntal. At a time when there is widespread admission that several development decades have brought many failures, while the development industry continues unabated, there is continuous and heightened self-criticism in development circles, a constant search for alternatives, a tendency towards self-correction and a persistent pattern of cooptation of whatever attractive or fashionable alternatives present themselves. Accordingly, the turnover of alternatives becoming mainstream has speeded up; the dialectics of alternative development and mainstream development has accelerated.

Green thinking about sustainability, a radical position twenty or so years ago, has long been institutionalized as 'sustainable development'. The informal sector, a twilight zone unnoticed by mainstream developers mesmerized by the state, has been put in the limelight by Hernan de Soto (1989) and embraced by establishment development agencies. The accompanying message of deregulation and government rollback of course beautifully matched the prevailing neoliberal outlook. NGOs, after decades of marginality, have become major channels of development cooperation. Governments go non-governmental by setting up Government Organized Non Government Organizations. In countries such as Mozambique and Bangladesh the resources of NGOs, domestic and international, exceed those at the disposal of government. Women's concerns, once an outsider criticism, have been institutionalized by making women and gender preferential parts of the development package. Criticism of foreign aid as development assistance has led to its being renamed 'development cooperation'. Capacity-building which used to be missing in conventional development support is now built in as a major objective. Mega-summits – in Rio, Cairo, Copenhagen, Beijing, Istanbul – have been forums for the alignment of official and unofficial discourses.

In other words, forms of alternative development have become institutionalized as part of mainstream development, and in some circumstances have become or overtaken mainstream development, to the point that MAD, or mainstream alternative development, might not be an odd notion. This turn of affairs is not at all incidental but a logical function of the way the overall development process is moving.

We can regard alternative development either as an open-ended poser, or as a set of ideas and practices that in time have themselves been institutionalized, and while critically scrutinizing the latter we can keep open the former. The advantage of alternative development as an open-ended poser is that it provides a flexible position of critique. Of course this principle can be adopted without any reference to 'alternative development'; instead development itself can be defined as 'constant consideration of alternatives' (e.g. Coetzee 1989: 11). The disadvantage is that without a theory alternative development is like a ship without a rudder.

Alternative Development Paradigm

While much alternative development thinking makes a diffuse impression, this has gradually been giving way to a sharper and more assertive positioning on account of several trends. (1) The enormous growth of NGOs in numbers and influence generates a growing demand for strategy and therefore theory. (2) The importance of environmental concerns and sustainability has weakened the economic growth paradigm and given a boost to alternative and ecological economics. (3) The glaring failure of several development decades further unsettles the mainstream paradigm of growth. (4) The growing challenges to the Bretton Woods institutions lead to the question whether these criticisms are merely procedural and institutional (for more participation and democratization) or whether they involve fundamentally different principles.

These diverse trends generate various lines of tension. One line of friction runs between the general alternative development preoccupation with local and endogenous development and the growing demand for *global* alternatives. Globalization under the sign of the unfettered market is denounced because it clashes with endogenous development, while the mushrooming of NGOs itself is a manifestation of the growing momentum of global civil society, in other words represents another arm of globalization. Another line of friction runs between diffuse alternative development and an alternative development paradigm, the former implying a soft and the latter a hard boundary with mainstream development, and theoretical openness or closure. These tensions find expression in more or less subtle differences among alternative development positions.

In view of the holistic aspirations of alternative development it would be desirable for disparate alternative development knowledge pools to be grouped together; yet in view of the different functions that alternative development fulfils – animating local development, guiding international NGO strategy, informing global alternatives – this will not necessarily happen. Alternative development serves dispersed discourse communities. International NGOs tend to look both ways, at local grassroots development *and* at global alternatives. These different functions overlap and intersperse and are not necessarily incompatible, but rhyming them requires making them explicit, which is not often done, and an effort at synthesis, which requires more reflection on local/global and micro/mega interconnections than is common in most alternative development literature.

Oddly, in view of the claim to an alternative development paradigm and its growing appeal, attempts to theoretically develop alternative development have been relatively few.[3] There may be several reasons for this. Alternative development tends to be practice oriented rather than theoretically inclined. The world of alternative development is not a 'library world'. Part of alternative development logic is that as development is people-centred, genuine development knowledge is also people's knowledge and what counts is local rather than abstract expert knowledge. With the local orientation of alternative development comes a certain regional dispersal in the literature, which looks like a scattered archipelago of primary local knowledges, with little overarching reflection. Besides, alternative development travels under many aliases – appropriate development, participatory development, people-centred development, human-scale development, people's self-development, autonomous development, holistic development; and many elements relevant to alternative development are developed, not under the banner of alternative development but under specific headings, such as participation, participatory action research, grassroots movements, NGOs, empowerment, conscientization, liberation theology, democratization, citizenship, human rights, development ethics, ecofeminism, cultural diversity, etc. Such dispersion does not facilitate generating a coherent body of theory. Many alternative development sources do not in any methodical way refer to one another but keep on generating alternatives from the ground up, in the process reinventing the wheel without zeroing in on fundamentals or generating 'expert opinion' and debate. In part this may be a matter of the 'alternative' character of alternative development, alternative in the sense of a habitus of subversion, an intuitive aversion to method, to systematization and codification, which implies a distrust of 'experts' and even of theory itself. This weakens the claim to deliver a different paradigm.

Alternative development is not necessarily anti-theoretical but it is intellectually segmented. The work of several alternative development authors can be contextualized in terms of their social location. David Korten is an NGO strategist who contributes both to local development and global alternatives. John Friedmann is primarily concerned with local and regional planning. Anisur Rahman mainly addresses local and grassroots development. Manfred Max-Neef and Hazel Henderson are alternative economists, the former engaged with local development and the latter with global alternatives. Training, teaching and research are other contexts in which alternative development is being articulated, across a wide spectrum from small local institutes to university programmes.[4]

While alternative development is often referred to as an alternative development model or paradigm, which implies an emphatic theoretical claim, what is delivered on this score is quite uneven. Critics of the Bretton Woods institutions as bulwarks of mainstream developmentalism increasingly claim to present a paradigm shift in development. The same elements keep coming back: 'equitable, participatory and sustainable human development' (e.g. Arruda 1994: 139). 'The new approach to development includes the values of equity, participation and environmental sustainability, as well as improving physical well-being' (Griesgraber and Gunter 1996a: xiv). Is this sufficient as the basis of a new paradigm? It concerns the 'how to's' of development rather than the nature of development as such. It identifies aspirations rather than attributes of development. As such it can easily be 'added on' to mainstream development discourse and indeed often is. Since mainstream development nowadays embraces and advertises the same values, the outcome is a rhetorical consensus rather than a paradigm break.

Rahman (1993) contrasts a *consumerist* view of development, which treats people as passive recipients of growth, with a *creativist* view, according to which people are the creative forces of development, the means as well as the end of development, for development is defined as people's self-development. This refers to a set of normative orientations, rather than to a different explanatory framework. Such elements may add up to a distinctive alternative development profile but not to a paradigm. The distinguishing element of alternative development should be found in the *redefinition* of development itself and not merely in its agency, modalities, procedures or aspirations.

Dissatisfaction with development-as-growth is an increasingly common position, not merely since the Club of Rome's report on *The Limits to Growth* (Meadows et al. 1972). Yet if development is not about growth, what is it? One option is to redefine development as *social transformation* (e.g. Addo et al. 1985). In itself development as transformation is vague because it is like saying that development is change – change from what to what, what kind of change? 'Good change', according to Robert Chambers (1983). Institutional transformation adds some concreteness but still needs context. Korten (1990) defines development as transformation towards justice, inclusiveness and sustainability. Again these are normative clauses, but ethics of development (e.g. Goulet 1992) does not necessarily add up to redefining development. Alternatively, might the character of alternative development be found in a distinctive *development style*? Max-Neef (1991: 86) mentions 'avoiding bureaucratization' and for Korten the surest way to kill a social movement is to throw money at it. But the downside of this position is the romanticization of social movements (as in post-development).

It may be argued that theory is a central concern of alternative development, for it is about the redefinition of development. Korten (1990: 113) notes that 'it is impossible to be a true development agency without a theory that directs action to the underlying causes of underdevelopment. In the absence of a theory, the aspiring development agency almost inevitably becomes instead merely an *assistance* agency engaged in relieving the more visible symptoms of underdevelopment through relief and welfare measures.' Indeed, 'an organization cannot have a meaningful development *strategy* without a development theory' (1990: 114). Korten (1990: 67) proposes a redefinition of development as follows:

> Development is a process by which the members of a society increase their personal and institutional capacities to mobilize and manage resources to produce sustainable and justly distributed improvements in their quality of life consistent with their own aspirations.

The same point in different wording: 'The heart of development is institutions and politics, not money and technology, though the latter are undeniably important' (144). 'The most fundamental issues of development are, at their core, issues of power' (214). The kind of issues that Gunnar Myrdal raised years ago in *Asian Drama* (1968), issues of land ownership and distribution of power, issues that during development decades have been papered over by community development and other fads, which made little or no difference in relation to poverty: these fundamentals are now put centre-stage.

This position may be distinctive enough to establish a break with conventional development. For Korten it constitutes a break with the various approaches that coopt alternative values by 'adding them on' to the growth model. 'The basic needs strategies that gained prominence during the 1970s, and are still advocated by organizations such as UNICEF, are a variant of, usually an add-on to, a classical growth-centered development strategy' (1990: 44). The same applies to the approaches that have been concerned with giving structural adjustment a 'human face'. 'The basic services for which they pleaded were best characterized as a facade, putting a more palatable face on actions that are based on flawed analysis and theory, rather than coming forward in support of more basic, but politically controversial reforms' (45). The report of the World Commission on Environment and Development on *Our Common Future* (1987), known as the Brundtland Report, is also criticized for merging sustainability and growth in the notion of 'sustainable growth' (166).

A further question is whether, beyond an alternative definition of development, alternative development has a distinctive methodology, epistemology and policy agenda. A review of alternative development positions on questions of agency, endogenous development, indigenous knowledge and development cooperation, may serve to fill in and give substance to an alternative development paradigm or profile and also to detect whether there are contradictory elements among them. Since the literature is extensive, uneven and dispersed this is only a provisional review.

Agency

With regard to agency there have been marked changes over time in alternative development thinking. Generally alternative development combines the aims of development and emancipation. As development 'from below' it is part of the general concern with civil society. In 1970s alternative development manifestos the forces that were to carry and implement 'another development' were the community and informal sector, or the 'third system'. Of the big three – state, market, society – the emphasis was entirely on society as the foundation for another development. Clearly at the time alternative development was a protest position against state-led development. The strength of NGO discourse on the other hand is also a weakness: neglecting the role of the state. As such the rise of NGOs may be viewed as *de facto* part of the neoliberal 'counterrevolution' in development (Toye 1987). When in the 1980s the private sector came to be viewed as the leading sector of development, the scope of alternative development widened to include the state. Thus Friedmann (1992) and others argue that a strong civil society and a strong state go together. A strong, activist state in this view does not necessarily mean a dominant state. In alternative development the role of the state is not viewed in the same way as in conventional development: the state is to act as an enabler, a facilitator of people's self-development. For the state to perform such a role democratization is implied.

What about the third of the big three – market forces? Gradually this is being roped in, moving beyond not only anti-state but also anti-market understandings of people-centred development. 'Step-by-step we have moved to a recognition that government, business and voluntary organizations all have essential roles in development' (Korten 1990: 95). Not only practices but also prescriptions increasingly involve synergies between government, NGOs and firms, and elements such as fair trade, corporate codes, socially responsible business and banking. Thailand's Five Star Partnership Programme integrates the efforts of government, NGOs, private sector, religious communities and academic institutions to facilitate community and provincial development. Sato and Smith (1996) present this as a practice exemplar as part of an alternative development paradigm. A trend at the other extreme is for the market logic to take over to the point that private aid, as part of the development industry, becomes a business undertaking (Sogge 1996).

NGOs

The struggle of alternative development, according to Smitu Kothari (1994: 50), is 'nothing short of reversing the conquest of society by the economy'. This calls to mind Sukhamoy Chakravarty's saying that the market is a good servant but a bad master (quoted in Hettne 1992). Where the state has little autonomy in relation to business interests, foreign or domestic, social forces can operate as a countervailing power. In a situation where various forces seek to influence or control the state – strategic business groups, foreign corporate interests, multilateral agencies – organized civil society can operate as a check on the 'privatization' of the state and the public sphere.

The political economy of *dependencia* involved Third World intellectuals relying on the state and on the emergence of a national bourgeoisie. As intellectuals of Third World nationalism and anti-imperialism, at times they played the part of alternative mandarins. What is the political economy of alternative development? Which political and social forces sustain the world of everyday and really-existing alternative development? Whom does alternative development discourse serve? Who are funding NGOs and alternative development consultants? (See e.g. Gow 1991, Sogge 1996.)

NGOs have become part of the development industry, another component in the package. The rise of NGOs during the 1970s and 1980s was both a by-product of and compensation for the wave of neoliberalism (Duffield 1996). Civil society, social movements and NGOs are a mixed bag, all the more because, mushrooming amidst the breakdown of regulation (or informalization), they are unregulated themselves. Some NGOs such as church organizations were active long before the development era. There are steep differences between NGOs as public service contractors and people-oriented NGOs (e.g. Korten 1990, Edwards and Hulme 1992). NGOs suffer similar problems (bureaucratization, hierarchy, scale, corruption, dependence) as any organization. If they are sites of power outside the reach of the state they are within the reach of donors, who in turn move within the orbit of their funders, state or private, and their cultural and discursive agendas (e.g. Black 1992 about the career of Oxfam). NGOs can function as parastatals, subcontractors of the state or Governmental NGOs, but outside the channels of accountability and control. NGOs can just as easily be conservative agencies, such as evangelical movements broadcasting the theology of quiescence or the prosperity gospel of individual achievement, charismatic movements propagating new forms of ritualism; not to mention agencies such as the Summer Institute of Linguistics which is on record as having served as a CIA conduit.

Development NGOs have been denounced as 'new missionaries' engaged in recolonization, as 'unguided missiles' (Hanlon 1991), or as 'the new East India Company' (Burne 1995). They have been accused of neutralizing popular resistance and facilitating popular acceptance of structural adjustment (Arrelano-Lopez and Petras 1994). NGOs can contribute to democratizing development (Clark 1991), serve as vehicles of transnational networking building global civil society (Henderson 1993), as liaisons in 'innovation networking' (Mytelka 1993), or channels of outside interference beyond the controls of normalized politics and international relations (e.g. African Rights 1994). The role of NGOs is now viewed with less naivety and more discrimination concerning the institutional, discursive, economic and political constraints under which they operate.

New Politics

Alternative development literature is sprinkled with pleas for unity. In an Indian context, for instance, Smitu Kothari (1994: 51) notes: 'The pervasive fragmentation of the entire democratic spectrum has to be replaced by coalescing our dispersed efforts'. In part this reflects nostalgia, not so much for *Gemeinschaft* but for the 'old politics' characterized by clearly divided camps and neat ideological boundaries. Laclau and Mouffe (1985) contrast this with hegemonic politics, which is characterized by unfixed identities and fragmented space, in which nodal points nonetheless matter. In hegemonic politics coalitions are not stable as in the old-time coalitions because the subjectivities are not as stable. Alternative development may involve novel coalition politics of new and old social movements, with a view to a new convergence of concerns and interests, in relation both to local and to global politics. The case for a 'convergence of radicalisms' (Shiviah 1994) fails to persuade because in these kind of pleas the interests, identities and subjectivities involved tend to be taken as static and given, rather than as constructed in the process of articulation.

In alternative development, agency can be defined narrowly or broadly; it can be defined loosely, in diffuse alternative development, or sharply, in the alternative development paradigm. At any rate, what is more appropriate than a static coalition politics or a new kind of political 'unity' is the idea of *synergies* among pluralistic actors, synergies that are flexible and mobile and do not require ideological consensus. Thus, the World Bank's NGO desk is making tripartite negotiations between government, NGOs and international institutions a feature of its approach. Defining development policy as public action (Wuyts et al. 1992) is an approach that involves synergies among diverse actors and across sectors.[5]

Endogenous Development

The notion of the 'endogenous' refers to a social, cultural and symbolic space. Endogenous development implies a refutation of the view of development = modernization – Westernization. Self-reliance, then, does not simply concern the means but the end of development: the goals and values of development are to be generated from within. 'Development is endogenous – there are no front runners to be followed' (Rahman 1993: 217). An implication is that modernity is viewed as generated *from within*. Modernization then is not a matter of importing foreign models but also the 'modernization of tradition'. Imported modernization means the destruction of existing social and cultural capital – as in the cliché modernization view of tradition as 'resistance to change', modernization as the development of enclaves (rooted in colonialism) and the resulting dualistic structure.[6] By contrast, modernization-from-within means the revalorization and adaptation of existing social and cultural capital. Rahman (1993) relates how traditional self-help groups in West Africa, the Naam, have taken on other functions. A broad stream of literature discusses many instances of grafting development on to 'traditional' organizations (e.g. Carmen 1996, Burne 1995, Pradervand 1989, Verhelst 1990). These instances open up our understanding of development as well as modernity. The 'modernization of tradition' releases local and popular energies in a way that the modernization approach of top-down mobilization and outside-in imposition could never achieve.

An endogenous outlook is fundamental to alternative development. Yet endogenism is difficult to turn into a 'hard' principle. Generally the boundary between inside and outside is one of the fundamental problems of development thinking (e.g. Gordon 1991). For what is the *unit* of development? The conventional framework used to be the 'society' (read nation; read state), a position that was challenged by Wallerstein (1979) who argued that the actual unit of development is the world-system (i.e. the zone integrated by a division of labour in the production of goods necessary for reproduction). Alternative development introduces a diffuse range of alternative sites of endogeneity: people, community, local, grassroots.[7] Who are the *people* in 'people power'? Is it 'people' or 'the people' – in which case we are back with 'society'? Or does it involve a class element, as in 'popular sectors'? If endogenous means within the community, it leads to the question of ethnodevelopment (see below). If endogenous means within society, it leads to the question of globalization and the blurring of borders. External change agents or *animateurs* often play an important role in stimulating local processes or acting as brokers: this is another limit to endogeneity as a horizon (a point made by Friedmann 1992).

How far to take endogenism? For instance, are Islamic approaches to development part of alternative development? They match the basic criteria of being endogenous, geared to basic needs, participatory and sustainable. Would this also apply to Islamist grassroots and social organizing (e.g. in Egypt, Turkey, or for that matter Algeria)? The community activities of Shiv Sena in Bombay – an extreme rightwing Hinduist organization – have been praised for their alternative development efforts (Esman and Upton 1984: 8). Organizations such as the

Tamil Tigers (LTTE) are also known to be effective community organizers. After endogenism the next stop may be ethnochauvinism.

Ethnodevelopment

Endogenous development implies that each society should find its own strategy. But what is a society? An idea originally advocated by Rodolfo Stavenhagen (1986), with reference to the indigenous peoples in Latin America, and taken up by Hettne (1990) is ethnodevelopment.[8] In the words of Friberg and Hettne (1985: 221), states are 'artificial territorial constructions' and 'small communities of human beings are the ultimate actors'. 'The concept of nation-state implies that the territorial boundaries of the state coincide with the boundaries of a culturally homogeneous nation. This is the exception rather than the rule in a world with about 1500 peoples or nations but only 150 states.' Therefore, 'The tribes and nations of the world are much more basic units of development, because they allow for the forging of a genuine consensus between their members. Normative convergence can only be obtained where people share a framework of social reasoning.' (ibid.).

Under the guise of alternative radicalism, this is not merely a nostalgic and con-servative but a reactionary programme. It evokes false and illusory notions of 'consensus' and group boundaries based on a reification of *ethnos* = community. Friberg and Hettne note that 'Modernization always implies the decline and disin-tegration of natural communities' (1985: 233). First, this narrows modernization to exogenous modernization, eliminates the idea of modernization-from-within and thus denies the very idea of endogenous development. Secondly, should one accept these criteria as part of alternative development, it would mean alternative development upholding the same arguments as rightwing opponents of multi-culturalism in the West (and not only in the West): in the name of 'natural com-munities', immigrants can be banned; in the name of 'cultural homogeneity' as a condition for sharing 'a framework of social reasoning', multiculturalism can be declared inoperable. 'Natural communities' is the terminology of blood and soil politics. It is the kind of terminology that the followers of Hindutva in India would embrace. Endogenous development hardened to ethnodevelopment is a pro-gramme for separate development, for neo-apartheid and Bantustan politics, a pro-gramme for inward-looking deglobalization in the age of accelerated globalization.

This is alternative development at its worst. It evokes the spectre of ethno-fundamentalism. The reasoning is insinuating: 1500 peoples, therefore 1500 nations-in-waiting? Once 'genuine consensus' among group members is the work-ing criterion, an infinitesimal process of fissure is on the cards. In the contempo-rary world of 'ethnic cleansing' this sounds unbelievably naive. There may be constructive ways of valorizing ethnicity, e.g. in conjunction with local culture and policies of decentralization. But a prerequisite for reconstructing ethnicity is deconstructing it, in the sense of recognizing its constructed character (Nederveen Pieterse 1996), and not recycling static notions such as 'natural com-munities' and blood and soil politics.

'Green authors tend to visualize the future as a world of cooperating and fed-erated natural communities without strong centre–periphery gradients between them' (Friberg and Hettne 1985: 223). A further perennial problem of visualizing a future of autonomous communities, as in Green notions of bioregionalism, is that the relationship *among* communities or regions, which are inevitably differentially endowed in terms of resources, is not settled (cf. Young 1991). Friberg and Hettne are not unaware of the dark side of populism and the possibility of ecofascism: they mention the resemblance of the Green movement to Fascist movements of the 1930s with a similar emphasis on nature and folk culture (1985: 226).

Methodology

The hallmark of alternative development methodology is participation. Participatory Action Research, Rapid Rural Appraisal as well as conscientization, critical pedagogy and empowerment are further elements in the alternative development repertoire. These elements are not specific or exclusive to alternative development. They have been developed in education (e.g. McLaren 1995), liberation theology and general development studies. Arguably what is specific to alternative development is the local and popular context in which they are applied. Participation is a deeply problematic notion; it is an improvement on top-down mobilization, but it remains paternalistic – unless the idea of participation is radically turned around, such that governments, international institutions or NGOs would be considered as participating in people's local development.[9]

Epistemology

Korten (1990) mentions the phenomenon of 'believing is seeing', or paradigms controlling perception. We tend to select and suppress information according to our beliefs. Alternative development in this sense claims a 'Copernican revolution' in understanding development. The key resource becomes not the country's aggregate GNP but people's creativity. This would also imply, for instance, that 'poverty' as such disappears as a clear-cut development indicator. Poverty as an indicator follows from the development-as-growth paradigm: 'the poor' are the target of development because they lack economic resources. But if development is not about growth but about institutional transformation, then the concern is not merely with economic capital but as much with social, cultural, symbolic and moral capital and in these respects poor people can be rich. This introduces different distinctions such as the 'rooted' and the 'uprooted' poor (Carmen 1996). Stereotypes of poverty as wholesale deprivation, the 'culture of poverty' etc., are disabling elements of development discourse. They evoke the notion of development as external intervention. The keynote of alternative development epistemology is local knowledge.

Indigenous Knowledge

Another keynote in alternative development and post-development thinking is critique of science. In India, the work of Ashis Nandy, Shiv Vishvanathan,

Claude Alvares and Vandana Shiva is part of a wider critique-of-science movement. Vandana Shiva (1991) criticizes the Enlightenment model and seeks to formulate 'an alternative development paradigm'. Critique of science is also well developed in Latin America. According to Escobar (1992b), Western science through development exercises a form of 'cultural violence on the Third World' and what is needed are 'alternative conceptions of knowledge'.

Critique-of-science movements involve dissident intellectuals, popular organizations and NGOs who oppose mainstream development expertise and policy, and network with movements in the West and Japan. Beck (1992) regards critique of science and technology as the main form of struggle in the 'new modernity' of 'risk society'. In view of the globalization of risk – such as global ecological hazards, the export of polluting industries and waste materials, the risks of biogenetic engineering, the spread of reproduction technologies – this is rapidly becoming a global contestation. In the South 'indigenous knowledge' is a countervailing position to Western science.

Tariq Banuri formulates a cultural critique of modernity focusing on what he calls the 'impersonality postulate of modernity: That impersonal relations are inherently superior to personal relations' (1990: 79). This yields a continuum of contrasting positions, with respect to ontology: from individualism to holism; with respect to cosmology: from instrumentalism to relational context; and epistemology: from positivism to hermeneutics. These contrasts parallel Carol Gilligan's (1982) distinction between masculine/feminine and impersonal/relational perspectives.[10] Banuri links a Foucauldian agenda of resistance and 'resurrection of subjugated knowledges' to a vision of the future in the South. He argues in favour not only of a 'decentralized polity, economy, and society' but also of epistemological decentralization.

The problem, however, with the poststructuralist turn in development thinking is the same with poststructuralism in general: the critique of the Enlightenment easily slips into adoption of the 'other Enlightenment' – romanticism and unreflected reverence for tradition and community; or a postmodern conservatism, which in the end is indistinguishable from anti-modern conservatism. Critique of science is inherent in late modernity and therefore also in development thinking in its present late phase; but it can take an unreflected or a reflexive form. If unreflected, it verges on anti-intellectualism, or possibly, intellectual anti-intellectualism. I will conclude this chapter (and this book: see Chapter 10) by arguing for a reflexive development, which involves a reflexive, rather than a rhetorical and wholesale critique of science.

The notion of indigenous knowledge has developed out of the regard for local knowledge (Chambers 1983; Brokensha et al. 1980; Hobart 1993). 'To ignore people's knowledge is almost to ensure failure in development' (Agrawal 1995b: 3). Indigenous knowledge, or the practical knowledge of people in other cultures, gives substance and depth to otherwise rhetorical categories such as endogenous development.[11] Yet it is difficult – as in the case of other alternative development orientations – to turn indigenous knowledge into a clear-cut principle in view of the absence of a hard boundary between indigenous and other forms of knowledge. After all, what is 'indigenous'? This is also a construction (like 'modernity')

and one that is not devoid of romantic overtones. Agrawal (1995a) makes a
persuasive case that there are no principled grounds on the basis of which indigenous knowledge can be distinguished from scientific knowledge. Rather than
pursuing indigenous knowledge *per se*, Agrawal advocates the combination and
blending of knowledge systems. This note of caution is not meant to neutralize
criticisms from an 'indigenous' point of view but is the kind of qualification that
is necessary if one wants to take these concerns seriously, for instance in relation
to questions such as indigenous intellectual property rights or traditional resource
rights (e.g. Posey 1994).

Development Cooperation

With redefining development comes a different assessment of international
development cooperation. The general trend is away from development assistance
to cooperation and partnership. As Korten notes, the consequences of development assistance or international aid have all too often been anti-developmental:
'it *reduces* capacities for sustained self-reliant development' (1990: 139). Conventional development assistance is a matter of 'moving money' rather than
'building capacity'. This involves the familiar distinction between relief (welfare)
and development: 'Where the needs are chronic, rather than temporary, increasing the amount of humanitarian assistance, especially food aid, is likely to exacer-
bate the problem' (ibid.).

The principle of people's sovereignty or popular legitimacy as the basis of
sovereignty involves a redefinition of development cooperation as principally a
matter of people-to-people relations in which governments play a mediating and
enabling role. Development cooperation then needs to be redefined as a process
of 'mutual empowerment' (Korten 1990: 146-7, cf. Duffield 1996).

If we would group the elements discussed above as an alternative development
model in contrast to a conventional development model centred on growth, the
result might be as shown in Table 6.1. Still the question remains whether this
would constitute an alternative development paradigm or profile; for now the
slightly more neutral terminology of models is adopted. Since the profiles in each
model differ over time, in several boxes multiple options are indicated.

Accepting these as the contours of an alternative development paradigm would
have several attractions. Alternative development ceases to be *any* alternative in
relation to mainstream development. Alternative development as a diffuse position might be effective for alternative development as critique but not as a programme to be implemented. An alternative development paradigm might help the
chances for alternative development to gain recognition and institutional support,
which is necessary if it is no longer about marginal local initiatives supported by
NGOs but if it aims to be a large-scale overhaul of development as such. If alternative development is about wide-ranging synergies between communities,
government agencies, international institutions and business, then its profile must
be both distinct enough and acceptable enough to generate support in institutional
circles and diverse communities of interest. Yet this raises different questions.

Table 6.1   *Development models*

Models	Growth	Social transformation
Objectives	Accumulation	Capacitation, human development
Resources	Capital, technology, trade, foreign investment, external expertise	Human resources, social capital, local knowledge
Features	Growth-led	Equity-led
Agency	State-led or market-led	People, community. Synergies between society, government, market
Epistemology	Science	Critique of science, indigenous knowledge
Modalities	Exogenous examples, demonstration effect, modernity vs. tradition, technology transfer	Endogenous development, modernization from within, modernization of tradition
Methods	Import substitution industrialization, export-led growth, growth poles, innovation, structural adjustment	Participation, sustainability, democratization
Social policy	Trickle-down. Safety net	Trickle-up. Social capacitation through redistribution
Development cooperation	Aid, assistance	Partnership, mutual obligation
Indicators	GDP	Green GDP, Human Development Index, institutional densities

A serious discussion of alternative development as a paradigm would involve its negotiation, renegotiation and fine-tuning in wide circles. This treatment cannot prejudge such a broad discussion; but what does arise is a more fundamental question: whether the notion of paradigm is applicable at all.

Paradigm Politics

The world is tired of grand solutions. (Manfred Max-Neef 1991: 110)

To match Kuhn's concept, a paradigm shift in development would have to meet three conditions: it must provide a metatheory, be accepted by a community of practitioners, and have a body of successful practice, including exemplars that can be held up as paradigms in practice. Sato and Smith (1996: 90) mention these requirements, but their brief chapter fails to deliver a metatheory. In my view more fundamental questions need to be asked. What is the status of a paradigm and is this concept and that of paradigm shift relevant to social science? A paradigm in the sense of Thomas Kuhn (1962) refers to the explanatory power of a theoretical model and its institutional ramifications for the structure and organization of science. The point of Kuhn's analysis is a critique of positivism, particularly in the natural sciences. Kuhn's position was that social science is 'pre-paradigmatic' because a scholarly consensus such as exists in physics or biology is not available in social science.

If we consider this more closely, in the social sciences positivism is largely a past station, except in some forms of economics. The interpretative character of social science has become widely accepted since phenomenology, hermeneutics and more recently the 'linguistic turn'. Also if one does not accept discourse analysis and deconstruction as analytic instruments, the time of blind faith in models and grand theories is left behind. It is generally understood that social sciences are of an extraordinary complexity because they involve political processes that are reflexive in nature, in the sense that social actors will act upon any theory, which is thus modified in action. Constructivism is widely accepted as a theoretical framework in relation to social phenomena as well as in relation to social science theories, which of course are also social phenomena. In constructivism, notions of paradigm and paradigm shift are built in. Pierre Bourdieu's analyses of social science in action are an example (1988) and so is his notion of reflexive sociology (Bourdieu and Wacquant 1992). It follows that in relation to reflexive social science the concept of paradigm does not hold and that social science is basically 'post-paradigmatic' or, at least, non-paradigmatic. In social science 'paradigm' may be used in a loose sense but it does not serve the same function of critique of positivism as in natural sciences, nor does it adequately describe the organization of science.

Recent years have witnessed an outburst of claims for new paradigms in social science, development studies included – a kind of new paradigm epidemic. Paradigm shift is a central theme of postmodernism (McHale 1992, Bauman 1992, Santos 1996) and also figures in claims for 'new science' (Capra 1988). Lipietz (1995) presents political ecology as a new paradigm. Hazel Henderson's work centres on paradigm shifts (1991, 1996a, 1996b). Mahbub ul Haq (1995) proposes a human development paradigm. Norman Long's (1994) 'actor-oriented paradigm' refers to a critique of structuralist approaches in development and a return to anthropological sensibilities.

What is the point of these exercises in a general context of reflexive, constructivist social science? It does signal a watershed, at minimum a more reflexive mentality in social science. But is borrowing from the natural sciences an appropriate move? One impression is that the claims to paradigm shifts primarily serve a political purpose. What is at issue is a claim for political unity and convergence: by emphasizing the intellectual convergence of diverse elements, the chances for political cohesion of diverse constituencies may be enhanced. Part of the appeal of Kuhn's paradigm shift is the element of revolution or a drastic break in intellectual and therefore political practice. But in fact in current usages paradigm is used in a broad and loose sense of an 'intellectual framework', similar to discourse and *episteme*, and not in Kuhn's more specific sense of an explanatory framework that defines the practice of 'normal science'. More often it concerns normative values rather than explanatory and metatheoretical frameworks.

Development, even though it hinges on theory as the beacon of policy, is more concerned with policy than explanatory frameworks. In development, the claim of a paradigm shift means that a policy framework has changed. Thus, ul Haq's human development paradigm refers to a set of normative orientations – equity, sustainability, productivity, empowerment – and not merely to a different explanatory framework. There are still further reasons why the notion of a paradigm shift may not apply to development or alternative development.

The first consideration is diversity in the South. If conventional developmentalism (growth, modernization, neoclassical economics) is no longer acceptable because of its linear logic and universalist pretension, why should an alternative development paradigm hold? There are now 'five Souths' (Group of Lisbon 1995: 47) and a wide range of local variations within each of these: how could a single paradigm encompass such a diversity of development paths, needs and circumstances? Besides, would a new orthodoxy really be desirable? Is what is needed not rather a post-paradigmatic perspective? The diffuseness of alternative development may also be an analytical advantage. Alternative development as a loosely interconnected ensemble of sensibilities and practices is more flexible in resonating with diverse situations than an alternative development paradigm. While a paradigm shift implies a revolution in relation to past work it means routinization in relation to future work. It would fix a practice of 'normal development'. In view of the diversity and flux of the development field such routinization may precisely not be what is desirable. In other words, the urge toward paradigm renewal may itself be inappropriate.

Further considerations in relation to an alternative development paradigm are the following.

❑ The various elements of the alternative development package are each meaningful but none of them can be turned into a firm, hard principle: it follows that alternative development as a paradigm cannot stand up either. The strength of alternative development positions is critical, rather than programmatic.

❑ The elements of the alternative development paradigm are contradictory. In effect endogenism as a principle annuls any general formulation of alternative development. 'If the people are the principal actors in the alternative development paradigm, *the relevant reality must be the people's own, constructed by them only*' (Rahman 1993: 220, emphasis in original). By this logic, how can there be a general alternative development theory, let alone a paradigm? There can only be a sprawling archipelago of local alternative perspectives.

❑ The valorization of indigenous knowledge has similar implications. Giving the alternative development paradigm the status of a metatheory – the usual way out of 'Zeno's paradox' ('the Cretan says that all Cretans are liars') – does not work in this case because it establishes outsiders as experts over insiders.

There is also an institutional dimension to this question. There may be political advantages as well as disadvantages to a sharp break with mainstream development. Sanyal (1994) argues that alternative development has withered because it has not found institutional support, which it has not because agencies, bureaucracies and ministries cannot handle sharp discontinuities in principles and practices (discussed further under 'Mainstream development' below).

The above considerations apply to the *broad* alternative development paradigm (*à la* Hettne, Rahman, Carmen and others) while the Bretton Woods challengers propose a much narrower alternative development paradigm of equitable, sustainable and participatory development. Here a different problem applies: the distinction between the *narrow* alternative development paradigm and mainstream development exists as a rhetorical claim only, for the sole distinctive feature is the insistence that development be equitable. This implies a critique of the trickle-down principle of neoclassical economics; but that too, even in the mainstream, is nowadays hardly a controversial point. This, then, is a clear instance of 'paradigm politics'.

Mainstream Development

Mainstream development here refers to everyday development talk in developing countries, international institutions and international development cooperation. It now seems a long time since development was defined as growth and simply measured by means of per capita GNP. Gradually, starting with basic needs and other heterodox approaches in the 1970s, development has been redefined as enlargement of people's choices and human capacitation (e.g. Sen 1985) and as if people, basic needs, health, literacy, education and housing matter. The Human Development Index (HDI) has become an influential standard. People-centred development is becoming a mainstream position.

This means that there is now considerable overlap between mainstream and alternative development, which share much the same rhetoric, ideals and definition of development: participation, work with the poor and vulnerable groups, local action. This overlap is not always apparent from alternative development discourses, which often tend to stereotype and fix mainstream approaches. This may be a matter of institutional lag or ignorance about changes in the mainstream; or a proclivity to antagonistic posturing in terms of 'us' and 'them', building up the alternative appeal by emphasizing the backwardness of the mainstream. Adherents of alternative development hold different views on the nature of the relationship between alternative and mainstream development. Two extreme positions are that alternative development is to be as distinct and separate from mainstream development as possible (e.g. most Bretton Woods challengers, Kothari, in some respects Korten), or that continuity between mainstream and alternative development both exists and is desirable (e.g. Wignaraja 1992). Most proponents of an alternative development paradigm posit a contradiction between growth and structural reform on the one hand and alternative development on the other. Ul Haq, as a proponent of human development (HD), does not see a contradiction between human development and structural reform. His human development paradigm is identical to the alternative development paradigm except that, characteristically, it includes *production* as a core value.

This also implies a tension between alternative and human development. The limitation of human development, according to some, is that critical concerns are being instrumentalized short of the overhaul of the development-as-growth model, so that in effect development business-as-usual can carry on under a different umbrella. What we see is still a 'fetishism of numbers' (Max-Neef 1991). Friedmann (1992) mentions, besides human and citizen rights, 'human flourishing' as the value orientation of alternative development, precisely to counteract its operationalization in indices such as the Human Development Index. This affirms that alternative development is about something beyond merely another set of measuring standards, which is a point worth making – but only if we *also* consider the importance of indices such as HDI in influencing policy frameworks (Henderson 1996b: 122, ul Haq 1995). Implementation is desirable, practicalities are prosaic, and institutions need measurements. Human flourishing exceeds but also requires human development. In analogy with Moser's (1991) argument on gender needs, one could say that alternative development is not only about practical but also about strategic needs, i.e. a profound redistribution of resources within societies and on a world scale. Except that the alternative development paradigm stakes an even larger claim: the total overhaul of development.

According to Rajni Kothari (1993b), alternatives have been coopted, resulting in 'a world without alternatives'. Kothari complains of 'deep cooptation': not only organizations but mentalities have changed, a critical edge has been lost. He observes 'the consumerism and commercialisation of diverse human enterprise, the basic crisis of vision – in a sense, an end of "alternatives" in the real and comprehensive sense of the term' (1993b: 136). This kind of pessimism, while understandable, seems somehow illogical: what reason is there to assume, short of a fundamental shift in human nature, that the creativity that has given rise to alternatives in one context will not find different avenues of expression, whatever the circumstances and indeed prompted by them? That emancipation can be successful should not be held against it – although it often is, as if a Sisyphean task were a seal of purity. But of course Kothari views cooptation not as success but as capitulation – but doesn't the record look much more varied?[12] Cooptation, besides being logical in view of the way the development field is structured, may be desirable if it means a greater chance that once-marginal views are implemented. There is cause to regret cooptation mainly if one regards alternative development as a position external to the system; but this kind of island mentality is as sterile as delinking as a national development strategy. Governments and NGOs are factually interdependent in terms of agenda setting and funding. The entire field is changing, including government organizations.

An intermediate option is the 'growth plus' approach: growth *plus* redistribution, participation, human development, or 'sustainable growth'. 'Redistribution with growth' was a prominent position in the 1970s (Chenery et al. 1974). Structural adjustment with a human face has been an in-between position (Jolly 1986). Korten (1990) views 'adding on' as a weakness of alternatives and seeks therefore to establish as sharp as possible a break with conventional positions. However, from the point of view of policy implementation and institutional acceptance, 'adding on' may rather be a source of strength, because for bureaucracies in welfare ministries and international agencies total breaks are much more difficult to handle than additional policy options (Sanyal 1994). In view of such political ramifications, is it necessary or wise to formulate alternative development as anti-growth? Ul Haq (1995) argues for continuity, rather than plain contradiction, between growth and human development (cf. Griffin and McKinley 1994). In his view the key issue is the *quality* of growth. Ul Haq builds on the 1970s redistribution with growth position; the difference is that, while arguing for theoretical continuity and policy refinement, he also claims the status of a new paradigm and a 'revolutionary' role for human development. A different consideration is that substantively the nature of economic growth itself is undergoing rethinking, also in the North. An increasingly prominent line of research concerns the links between growth and social development and the idea that social capital is crucial to economic development (see Chapter 8).

Conclusion

Development is not what it used to be. It might be argued that the big hiatus in development now no longer runs between mainstream and alternative development but within mainstream development. Mainstream development now incorporates many alternative development elements and practices. It is the vast stretch of contemporary mainstream development, from the Bretton Woods institutions all the way to grassroots empowerment, that makes for its cacophonic, schizophrenic character. Broadly speaking, the divide now runs between human and alternative development, on the one hand, and the number-crunching approach to development, the positivism of growth, on the other. Institutionally this rift runs between the UN agencies and the IMF, with the World Bank increasingly – and precariously – straddled somewhere in the middle.

The differences between alternative and human development are significant enough but not as wide as those between them and the 'Washington consensus' (or what remains of it). By comparison to alternative development, human development is better positioned institutionally, from the UN system to economics and social welfare ministries in the South; on the other hand, it tends to be bureaucratic in outlook. The bottom line agency of the human development approach is the state, whereas the agency of alternative development is local, grassroots and social movement activism. To alternative development there is a protest element, a polemics against development-business-as-usual which represents a 'local' and grassroots take on development that is probably irreplaceable: witness contributions such as participatory action research. Alternative development brings anthropology into development. Yet alternative development cannot walk away from the role of the state. Education and health care policies cannot be left to local alternative development. Economic development requires state action. This is realized in more recent alternative approaches, which argue that a strong civil society needs a strong state (as in Friedmann 1992, Brohman 1996). This also follows from the need to combine micro and macro approaches to development. Human development provides an enabling perspective on the developmental role of the state. Thus, alternative and human development together represent a combination of local, grassroots and state perspectives. Both approaches also involve different perspectives on global reform. Neither is complete: alternative development cannot do without the state; human development cannot flourish without an active civil society, nationally and internationally. After all, what matters is the direction and character of overall development. In comparison to this question the differences between alternative and human development are relatively minor. The key issue is the relationship between social and human development and the policies followed by the Bretton Woods institutions.

Notes

1 The notion of counterpoint has been inspired by Wertheim's theory of emancipation (1974; cf. Nederveen Pieterse 1989, Ch. 3, 'Counterpoint and emancipation').

2 In the 1995 edition of his book, Hettne fine-tunes his position on alternative development in terms of three principles: 'The principle of territorialism as a counterpoint to functionalism. The principle of cultural pluralism as a counterpoint to standardized modernization. The principle of ecological sustainability as a counterpoint to "growth" and consumerism' (1995: 199). These reformulations are hardly improvements. Territorialism involves a spatial demarcation of development that is as problematic as the ideas on ethnodevelopment (discussed below). Cultural pluralism is now widely accepted and thematized in the culture and development approach (Ch. 5 above). Contrasting sustainability and growth is crude; ul Haq's (1995) point that what matters is not growth but the quality of growth is more to the point. I owe these quotes to a review of Hettne's book by Gasper (1996).

3 Sources include Dag Hammarskjöld Foundation (1975), Nerfin (1977), Wolfe (1981), Klauss and Korten (1984), Drabek (1987), Korten (1990), Hettne (1990), Max-Neef (1991), Friedmann (1992), Rahman (1993), Carmen (1996) and a wide array of articles in books and journals (such as *International Foundation for Development Alternatives*, which dissolved in the early 1990s, and *Alternatives*). Critiques of alternative development are Latouche 1993, Sanyal 1994 and Cowen and Shenton (1996: 457-72).

4 This is the context of Carmen (1996), Coetzee (1989), Guha and Vivekenanda (1985) and also of my work. I teach in an MA programme on Politics of Alternative Development Strategies at a graduate school in development studies. As an anthropologist by original training and after years living in countries in the South, my interests span the range from local development to global alternatives.

5 Brown and Ashman 1996, 1999 discuss various factors that make intersectoral cooperation fail or succeed.

6 New modernization theory as So (1990) notes does take into account traditions as sources of innovation and not just as 'resistance to change'.

7 Sundaram (1994) draws a distinction between 'development from below', which he views as the domain of local, district or regional government, and 'development from within' as the terrain of the village or grassroots. This distinction between endogenous (local government) and within (village) is rather unusual. I owe this reference to Aurora Galindo.

8 Independent of these sources Somjee (1991: 153-7) also uses the term ethnodevelopment but here it means so much as people's development.

9 Carmen 1996 makes this point. See also critiques of participation by Estava 1985 and the treatment by Stiefel and Wolfe 1994. The concepts of participation, empowerment, resistance and emancipation are critically discussed in Nederveen Pieterse 1992b.

10 Western social theories, according to Banuri (1990), view everything – exchange, production, jurisprudence, education, political science, etc. – through the prism of impersonality. The cognitive shift from the personal to the impersonal parallels a shift from internal to external constraints: it represents an advantage for centralized institutions, structures of surveillance and control in knowledge, politics, and architecture. Banuri cites Ashis Nandy's definition of progress as 'an expansion the awareness of oppression' (1990: 91). Gilles Deleuze said about Foucault: 'You have taught something absolutely fundamental: The indignity of speaking on someone else's behalf' (quoted in Banuri 1990: 96). From this follows a critique of the role of the expert: 'It is not for the outside expert to insist that the goals which he or she thinks worth pursuing are the ones which should be pursued by all

societies … the crisis if any stems precisely from the centralized intervention itself' (ibid.: 97). He concludes that 'the main task of the theorist … is to help strengthen resistance against oppressive institutions'. See the critique of Cowen and Shenton (1996: 453-61) on the ironies of this position.

11 A relevant journal is *Indigenous Knowledge and Development Monitor*. In 1993 a Foundation for the Promotion of Indigenous Knowledge Based Development was set up in Mysore, India, along with a Centre for Advanced Research of Indigenous Knowledge Systems. See also Goonatilake 1999.

12 Tony Chiejina (1993) compares Kothari's earlier articles, as founding editor of *Alternatives* in 1975 and subsequently, with his 1993 position. Elsewhere Kothari (e.g. 1993a) is more positive about citizen movements and organizations, recognizing their socially innovative contributions.

7
AFTER POST-DEVELOPMENT

> The idea of development stands like a ruin in the intellectual landscape. Delusion and disappointment, failures and crime have been the steady companions of development and they tell a common story: it did not work. Moreover, the historical conditions which catapulted the idea into prominence have vanished: development has become outdated. (Wolfgang Sachs 1992b: 1)

Along with 'anti-development' and 'beyond development', post-development is a radical reaction to the dilemmas of development. Perplexity and extreme dissatisfaction with business-as-usual and standard development rhetoric and practice, and disillusion with alternative development are keynotes of this perspective. Development is rejected because it is the 'new religion of the West' (Rist 1990a), it is the imposition of science as power (Nandy 1988), it does not work (Kothari 1988), it means cultural Westernization and homogenization (Constantino 1985) and brings environmental destruction. It is rejected not merely on account of its results but because of its intentions, its worldview and mindset. The mindset of economism implies a reductionist take on existence. Thus, according to Sachs, 'it is not the failure of development which has to be feared, but its success' (1992b: 3).

Post-development starts out from a basic realization: that attaining a middle-class life style for the majority of the world population is impossible (Dasgupta 1985). In time this has led to a position of total rejection of development. In the words of Gustavo Esteva,

> If you live in Mexico City today, you are either rich or numb if you fail to notice that development stinks... The time has come to recognize development itself as the malignant myth whose pursuit threatens these among whom I live in Mexico.... the 'three development decades' were a huge, irresponsible experiment that, in the experience of a world-majority, failed miserably. (1985: 78)

Post-development overlaps with Western critiques of modernity and techno-scientific progress, such as critical theory, poststructuralism and ecological movements. It parallels alternative development and cultural critiques of development. It stands to development as 'deep ecology' does to environmental management. There are different strands to this way of looking at development. *Anti-development* is rejectionism inspired by anger with development business-as-usual. *Beyond development* ('au delà de développement') combines this aversion with looking over the fence. In *post-development*, these are combined with a Foucauldian methodology and theoretical framework of discourse analysis and a politics inspired by poststructuralism. These positions are not all consistent and besides, as a recent approach, post-development thinking is not theoretically developed. The overlap among these sensibilities is sufficient to group them together here under the heading of post-development.

Development is the management of a promise — and what if the promise does not deliver? Living in Chiapas or other oppressed and poor areas, chances are that development is a bad joke. The question is what is done with this assessment. Post-development is not alone in looking at the shadow of development; all critical approaches to development deal with its dark sides. Dependency theory raises the question of global inequality. Alternative development focuses on the lack of popular participation. Human development addresses the need to invest in people. Post-development focuses on the underlying premises and motives of development, and what sets it apart from other critical approaches is its rejection of development. The question is whether this is a tenable and fruitful position.

In the 1980s these views crystallized around the journal *Development: Seeds for Change*. They have been taken up by intellectuals in Latin America (Esteva, Escobar), India (see Dallmayr 1996 on the 'Delhi school'), Pakistan (Rahnema and Bawtree 1997), Malaysia (Just World Trust 1995), France (Latouche 1993), Switzerland (Rist 1997), Germany (Sachs 1992a), Belgium (Verhelst 1990), England (Seabrook 1994), Ireland (Tucker 1999), Japan (Lummis 1991). They have become prominent since they coalesce with ecological critiques and ecofeminism (Mies 1986, Shiva 1988b) and through bestsellers such as Sachs' *Development Dictionary*.

First we will consider some of the overt positions of post-development – the problematization of poverty, the portrayal of development as Westernization, and the critique of modernism and science. The argument then turns to the methodological dimension of discourse analysis of development. We will then look at the difference between alternative development and 'alternatives to development'. The reasons why this difference is made out to be so large are, in my interpretation, anti-managerialism and dichotomous thinking. This exposition closes with a discussion of the politics of post-development and a critical assessment.

Problematizing Poverty

An insight that runs through post-development is that poverty is not to be taken for granted. In the words of Vandana Shiva:

> Culturally perceived poverty need not be real material poverty: subsistence economies which serve basic needs through self-provisioning are not poor in the sense of being deprived. Yet the ideology of development declares them so because they don't participate overwhelmingly in the market economy, and do not consume commodities provided for and distributed through the market...(1988b: 10)

Poverty is in the eye of the beholder. Sachs (1999) distinguishes between *frugality*, as in subsistence economies; *destitution*, which can arise when subsistence economies are weakened through the interference of growth strategies; and *scarcity*, which arises when the logic of growth and accumulation has taken over and commodity-based need becomes the overriding logic. In this early work, Sachs' policy recommendation is to implement growth strategies with caution, building on frugal lifestyles. This matches the recommendations made by 'ecological developers' all along, such as the agronomist René Dumont (1965, 1974), to follow growth strategies in tandem with appropriate technology and maximum use of local resources. But the rejection of either growth or development does not follow.

'Poverty' is not simply a deficit, for that is simply to adopt the commodity-based perspective of the North; 'poverty' can also be a resource. Attributing agency to the poor is a common principle in alternative approaches such as con-scientization à la Paulo Freire, human-scale development (Max-Neef 1982, 1991, Chambers 1983), participatory action research and the actor-oriented approach. According to Rahnema, poverty is real enough, but is also a culturally and historically variable notion. 'The way planners, development actomaniacs and politicians living off global poverty alleviation campaigns are presenting their case, gives the uninformed public a distorted impression of how the world's impoverished are living their deprivations. Not only are these people presented as incapable of doing anything intelligent by themselves, but also as preventing the modern do-gooders from helping them' (1992: 169). This is a different issue: it concerns the representation of poverty. By way of counterpoint, Rahnema draws attention to 'vernacular universes' that provide hope and strength; to the spiritual dimension ('Most contemporary grassroots movements have a strong spiritual dimension'; 171); and to 'convivial poverty', 'that is, voluntary or moral poverty' (171). This suggests affinity with the lineage of the Franciscans, liberation theology and Gandhian politics.

In this view, it is the economism of development that is truly pauperizing. While these considerations may be valid up to a point, a consequence is that poverty alleviation and elimination – for what these efforts are worth – slip off the map. Another problem is that less market participation does not necessarily imply more social participation – lest we homogenize and romanticize poverty, and equate poverty with purity (and the indigenous and local with the original and authentic). The step from a statistical universe to a moral universe is worth taking, but a moral universe also involves action, and which action follows?

Development = Westernization

> The debate over the word 'development' is not merely a question of words. Whether one likes it or not, one can't make development different from what it has been. Development has been and still is the *Westernisation of the world*. (Serge Latouche 1993: 160; emphasis in original)

According to Escobar, the problem with 'Development' is that it is external, based on the model of the industrialized world and what is needed instead are 'more endogenous discourses'. The assertion of 'endogenous development' calls to mind dependency theory and the 'foreign bad, local good' position (Kiely 1999). According to Rajni Kothari, 'where colonialism left off, development took over' (1988: 143).[1] This view is as old as the critique of modernization theory. It calls to mind the momentum and pathos of decolonization, the arguments against cultural imperialism, CocaColonization, McDonaldization, Disneyfication and the familiar cultural homogenization thesis according to which Western media, advertising and consumerism induce cultural uniformity.

All this may be satisfying, like the sound of a familiar tune, but it is also one-sided and old-fashioned. In effect, it denies the agency of the Third World. It denies the extent to which the South also owns development. Several recent development perspectives originate to a considerable extent in the South, such as dependency theory, alternative development and human development. Furthermore, what about 'Easternization', as in the East Asian model, touted by the World Bank as a development miracle? What about Japanization, as in the 'Japanese challenge', the influence of Japanese management techniques and Toyotism (Kaplinsky 1994)? At any rate, 'Westernization' is a lumping concept that ignores diverse historical currents. Latouche and others use the bulky category 'the West', which in view of steep historical differences between Europe and North America is not really meaningful. This argument also overlooks more complex assessments of globalization. A more appropriate analytic is polycentrism. Then, the rejoinder to Eurocentrism is not Third Worldism but a recognition that multiple centres, also in the South, now shape development discourse (e.g. Amin 1989; Chapter 2 above).

Critique of Modernism

Part of the anti-Western sentiment is anti-modernism. No doubt development suffers from a condition of 'psychological modernism', has erected monuments to modernism, vast infrastructure and big dams – placing technological progress over human development. States in the South have used science as instruments of power, creating 'laboratory states' (Visvanathan 1988), as in Rajiv Gandhi's high-tech modernization drive in India and Indonesia's experiment in aircraft technology. In Latin America, the work of the *cientificos* is not yet complete. Brazil's commitment to high modernism is on display in Brasilia (Berman 1988). Islamabad in Pakistan is another grid-planned capital city without heart or character. The 1998 nuclear tests in South Asia are another rendezvous of science and *raison d'état* (Subrahmanyam 1998). For Gilbert Rist development thinking represents the 'new religion of the West' (1990a), but indeed the worship of progress is not reserved to the West.

Aversion to modernism also exists in the West; rationalism is one face of the Enlightenment and romanticism is another. There are many affinities and overlaps between critical theory and the counterculture in the West (Roszak 1973, Berman 1988, Toulmin 1990) and anti-modernism in the South. Schumacher ('small is beautiful') found inspiration in Buddhist economics (Wood 1984) and Fritjof Capra in Eastern mysticism, while Ashis Nandy's outlook has been shaped by Freud, the Frankfurt School and Californian psychology.

Part of the critique of modernism is the critique of science. A leitmotif, also in ecological thinking, is to view science as power. 'Science' here means Cartesianism, Enlightenment thinking and positivism, an instrument in achieving mastery over nature. Critique of Enlightenment science runs through the work of Vandana Shiva (1991). But this is not a simple argument. For one thing, science has been renewing itself, for example in quantum physics and chaos theory, and undergoing paradigm shifts leading to 'new science'. In addition there are countertrends within science, such as the methodological anarchism of Feyerabend and the work of Latour (1993). In social science, positivism is no longer the dominant temperament; increasingly the common sense in social science is constructivism. In economics positivism prevails, but is also under attack. Thus, for Hazel Henderson economics is not science but politics in disguise (1996b). A clear distinction should be made between *critique of science* and *anti-science*. Acknowledging the limitations of science, the role of power/knowledge and the uses made of scientific knowledge does not necessarily mean being anti-science. Critique of science is now a defining feature of new social movements North and South (Beck 1992). Ecological movements use scientific methods of monitoring energy use, pollution and climate changes. 'Green accounting' and 'greening the GDP' use scientific standards, but for different ends than previously.[2] Anti-development at times sounds like twentieth-century Luddism, with more rhetoric than analysis and not altogether consistent (e.g. Alvares 1992).[3] From a Third World point of view as well there are other options besides anti-science (e.g. Goonatilake 1999).

It is more appropriate to view modernism as a complex historical trend, which is in part at odds with simple modernization. Thus, the dialectics of modernity are part of modernity, which has given rise to critical modernism and reflexive modernity (Beck 1992). Ironically, the aversion of modernism is also an expression of high modernism, advanced modernity and postmodernism (Lee 1994; cf. Chapters 9 and 10 below).

Development as Discourse

According to Escobar, the 'discourse of Development', like the Orientalism analysed by Edward Said, has been a 'mechanism for the production and management of the Third World... organizing the production of truth about the Third World' (1992b: 413-14). A standard Escobar text is: 'development can best be described as an apparatus that links forms of knowledge about the Third World with the deployment of forms of power and intervention, resulting in the mapping and production of Third World societies' (1996: 213).

Discourse analysis forms part of the 'linguistic turn' in social science. It involves the careful scrutiny of language and text as a framework of presuppositions and structures of thought, penetrating further than ideology critique. Prominent in literature criticism, discourse analysis has been applied extensively in cultural studies, feminism, black studies, and now in social science generally. Discourse analysis contributes to understanding colonialism as an epistemological regime (Mitchell 1988), it can serve to analyse the 'development machine' (Ferguson 1990) and development project talk (Apthorpe and Gasper 1996, Rew 1997) and has become a critical genre in development studies (Crush 1996a, Grillo and Stirrat 1997). Discourse analysis applied to development is the methodological basis of post-development, which in itself it is not specific to post-development; what is distinctive for post-development is that from a methodology, discourse analysis has been turned into an ideological platform.

Escobar (1992b: 419) concurs with Gustavo Esteva that development is a 'Frankenstein-type dream', an 'alien model of exploitation' and besides reflects urban bias. 'The dream of Development is over' and what is needed is 'Not more Development but a different regime of truth and perception' (ibid.: 412-14). Escobar refers to a 'group of scholars engaging in the most radical critique of Development' viewed as the 'ideological expression of postwar capital expansion'. In this view, World Bank studies and documents 'all repeat the same story'. 'Development colonized reality, it became reality'. It 'may be now a past era'. 'The dream of Development is over' (419). To 'establish a discontinuity, a new discursive practice' it is appropriate to 'undertake an archaeology of Development' (414-15). To effect change means to effect a 'change in the order of discourse', to open up the 'possibility to think reality differently'. The grassroots orientation disrupts the link between development, capital and science and thus destabilizes the 'grid of the Development apparatus' (424).

Escobar's perspective provides a broad and uneven *mélange*, with exaggerated claims sustained by weak examples. Broad in combining vocabularies: poststructuralism, social movement theory and development. Uneven in that the argument centres on anti-development but makes no clear distinction between anti-development and alternative development. Exaggerated in that his position hinges on a discursive trick, a rhetorical ploy of equating development with 'Development'. This in itself militates against discourse analysis, caricatures and homogenizes development, and conceals divergencies within development. His perspective on actual development is flimsy and based on confused examples, with more rhetoric than logic. For instance, the claim that the World Bank stories are 'all the same' ignores the tremendous discontinuities in the Bank's discourse over time (e.g. redistribution with growth in the 1970s, structural adjustment in the 1980s, and poverty alleviation and social liberalism in the 1990s). And while Escobar and Esteva associate 'Development' with urban bias, World Bank and structural adjustment policies in the 1980s have been precisely aimed at correcting 'urban parasitism', which for some time had been a standard criticism of nationalist development policies (a classic source is Lipton 1977).

Alternatives *to* Development

Many concerns of post-development are not new and are shared by other critical approaches to development. Post-development parallels dependency theory in seeking autonomy from external dependency, but now taken further to development as a power/knowledge regime. Post-development faith in the endogenous resembles dependency theory and alternative development, as in the emphasis on self-reliance. While dependency thinking privileges the nation state, post-development, like alternative development, privileges local and grassroots autonomy. Alternative development occupies an in-between position: with post-development it shares the radical critiques of mainstream development but it retains belief in and accordingly redefines development. The record of development is mixed and includes achievements (as noted in human development), so what's the point of rejecting it *in toto*? In many ways the line between alternative and post-development is quite thin, again except for the rejection of development.

Scanning 'the present landscape of Development alternatives' looking for 'a new reality', Escobar is 'not interested in Development alternatives, but rather in alternatives to Development'. Alternative development is rejected because 'most of the efforts are also products of the same worldview which has produced the mainstream concept of science, liberation and development' (Nandy 1989: 270). Latouche (1993: 161) goes further: 'The most dangerous solicitations, the sirens with the most insidious song, are not those of the "true blue" and "hard" development, but rather those of what is called "alternative" development. This term can in effect encompass any hope or ideal that one might wish to project into the harsh realities of existence. The fact that it presents a friendly exterior makes "alternative" development all the more dangerous.' This echoes Esteva's fulmination against those who 'want to cover the stench of "Development" with "Alternative Development" as a deodorant' (1985: 78).

Latouche examines 'three principal planks of alternative development: food self-sufficiency; basic needs; and appropriate technologies' and finds each of them wanting (1993: 161). In fact these are part of 'another development' in the 1970s and are no longer specific to alternative development in the 1990s, if only because they have entered mainstream development discourse. Latouche maintains that 'The opposition between "alternative development" and *alternative to* development is radical, irreconcilable and one of essence, both in the abstract and in theoretical analysis.... Under the heading of "alternative development", a wide range of "anti-productivist" and anti-capitalist platforms are put forward, all of which aim at eliminating the sore spots of underdevelopment and the excesses of maldevelopment' (159).

At this point other arguments come into the picture: anti-managerialism and dichotomous thinking. These are not necessarily part of the explicitly stated post-development view, but they might explain the size of the gap between alternative development and post-development.

Anti-managerialism

Development thinking is steeped in social engineering and the ambition to shape economies and societies, which makes it an interventionist and managerialist discipline. It involves telling other people what to do – in the name of modernization, nation building, progress, mobilization, sustainable development, human rights, poverty alleviation, and even empowerment and participation (participatory management). Through post-development runs an anti-authoritarian sensibility, an aversion to control and perhaps an anarchist streak. Poststructuralism too involves an 'anti-political' sensibility, as a late-modern scepticism. If the public sphere is constructed through discourse and if any discourse is another claim to truth and therefore a claim to power, what would follow is political agnosticism. This also arises from the preoccupation with autonomy, the problem of representation and the indignity of representing 'others'.[4]

Douglas Lummis declares an end to development because it is inherently anti-democratic (1991, 1994). Viewing development through the lens of democratization is pertinent enough, not least in relation to the Asian authoritarian developmental states. Nowadays development managerialism not only involves states but also international financial institutions and the 'new managerialism' of NGOs. All of these share a lack of humility, a keynote of the development power/knowledge complex. In post-development there is suspicion of alternative development as an 'alternative managerialism' – which may make sense in view of the record of many NGOs (e.g. Sogge 1996). So what to do? Emery Roe's response, in a discussion of sustainable development as a form of alternative managerialism, is 'Nothing' (1995: 160).

However, as Corbridge argues, 'an unwillingness to speak for others is every bit as foundational a claim as the suggestion that we can speak for others in an unproblematic manner' (1994: 103, quoted in Kiely 1999: 23). Doing 'nothing' comes down to an endorsement of the status quo (a question that returns under the politics of post-development below). Gilbert Rist in Geneva would argue: I have no business telling people in Senegal what do, but people in Switzerland, yes.[5] This kind of thinking implies a compartmentalized world, presumably split along the lines of the Westphalian state system. This is deeply conventional, ignores transnational collective action, the relationship between social movements and international relations, the trend of post-nationalism and the ramifications of globalization. It completely goes against the idea of global citizenship and 'global civil society'. Had this been a general view, the apartheid regime in South Africa would have lasted longer. Under the heading of 'post' thinking, this is actually profoundly conservative.

Dichotomous Thinking

Post-development thinking is fundamentally uneven. For all the concern with discourse analysis, the actual use of language is sloppy and indulgent. Escobar plays games of rhetoric: in referring to development as 'Development' and thus suggesting its homogeneity and consistency, he essentializes 'development'. The same applies to Sachs and his call to do away with development: 'in the very call for banishment, Sachs implicitly suggests that it is possible to arrive at an unequivocal definition' (Crush 1996b: 3). Apparently this kind of essentializing of 'development' is necessary in order to arrive at the radical repudiation of development, and without this anti-development pathos, the post-development perspective loses its foundation.

At times one has the impression that post-development turns on a language game rather than an analytic. Attending a conference titled 'Towards a post-development age', Anisur Rahman reacted as follows: 'I was struck by the intensity with which the very notion of "development" was attacked. ... I submitted that I found the word "development" to be a very powerful means of expressing the conception of societal progress as the flowering of people's creativity. Must we abandon valuable words because they are abused? What to do then with words like democracy, cooperation, socialism, all of which are abused?' (1993: 213-14)

There are several problems with this line of thinking. First, some of the claims of post-development are simply misleading and misrepresent the history of development. Thus, Esteva and several others in the *Development Dictionary* (Sachs 1992a) refer to Truman in the 1940s as the beginning of the development era. But this is only one of the beginnings of the application of development to the South, which started with colonial economics; besides, development has an older history – with the latecomers to industrialization in Central and Eastern Europe, and in Soviet economic planning.

Second, dichotomous thinking, pro- and anti-development, underrates the dialectics and the complexity of motives and motions in modernity and development. Even though at given points particular constellations of thinking and policy seem to present a solid whole and façade, there are inconsistencies underneath and the actual course of development theory and policy shows constant changes of direction and numerous improvisations. Thus, some speak of 'the chaotic history of development theory' (Trainer 1989: 177) and 'the fashion-conscious institutional language of development' (Porter 1996; Chapter 3 above).

Third, post-development's take on real existing development is quite narrow. The instances cited in post-development literature concern mainly Africa, Latin America and India; or reflections are general and no cases are discussed (as with Nandy). The experience of NICs in East Asia is typically not discussed: 'the assertion that "development does not work" ignores the rise of East Asia and the near doubling of life expectancy in much of the Third World' (Kiely 1999: 17).

Politics of Post-development

Strip away the exaggerated claims, the anti-positioning, and what remains is an uneven landscape. Eventually the question to ask is, what about the politics of post-development: fine points of theory aside, what is to be done? Post-development does make positive claims and is associated with affirmative counterpoints such as indigenous knowledge and cultural diversity. It opts for Gandhian frugality, not consumerism; for conviviality, *à la* Ivan Illich, for grassroots movements and local struggles. But none of these are specific to post-development nor do they necessarily add up to the conclusion of rejecting development.

Forming a position in relation to post-development might proceed as follows. Let's not quibble about details and let's take your points on board and work with them. What do you have to offer? This varies considerably: Sachs (1992a) is a reasonable refresher course in critiques of development. Latouche's arguments are often perceptive and useful, though they can also be found in alternative development sources (such as Rahman 1993, Pradervand 1989) and are mostly limited to sub-Saharan Africa. A commonsense reaction may be: your points are well taken, now what do we do? The response of Gilbert Rist is that alternatives are not his affair.[6] The general trend in several sources is to stop at critique. What this means is an endorsement of the status quo and, in effect, more of the same, and this is the core weakness of post-development (cf. Cowen and Shenton 1996).

If we read critiques of development dirigisme, such as Deepak Lal's critique of state-centred development economics – which helped set the stage for the neoconservative turn in development – side by side with post-development critiques of development power, such as Escobar's critique of planning, the parallels are striking.[7] Both agree on state failure, though for entirely different reasons. According to Lal, states fail because of rentseeking; Escobar's criticisms arise from a radical democratic and anti-authoritarian questioning of social engineering and the faith in progress. But arguably, the net political effect turns out to be much the same. In other words, there is an elective affinity between neoliberalism and the development agnosticism of post-development.

Escobar offers one of the more forward post-development positions but is also contradictory. On the one hand he caricatures 'Development' and argues for 'alternatives to Development', and on the other he pleads for redefining development. Other positions, such as that of Sachs, are both more limited and more consistent – all past and no future. *The Development Dictionary* features critiques of the market, state, production, needs, etc., which are historically informed but overstate their case and offer no alternatives, and ultimately fall flat. Recognizing the power/knowledge nexus in discourse, Escobar proposes 'the formation of nuclei around which new forms of power and knowledge can converge' (424). Basic to his approach is the 'nexus with grassroots movements'. He evokes a 'we' that, following Esteva (1985), comprises 'peasants, urban marginals, deprofessionalized intellectuals'. What they share is an 'interest in culture, local knowledge', 'critique of science' and 'promotion of localized, pluralistic grassroots movements'. In another passage, grassroots movements include: women, ecological movements, peasants, urban marginals, civic movements, ethnic minorities, indigenous peoples, popular culture, youth movements, squatter movements, Christian base communities. Their common features, according to Escobar, are that they are 'essentially local', pluralistic, and distrust organized politics and the development establishment.

As nodal points Escobar mentions three major discourses – democratization, difference and anti-Development – which can serve as the 'basis for radical anti-capitalist struggles'. What is 'needed is the expansion and *articulation* of anti-imperialist, anti-capitalist, anti-productivist, anti-market struggles' (1992b: 431). Again, as in 1980s alternative development discourse, this is the aspiration to construct a grand coalition of opposition forces, now combined with a Foucauldian search 'toward new power-knowledge regimes' (432). The desire for a grand oppositional coalition involves the evocation of a 'we' that, in the desire for discontinuity, claims to capture all social movements in the 'Third World', now under the heading of anti-Development. 'Many of today's social movements in the Third World are in one way or another mediated by anti-Development discourses ... although this often takes place in an implicit manner' (431). In the West, social movements militate against commodification, bureaucratization and cultural massification; in the Third World, according to Escobar, they militate 'against bureaucratization achieved by Development institutions (e.g. peasants against rural development packages, squatters against public housing programmes), commodification, capitalist rationality brought by Development technologies' (431).

This is clearly a biased representation: social movements in the South are much too diverse to be captured under a single heading. Many popular organizations are concerned with access to development programmes, with inclusion and participation, while others are concerned with alternative development and renegotiating development, with decentralization, or alternative political action. 'Anti-development' is much too simple and rhetorical a description for the views of the 'victims of development'. Indeed 'victims of development' is too simple and biased a label (cf. Woost 1997). This view suffers from the same problems as early alternative development arguments: it underestimates the desire for and appeal of development and engages in 'island politics' or politics of marginality. Besides, it is contradictory. In its reliance on deprofessionalized intellectuals and distrust of experts, post-development rubs shoulders with anti-intellectualism, while it also relies on and calls for 'complex discursive operations'. Post-development no longer focuses on class interests and is postmarxist in outlook, yet Escobar also reinvokes radical anti-capitalist struggles. Like some forms of alternative development, post-development involves populism, now seasoned by an awareness of the articulation effect; yet its striving for a new articulation of anti-imperialist, anti-capitalist and other movements is populist.

At the same time, the political horizon of post-development is one of resistance rather than emancipation. Made up of resistance à la Scott, it participates in the 'romance of resistance' (Abu-Lughod 1990). Its other component is local struggles à la Foucault. Earlier I argued that in post-development discourse analysis is used not merely as an analytical instrument but as an ideological tool (Chapter 1); this becomes apparent when it comes to politics. As many have argued (Said 1986, Hoy 1986), Foucault's imagination of power is an imagination without exit. Foucault engages in a 'monologue of power' (Giri 1998: 198). In the footsteps of this logic, post-development takes critique of development to the point of retreat. Retreat from business-as-usual can be a creative position from which an alternative practice may grow. Thus critical theory and its negation of the negation, though pessimistic in outlook, has served as a point of reference and inspiration, for instance to social movements of the 1960s. But the imaginary of power that inspires post-development leaves little room for forward politics.

The quasi-revolutionary posturing in post-development reflects both a hunger for a new era and a nostalgia politics of romanticism, glorification of the local, grassroots, community with conservative overtones. Different adherents of post-development advocate different politics. Escobar opts for a 'romance of resistance'. The politics of Gilbert Rist are those of a conventionally compartmentalized world. Rahnema opts for a Confucian version of Taoist politics (discussed in Chapter 9 below). Ray Kiely adds another note: 'When Rahnema (1997: 391) argues that the end of development "represents a call to the 'good people' everywhere to think and work together", we are left with the vacuous politics of USA for Africa's "We are the World". Instead of a politics which critically engages with material inequalities, we have a post-development era where "people should be nicer to each other"' (1999: 24).

In the *Power of Development*, Jonathan Crush offers this definition: 'This is the power of development: the power to transform old worlds, the power to imagine new ones.' The context is a comment on a colonial text: 'Africans become objects for the application of power rather than subjects experiencing and responding to the exercise of that power' (1996b: 2). Crush comes back once more to the power of development: 'The power of development is the power to generalize, homogenize, objectify' (22). There is a disjuncture between these statements. While the first is, or seems to be, affirmative, the other two are negative. Clearly something is lost in the process. It is what Marx called, and Schumpeter after him, the process of 'creative destruction'. What happens in post-development is that of 'creative destruction' only destruction remains. What remains of the power of development is only the destructive power of social engineering. Gone is the recognition of the creativity of developmental change (cf. Goulet 1992). Instead, what post-development offers, besides critique, is another series of fashionable interpretations. Above all it is a cultural critique of development and a cultural politics (Fagan 1999). This reflects on more than just development: 'development' here is a stand-in for modernity and the real issue is the question of modernity.

Coda

Post-development is caught in rhetorical gridlock. Using discourse analysis as an ideological platform invites political impasse and quietism. In the end post-development offers no politics besides the self-organizing capacity of the poor, which actually lets the development responsibility of states and international institutions off the hook. Post-development arrives at development agnosticism by a different route but shares the abdication of development with neoliberalism. Since most insights in post-development sources are not specific to post-development (and are often confused with alternative development), what is distinctive is the rejection of development. Yet the rejection of development does not arise from post-development insights as a *necessary* conclusion, that is, one can share its observations without arriving at this conclusion: in other words, there is no compelling logic to post-development arguments.

Commonly distinguished reactions to modernity are neotraditionalism, modernization and postmodernism (e.g. McEvilley 1995). Post-development belongs to the era of the 'post' – poststructuralism, postmodernism, postcolonialism, postmarxism (postcapitalism?). It is premised on an awareness of endings, on 'the end of modernity' and, in Vattimo's words, the 'crisis of the future' (1988). Post-development parallels postmodernism both in its acute intuitions and in being directionless in the end, as a consequence of the refusal to translate, or lack of interest in translating, critique into construction. At the same time it also fits the profile of the neotraditionalist reaction to modernity. There are romantic and nostalgic strands to post-development and its reverence for community, *Gemeinschaft*, the traditional and there is an element of neo-Luddism in the attitude toward science and technology. The overall programme is one of resistance rather than transformation or emancipation.

Post-development is based on a paradox. While it is clearly part of the broad critical stream in development, it shows no regard for the progressive potential and dialectics of modernity – for democratization, soft power technologies, reflexivity. Thus, it is not difficult to see that the three nodal discourses identified by Escobar – democratization, difference and anti-development – *themselves* arise out of modernization. Democratization continues the democratic impetus of the Enlightenment; difference is a function of the transport and communication revolutions, the world becoming 'smaller' and societies multicultural; and anti-development elaborates the dialectics of the Enlightenment set forth by the Frankfurt School. Generally, the rise of social movements and civil society activism, North and South, is also an expression of the richness of overall development, and cannot be simply captured under the label 'anti'. Post-development's source of strength is a hermeneutics of suspicion, an anti-authoritarian sensibility, and hence a suspicion of alternative development as an 'alternative managerialism'. But since it fails to translate this sensibility into a constructive position, what remains is whistling in the dark. What is the point of declaring development a 'hoax' (Norberg-Hodge 1995) without proposing an alternative?

Alternative development thinking primarily looks at development from the point of view of the disempowered, from bottom-up, along a vertical axis. It combines this with a perspective on the role of the state; in simple terms: a strong civil society needs a strong state (Friedmann 1992). Post-development adopts a wider angle in looking at development through the lens of the problematic of modernity. Yet, though its angle is wide, its optics is not sophisticated and its focus is blurred. Its take on modernity is one-dimensional and ignores different options for problematizing modernity, such as 'reworking modernity' (Pred and Watts 1992), or exploring modernities in the plural (Nederveen Pieterse 1998b). More enabling as a position is reflexive modernity and a corollary in relation to development is reflexive development (Chapter 10 below).

In my view post-development and 'alternatives to development' are flawed premises – flawed not as sensibilities but as positions. The problem is not the critiques, which one can easily enough sympathize with and which are not specific to post-development, but the companion rhetoric and posturing, which intimate a politically correct position. 'Alternatives to development' is a misnomer because no alternatives to development are offered. There is no positive programme; there is critique but no construction. 'Post-development' is misconceived because it attributes to 'development' a single and narrow meaning, a consistency which does not match either theory or policy, and thus replicates the rhetoric of developmentalism, rather than penetrating and exposing its polysemic realities. It echoes the 'myth of development' rather than leaving it behind. Post-development makes engaging contributions to collective conversation and reflexivity about development and as such contributes to philosophies of change, but its contribution to politics of change is meagre. While the shift toward cultural sensibilities that accompanies this perspective is a welcome move, the plea for 'people's culture' (Constantino 1985) or indigenous culture can lead, if not to ethnochauvinism and 'reverse orientalism' (Kiely 1999: 25), to reification of both culture and locality or people. It presents a conventional and narrow view of globalization, equated with homogenization. On a philosophical level we may wonder whether there are alternatives to development for *homo sapiens* as the 'unfinished animal', i.e. to development writ large, including in the wide sense of evolution.

Notes

1 Elsewhere Kothari addresses development in more affirmative ways.

2 Modernism and science are also discussed in Chapter 9.

3 Alvares (1979) proposes appropriate technology as an alternative approach.

4 In some ways this matches the weary anti-politics sensibility of intellectuals in Eastern Europe (Konrád 1984). On representations of others, according to Crush, 'The current obsession with Western representations of "the Other" is a field of rapidly diminishing return' (1996b: 22).

5 In correspondence with the author.

6 At a seminar at the Institute of Social Studies, The Hague.

7 Both papers are reproduced side by side in Corbridge 1995.

8

EQUITY AND GROWTH
REVISITED: A SUPPLY-SIDE
APPROACH TO SOCIAL
DEVELOPMENT

Does combining a variety of arguments on the relationship between equity and growth yield new insight? Redistribution with growth, prominent in the 1970s, is currently being revisited. East Asian experiences can also be considered with a view to equity. Human development makes a strong case for combining equity and growth along the lines of human capital, but leaves the social dimension unexplored. Studies of welfare states add finesse to equity-growth arguments. Sociology of economics addresses questions of embeddedness, social capital, networks and trust, which are relevant in this context. By adding novel elements, this chapter seeks to arrive at a new overall perspective on social development.

On the occasion of the World Summit for Social Development in Copenhagen in 1995, benevolent statements were issued on the relationship between growth and equity, such as 'Economic growth and social development impinge on each other, i.e. broadly effective social progress is not possible without a socially oriented economic and finance policy' (*Development & Cooperation*, 1, 1995: 12). Here an attempt is made to probe such rhetorical statements to find a core of policy-relevant thinking.

'Social orientation' can have several meanings. In the framework of Copenhagen the dominant tendency has been to relegate questions of social development to poverty alleviation. What may be necessary however is to challenge the Washington consensus in development not merely in policy terms, resulting in an adjustment (but not a structural adjustment) of structural adjustment, but also in intellectual terms. Revisiting Keynesian management strategies (Singer 1996) may be important but one wonders whether they are a viable option in the context of accelerated globalization. Here I explore the equity-growth argument.

First let me briefly refer to two alternative positions: *rejecting growth* or, alternatively, pursuing *equity without growth*. A prominent set of positions for various reasons rejects growth, such as ecological views, according to which more is not better, and alternative development views, according to which what matters is not growth but development that is equitable, sustainable and participatory. In many instances this view is accompanied by a repudiation of growth *per se*. A further position is post-development, which repudiates not only growth but also development as such. A general problem with these positions (discussed in

Chapters 6 and 7 above) is that the target is too wide: what should be at issue is not growth as such but the quality of growth. Exploring this is the point of juxtaposing growth and social development. Clearly 'growth' is a deeply problematic category. The mere question of how growth is defined and measured raises numerous problems. On the other hand, simply rejecting growth may leave us with too narrow a position and too narrow a political coalition to implement whatever policies seem desirable.

At a general level it may be argued that what many people desire is not growth but change, qualitative transformation. Marshall Berman (1988: 47) refers to 'the desire for development'. It seems that the point is not to go against this desire, or complex of desires, not to adopt a confrontational approach, a politics of purity or abstinence, which would invoke resistance; but to transform and channel desire, or, at risk of sounding patronizing, an education rather than a suppression of desire. The marketplace represents powerful and dynamic forces in society, which resonate with deep-seated drives – not merely to 'accumulate, accumulate' but also to 'change, change' and 'improve, improve'. Market forces alienate and marginalize many in society, but is the appropriate response to marginalize, alienate or ignore market forces in return? A wiser course may be to explore what common ground exists between the market and social development, or the scope for a social market approach. The target is not the market but the unregulated market.

A different option is to pursue equity without growth. This kind of approach has been referred to as 'support-mediated security' (Drèze and Sen 1989).[1] This may give us the 'Kerala model' – a constellation of advanced social policies and comparatively high levels of education, health and female empowerment. From the mid-1970s, as Kerala was acquiring international model status, it was slipping into a major crisis, including 'severe stagnation in the spheres of material production, soaring unemployment, acute fiscal crisis and erosion of sustainability of the social welfare expenditures' (Isaac and Tharakan 1995: 1995).[2] Growing unemployment may be due to the fact that investors shun a state where the unions, with the backing of state government, are too strong; that at least is the position of the local rightwing backlash, which coincides with international press comments (e.g. Straaten 1996). This refers us to the familiar chronicles of Western welfare states in the era of post-Fordism and globalization and the question of 'social dumping'. Still, aside from the deeply politicized question of how to account for the Kerala crisis, one conclusion is that 'in the absence of economic growth it is difficult to sustain, much less expand, welfare gains' (Isaac and Tharakan 1995: 1993).

So we turn to equity with growth, summed up under the heading of social development. The point here is not to make a case for social development in *moral* terms, in the name of solidarity, compassion or decency. Thus, according to Galbraith (1996), 'In the good society there must not be a deprived and excluded underclass'. It is not that such moral considerations are irrelevant but they are of limited purchase. Moral economies and discourses are unevenly distributed so that achieving a political consensus purely on moral grounds is unlikely. Moral arguments invite trade-offs – the appeal of moral policy may be outweighed by the importance of economic growth. Since in conventional views growth is supposed to trickle down, morality would be merely a matter of time: in time growth policies will generate moral outcomes. Hence moral considerations tend to be practically outflanked and too easily neutralized by growth policies.

Neither is the point to make a *political* case for social development. Social and welfare policies enhance political stability and legitimacy but they also invite trade-offs – between political legitimacy and political efficacy or state autonomy. A classic position is that collective demands are to be restrained so that collective interests will not crowd out state autonomy and state capacity to take reform measures. The absence of social development may prompt uncontrolled informalization, including ethnic and religious mobilization and a growing underground economy. These are important considerations but they are not the main line of argument followed here.

Rather, the point is to consider the case for social development on *economic* grounds, in relation to growth itself. Or, to examine the case whether, how, to what extent and under which circumstances social development is good for growth, beneficial to business. Phrasing it in contemporary language, the point is to explore the scope for a market-friendly social development. This line of thinking involves classic debates – on the welfare state, on the 'big trade-off' between equality and efficiency (Okun 1975), on modernization and equality. Here this question is revisited by considering several lines of research and bodies of literature, to see what the present scope is of social development arguments and whether their combination yields new insight. This may be worth doing considering that 'there is no very strong tradition of doing macroeconomics as if poor people and social processes mattered' (Taylor and Pieper 1996: 93).

Relevant lines of research include the following. (1) Redistribution with growth. Prominent in the 1970s, these views are currently being revisited. (2) Lessons from East Asia. Usually discussed with a view to the role of state intervention, they can also be considered with a view to equality and equity. (3) Human development. This approach makes a strong case for combining equity and growth along the lines of human capital, but leaves the social dimension and social capital unexplored. (4) Lessons from welfare states. (5) New institutional economics provides institutional analyses and sociology of economics addresses questions of embeddedness, social capital, networks and trust. Other bodies of literature are relevant to social development – such as comparative studies of social security, the regulation school, post-Fordism, associational democracy – but fall outside this treatment. The point of this exercise is to find out what they add up to when various arguments on equity and growth are grouped together and, by adding novel elements that are not usually combined with social development, to arrive at a new overall perspective.

Social Development

It is appropriate first to delineate in what sense social development is used here. One narrow meaning of social development is public welfare policies of health, education and housing. This approach, as Midgley (1995) points out, suffers from compartmentalization: the separation of social policies from development policies. The Copenhagen summit was not free of this tendency: social development often referred to or ended up in the basket of poverty alleviation (cf. UNRISD 1995). For the same reason, the present argument does not concern the social economy, progressive market or socially responsible business, cooperatives or fair trade (e.g. Ekins 1992). Not because they are not important, but because they represent a compartmentalized or at least a partial approach. The focus is on the overall economy rather than on particular segments. Secondly, social development can be used in a disciplinary sense, if it is distinguished from in particular economic development (e.g. Booth 1994a).[3] The third option, which is followed here, is to view social development in a substantive and comprehensive manner with equal emphasis both on 'social' and on 'development': in other words an integrated approach to social concerns and growth strategies.

Midgley defines social development as 'a process of planned social change designed to promote the well-being of the population as a whole in conjunction with a dynamic process of economic development' (1995: 25). Here the notion of planning carries dirigiste overtones (while in effect Midgley argues for 'managed pluralism'), which raises the question of the agency of social development.

The dominant discourse of social development used by governments, international institutions and many NGOs is as a terrain of social policy: which means a social engineering, managerial approach to social development. This is apparent if we leaf through the reports submitted to the World Summit for Social Development.[4] The bodies of literature reviewed here reflect this general tendency, except for sociology of economics, which looks at the social from the ground up. We might term this a society-centred approach to social development or, possibly, social development from below. Actual social security concerns much more than government social policy, such as family and local networks (e.g. Hirtz 1995, DSE 1994). As Ann Davis (1991: 84) remarks, 'Of course, social work agencies are only one way of replenishing family and friendship networks'. When social security falls outside conventional social policy, how could a conventional approach to social development be adequate? Accordingly, implicit in 'social development' are multiple layers of meaning: whether social development is compartmentalized or linked to development; whether it is managerial, from above, or society-centred, from below.

Redistribution with Growth

In the 1970s growth and redistribution literature several currents of thought came together. Adelman and Morris (1967) developed an approach to social development influenced by modernization theory; their social development index may be read as a modernization index.[5] At a time when Keynesian demand management played a prominent part, Gunnar Myrdal adopted a productivist or supply-side approach. According to Myrdal, 'welfare reforms, rather than being costly for society, actually lay the basis for more steady and rapid economic growth' (quoted in Esping-Andersen 1994: 723; cf. Myrdal 1968). In presenting redistribution as a *precondition* to growth, Myrdal followed a Swedish tradition. 'The unique contribution of Swedish socialism was its idea of "productivist" social policy. Its leading theoreticians stood liberalism on its head, arguing that social policy and equality were necessary preconditions for economic efficiency, which, in turn, was a prerequisite for the democratic socialist society' (Esping-Andersen 1994: 713)

The Swedish concept of a 'productivist social justice' in which 'the welfare state invests in optimizing people's capacity to be productive citizens' contrasts with 'the strong Catholic influence in Continental European welfare states [which] has resulted in a policy regime that encourages women to remain within the family' (1994: 722). The productivist approach to social justice addresses the standard criticism of Keynesian policies that they concern demand only and ignore supply factors. We find echoes of productivist arguments in human development (below) and the regulation school.

In a well-known World-Bank sponsored study, Hollis Chenery and associates (1974) argued that egalitarian and developmental objectives are complementary, a position that favoured redistribution of income and assets to the poorest groups. If we now reread *Redistribution with Growth* and sequel studies (such as Adelman and Robinson 1978), we see that they are inspired by dissatisfaction with the mainstream course followed during the first development decade. This egalitarian approach was outflanked and clipped by the rise of monetarism, supply-side economics and neoconservativism in the 1980s. It makes sense to revisit these arguments taking into account subsequent trends and addressing the misgivings about dirigisme, rents and rent seeking, welfarism and dependency.

In the 1990s the idea of redistribution with (or for) growth regained ground in mainstream development policy, with some new inflections: a general concern with social indicators in measuring development, to the point of redefining development itself; an emphasis on human capital; and a growing critique of trickle-down. A World Bank report to the Copenhagen summit, *Advancing Social Development*, notes: 'How growth affects poverty depends greatly on the initial distribution of income. The more equal the distribution of income to start with, the more likely it is that poverty will be reduced for a given increase in average income' (1995: 4-5). Hence the World Bank recognition of the importance of safety nets for the poor when implementing deficit reduction (23). This World Bank package includes 'promoting labor-demanding growth, investing in people, providing safety nets, and improving governance' (48). In this fashion social development is assimilated as part of structural reform – as a supplementary safety net, as structural adjustment with a human face, or as 'stage two' of structural reform and the political stabilization of reform policies.

In view of the importance of the initial distribution of income and its effect on poverty alleviation, would merely installing safety nets be logical or adequate? It would seem that to achieve these effects more far-reaching measures are called for. In addition what is at issue are structural reform policies themselves and their underlying economic rationale. The actual challenge is to examine the nexus not merely between income distribution and poverty alleviation but between equity and growth. Redistribution with growth, in a mix of productivist and demand management elements, also informs South Africa's Reconstruction and Development Programme (cf. Moll et al. 1991).

Lessons of East Asia

Equitable development policies are widely recognized as a crucial factor in East Asian development. Thus, 'there is substantial evidence to suggest that equity in income distribution and decent welfare systems are friends not enemies of growth, a pattern strikingly clear for Japan, Taiwan, Hong Kong, Korea and Singapore where equity and growth have gone hand in hand' (Weiss 1996: 195). World Bank studies acknowledge that one of the initial conditions for rapid growth in East Asia

> was the relative *equality of income* in the first generation NIEs [Newly Industrialising Economies]. This factor was more of a change brought about by policy than an inheritance. Most other low- and middle-income countries were not able to achieve similar equality of income or assets. Large land reform schemes in both Korea and Taiwan, China, did away with the landholding classes and made wage income the main source of advancement. Public housing investments in Singapore and Hong Kong were early priorities of governments bent on maintaining a national consensus on development policies. (Leipziger and Thomas 1995: 7)

This point is often noted: 'some of the advantages of the rapidly growing East Asian countries were their unusually low initial income inequality in 1960 and their labor-demanding pattern of growth, which tended to reduce income inequality over time' (World Bank 1995: 5).

Education policies are part of this equation. The World Bank study on *The East Asian Miracle* 'shows that the single most important factor in launching the miracle countries on a path of rapid, sustained economic growth was universal or near-universal primary school enrolment... In 1960 Pakistan and Korea had similar levels of income, but by 1985 Korea's GDP per capita was nearly three times Pakistan's... In 1960 fewer than a third of the children of primary school age were enrolled in Pakistan while nearly all were enrolled in Korea' (ibid.: 34).

Such evidence is less conclusive in relation to the late NICs in Southeast Asia. In Malaysia between 1970 and 1990, the New Economic Policy established an interethnic trade-off between Bumiputras and Chinese (economic gains for the Malays and political citizenship rights for the Chinese, without infringement on their economic position) that was made possible by rapid growth rates and foreign investment, and that resulted in equity among Malays and Chinese (but excluding inhabitants of Sabah and Sarawak, the indigenous Orang Asli, and Indians) (Gomez 1994, Jomo 1995). Policies pursuing equity and growth have been less in evidence in Thailand, play a minor part in Indonesia and have been absent in the Philippines.

While the elements of equity in the growth path of East Asian NIEs are noted in World Bank and other studies, they are not often highlighted. In Leipziger and Thomas' *Lessons of East Asia* they figure in the text but not in their 'Development Checklist', which features items such as selective industrial policies and directed credit (1995: 2). Debates on the East Asian NICs have concentrated on the question of the efficacy of government interventions – as the primary challenge to neoclassical economics and its emphasis on trade liberalization as the clue to Asian economic success. The question of the 'governed market' (Wade 1990) or 'governed interdependence' (Weiss 1996) and the everlasting debate on state or market (Wade 1996) has tended to overshadow other issues such as equity and growth. In an Asian perspective on the 'East Asian Miracle' study, equity and growth, or 'shared growth', is mentioned in passing while the emphasis is on the institutional capacities of government (Ohno 1996: 20, Iwasaki et al. 1992).

The emphasis on the authoritarian character of Asian regimes (which is itself a variation on the well-worn theme of 'Oriental despotism') biases the discussion. References to Confucianism and 'Asian values' are not particularly helpful either. The first distinctive feature of East Asian authoritarian government is that it has been *developmental* – unlike, say, Somoza's authoritarianism or that of predatory states; the second is that in significant respects it has been *cooperative* in relation to market and society – unlike Pinochet's regime in Chile. The third is that it has not only disciplined labour but also capital. What has been overlooked or downplayed is the coordinating character of government intervention in East Asia and the ingenious political and social arrangements which have been devised in order to effect social policies in a market-friendly fashion, or vice versa, to effect market support strategies in a society-friendly fashion (Weiss 1996, Ohno 1996). Specific examples include state support for small and medium-size businesses in Taiwan (Hamilton and Woolsey Biggart 1992), Singapore's housing policy (Rodan 1989, Hill and Kwen Fee 1995) and Malaysia's new economic policy. China's experiences in combining the market economy and social development are also worth examining (Gao 1995, Griffin 2000b).

Human Development

> Empowerment is not only democratic, it is efficient. (Griffin and McKinley 1994)

The human development (HD) perspective takes the further step of making a general case for the nexus between equity and growth. According to Keith Griffin (1996: 15-17), 'under some circumstances, the greater is the degree of equality, the faster is likely to be the rate of growth'. His considerations include the cost of the perpetuation of inequality and that inequality undermines political legitimacy while 'modern technology has destroyed the monopoly of the state over the means of violence'. Furthermore, 'measures to reduce inequality can simultaneously contribute to faster growth'.

> There is much evidence that small farms are more efficient than either large collective farms of the Soviet type or the capitalist latifundia one finds in Latin America and elsewhere. A redistributive land reform and the creation of a small peasant farming system can produce performances as good if not better than those of other agricultural systems. The experience of such places as China and Korea is instructive… what is true of small farms is equally true of small and medium industrial and commercial enterprises. An egalitarian industrial structure, as Taiwan vividly demonstrates, can conquer world markets. (Griffin 1996: 17; cf. Fei et al. 1979)

Further elements mentioned by Griffin are investments in education – 'There is probably no easier way to combine equality and rapid growth. The whole of East Asia is testimony to the veracity of this proposition' – and the liberation of women. 'A final example of the falsity of the great trade-off is the liberation of women. Equal treatment of women would release the talent, energy, creativity and imagination of half the population' (ibid.: 17; cf. Buvini et al. 1996).

A broadly similar case is made by ul Haq, who mentions 'four ways to create desirable links between economic growth and human development' (1995: 21-2): investment in education, health and skills; more equitable distribution of income; government social spending; and empowerment of people, especially women. Ul Haq proposes a HD paradigm of equity, sustainability, productivity, and empowerment (1995: 16). It is the element of productivity that sets this paradigm apart from the alternative development paradigm. This refers to the supply-side factor as the nexus between equity and growth.

This position is not necessarily controversial from the point of view of neo-classical economics. HD owes its definition to the emphasis on the investment in human resources, human capital, which is prominent in the East Asian model and Japanese perspectives on development and is now a mainstream development position. The growing knowledge intensity of economic growth, as in innovation-driven growth and the emphasis on R&D and technopoles, reinforces the argument that investment in human capital fosters growth. Ul Haq rejects the idea that adjustment and HD would be antithetical, either conceptually or in policy: 'Far from being antithetical, adjustment and growth with human development offer an intellectual and policy challenge in designing suitable programmes and policies... The challenge of combining these two concerns is like that of combining the conflicting viewpoints of the growth school and the distribution school in the 1970s' (1995: 7-8). The same reasoning informed 'structural adjustment with a human face' (Jolly 1986).

It is not difficult to find confirmation for human capital arguments in neoclassical economics:

> welfare economics and human capital theory provide important market-conforming justifications for a range of social policies, most notably for public health and education... neoclassical economics is inherently theoretically elastic. The theory of market failure may, in fact, justify a 'residual' welfare state, while information failure theory can be applied to argue for a fully fledged, comprehensive welfare state. (Esping-Andersen 1994: 712)

Nevertheless, the author continues, neoclassical economics emphasizes the efficiency trade-offs associated with welfare policies, specifically negative effects on savings (and hence investments), work incentives, and institutional rigidities (as with respect to labour mobility). In other words, neoclassical economics can both acknowledge and deflect welfare arguments by treating them as subsidiary to growth as the primary objective, so that in the end welfare policies end up on the backburner. The key aim should be, rather, to zero in on those elements in the equity-growth debate which are controversial or which open up the framework of neoclassical economics.

The HD approach skirts rather than confronts this issue. This follows from the fact that HD follows the human capital argument, which is part of rather than outside the paradigm of neoclassical economics. In addition, in assuming the *individual* as the unit of human development HD shows that its intellectual roots are in liberalism.[6] HD may also be interpreted as the lessons of East Asia translated into general policy. As such one way of reading it is as a meeting point between the authoritarian state and the neoliberal market, with the state acting as the supplier of human skills to the market, through human resource development programmes, packaged to achieve effective global competition. Merging social concerns and market concerns is excellent, but the question is, on which terms? According to ul Haq there is no contradiction in principle between structural reform and HD, it is only a matter of designing the right policy mix. This means that HD may be institutionally and ideologically acceptable to all sides. Since HD does not challenge but goes along with market logic, it does not in a principled way address the problem of the unregulated market.

HD has been inspired by Amartya Sen's capabilities approach to development (1985). An obvious question is, if capacitation is the objective and measure of development, then who defines capacity, ability, or human resources? What about the disabled, unwed mothers, the aged? What about human traits that *cannot* be translated into economic inputs, resources?[7] Besides, if capacitation and the enlargement of people's choices are the yardstick of development, as HD would have it, should we also consider say the Medéllin Cartel a form of capacitation and enlargement of people's choices? As Gasper (1997) argues, to Sen's capabilities approach there is no moral dimension. To the extent, then, that HD does not challenge neoliberalism and the principle of competitiveness but endorses it, HD may enable development business-as-usual to carry on more competitively under a general 'humane' aura. Then, social development, if sharpened, redefined and renewed in a wider framework, may be a more inclusive and enabling perspective than HD.

Lessons of Welfare States

Looking at social development side by side with the welfare state serves two purposes. It bridges the increasingly artificial divide between developed and developing countries and it helps to clear the path from economic generalizations to institutional and political questions. It might also, on the other hand, confuse issues: equity-growth policies do not necessarily have to take the form of the welfare state, which is a specific institutional arrangement.

It is not difficult to find econometric confirmation for the general positive correlation between equity or equality and growth: 'virtually every single statistical study concludes growth is positively related to equality' (Esping-Andersen 1994: 723); 'most econometric studies conclude that inequality is harmful to growth' (725). However, aside from methodological limitations, a fundamental theoretical fallacy is implicit in this approach. Ironically, this echoes the fallacy inherent in neoclassical economics, namely the tendency to abstract economic factors from institutional and political dynamics. According to Esping-Andersen, 'the narrowly economic framework of the neoclassical model' is the reason for 'the curious gap between theoretical claims and empirical findings': 'The model is consistent only when it leaves out political and social variables; studies that incorporate them invariably produce contradictory results' (724).

The welfare state may also be thought of as a particular way in which the economy is embedded in society. 'The welfare state is not something opposed to or in some way related to the economy; it is an integral element in the organic linkage of production, reproduction and consumption... what we think of as the postwar welfare state is but one crucial regulatory element in the Fordist system of mass production' (Esping-Andersen 1994: 716-17). The failure of welfare states lies not so much in fiscal strain but can rather be seen as a 'manifestation of a mounting incompatibility between a fossilized welfare state, on one hand, and a rapidly changing organization of production and reproduction, on the other hand' (717). This refers to a series of shifts – toward service production, of industrial production to NICs, from standardization to flexibility, and from the Fordist family to women's economic independence, dual-earner households and non-linear life patterns. In welfare arrangements, this may involve shifts toward the Schumpeterian workfare state (Jessop 1994) and toward welfare pluralism (Mishra 1996).

The reorganization of production is a function of new technologies and changing consumer demand (flexible accumulation) as well as globalization and the rise of the NICs. The crisis of welfare states, then, is also, in part, the other side of the coin of East Asian economic success. For instance, 'the redistributive Keynesian demand-stimulus policy, which served very well to assure adequate demand for domestically produced mass-consumption goods ... became increasingly counterproductive when such goods originated in Taiwan and Korea' (Esping-Andersen 1994: 717). This suggests that the framework in which equity and growth are conventionally considered – the society or nation state – needs to be opened up, eventually to a global scope.[8]

Studies of welfare states highlight their diversity. This includes distinguishing between residual welfare states (USA), lean welfare states (Switzerland, Japan), productivist welfare states (Scandinavia), and the Rhineland welfare states which tend to uphold status differences rather than being egalitarian. These distinctions may be merged with dynamic arguments on the relationship between equity and growth.

Arguments on the relationship between equity and growth coined in general terms are superseded by 'more complex, interactive models that posit curvilinear relationships between welfare states and economic performance' (Esping-Andersen 1994: 723). Such arguments suggest that up to a certain point the welfare state will have a positive influence on economic growth but that this then turns increasingly negative. Another curvilinear model suggests that 'full employment is best secured in countries where collective institutions (and the Left) are either very weak or very strong... In the former case, labor market clearing is largely left to naked market forces; in the latter, to political management' (724). Accordingly,

> the effect of a welfare state cannot be understood in isolation from the political-institutional framework in which it is embedded ... there may exist a trade-off between equality and efficiency in countries where the welfare state is large and very redistributive but in which the collective bargaining system is incapable of assuring wage moderation and stable, nonconflictual industrial relations. Thus, in concrete terms, a Swedish, Norwegian, or Austrian welfare state will not harm growth, while a British one will (even if it is smaller)... if we turn to a dynamic interpretation, the evidence suggests that as long as a large and redistributive welfare state is matched by neocorporatist-style

political exchange mechanisms, equality and efficiency are compatible; when the capacity for harmonious political bargains ceases to function, the same welfare state may threaten economic performance. (725-6)

One line of argument is that once a certain level has been reached growth yields diminishing returns in terms of welfare and wellbeing (Daly and Cobb 1994). This calls to mind an earlier argument of Keynes on diminishing returns of the pursuit of surplus (Singer 1989).

Similar dynamic and curvilinear arguments have been made in relation to 'social capability': 'a country's potential for rapid growth is strong not when it is backward without qualification, but rather when it is technologically backward but socially advanced' (Temple and Johnson 1996: 2). How to define and measure 'social capability'? Putnam (1993) looks at associational membership and survey measures; Myrdal (1968) considered levels of mobility, communication and education. Temple and Johnson (1996: 1) are concerned with the 'social factors that play a role in the speed of catching up' and they define social capacity narrowly as 'the capacity of social institutions to assist in the adoption of foreign technology' (3). They follow the Adelman and Morris index of social development and conclude from their findings that the 'relative importance of investments in physical capital and schooling appears to vary with the extent of social development' (41).

Social Capital

This brings us to the wider question of the institutional embeddedness of social policies. At the end of the day arguments about equity and growth cannot be made in generic terms. They are political questions or, more precisely, for their economic rationale to be operative they depend on institutional arrangements and political settlements. New institutional economics focuses on the institutional requirements for economic growth such as legal frameworks and structures of rights, while the growing body of work on sociology of economics examines the embeddedness of economic behaviour.

The standard literature on social development is, as mentioned before, dominated by questions of social policy. Literature on economic performance increasingly turns towards social issues (e.g. Granovetter 1992, Stewart 1996), but on an entirely different wavelength. Since the two fields hardly meet it is an interesting exercise to consider their possible intersections. They concern two dimensions of social development: social policy and the economic significance of social networks and relations of trust, which is often summed up under the heading of social capital. Social capital refers to a widely ramifying range of arguments, with various possible intersections with social development, depending on which angle on social capital one adopts.[9]

For Bourdieu (1976) a key concern is that of the relations among economic, social, cultural and symbolic capital, which he regards as cumulative and interchangeable. Current interest is more concerned with social capital as a clue to economic capital, an asset in the process of accumulation. Social capital in this sense may be appropriated in a rightwing perspective, in which civil society serves as a counter (rather than as a complement) to the state. According to Fukuyama (1995: 103), 'The character of civil society and its intermediate associations, rooted as it is in nonrational factors like culture, religion, tradition, and other premodern sources, will be key to the success of modern societies in a global economy.' Building intermediate associations may be an alternative to the role of government and to 'social engineering', which are held to be a dead end. Leftwing takes on social capital make a similar case, but this time aiming to address not state failure but market failure. With a view to the success of corporatist strategies in East Asia and continental Europe, various forms of 'concertation' may be recommended as redress for market failure. Communitarianism emphasizes building community and civic virtue. In Britain, rethinking social democracy combines ideas about rebuilding community, the social market or social economy (Sheffield Group 1989) and 'stakeholder capitalism' (Hutton 1995) with the renewal of democracy, as in associative democracy (Hirst 1993, Amin 1997).

These concerns overlap with an extensive literature on industrial districts and local economic development, which goes beyond agglomeration economies and transaction cost arguments to incorporate relations of trust (Harrison 1992, Ottati 1994) and institutional densities (Amin and Thrift 1993) as elements that go into the making of regional economic performance. Politics of place may also involve local culture as a dimension of economic performance (Hanloe et al. 1990; Lash and Urry 1994). Analyses of the 'Third Italy' from the point of view of associative economics also refer to local democracy as an economic asset. This may take the form of a New Left productivism, centred on 'the popular construction of cooperation through citizenship and authentic participation, in politics and the workplace' (Amin 1997: 316). In this context the informal economy may be viewed as a permanent arrangement, which may be further developed, for instance in the form of labour exchange networks (e.g. exchanging child care for gardening), in combination with an active and capacious state.

These rightwing and leftwing takes on social capital are both upbeat, optimistic, in viewing social capital as an avenue either to outflank the state or to combine strong civil society, strong state, strong economy. Social capital has thus become a new terrain of rhetorical positioning and ideological contestation, which calls for greater analytic clarity.

Quite influential in putting social capital on the map has been Putnam's (1993) study of the course of administrative decentralization in Italy since the 1970s. According to Putnam, those regions in Italy, in the north, which have a historical legacy of civic associations and participatory local government have reacted well to administrative decentralization in terms of regional government and economic performance; while the Mezzogiorno, which has been governed historically along centralized and vertical lines, shows high rates of failure both in administration and economic achievement. His conclusions come down on the side of 'history as destiny' and carry a conservative bias. Putnam's work has been criticized for misconstruing 'path dependency', misreading Italian history and stereotyping the South (Levi 1996, Sabetti 1996). Besides, this approach leaves no room for the possibility of nurturing or generating social capital. The record of several countries shows that the vicious circle can be broken. In East Asia policy interventions have been able to create economically enabling political and institutional conditions within reasonably short time spans, even in countries that had been used to vertical and centralized government. In other words, levels of trust are not simply historical givens but can be fostered through an appropriate policy mix. Policy performance can be a source of trust, not just a result.

Notions such as social capital and the social market carry a double meaning: they refer to the socialization of the market and at the same time to the instrumentalization or commodification of social relations. The notion of 'trust as a commodity' exemplifies this double move (Dasgupta 1988). Likewise there are different dimensions to embeddedness. At a general level the point is that the economy is embedded in society; down the ladder of abstraction, any market relationship is embedded in a specific social configuration. A few considerations may clarify the range of applicability of social capital. (1) Social capital is particularistic. To networks there are boundaries, and boundaries are exclusionary. 'Neighborhoods... are a source of trust and neighborhoods are a source of distrust. They promote trust of those you know and distrust of those you do not, those not in the neighborhood or outside the networks' (Levi 1996: 51). The other side of embeddedness is exclusion; the other side of trust is risk. Social capital then may be a strategy of risk management. (2) Social exclusion and closure facilitate trust and cooperation by ensuring the predictability of relations and preventing the leakage of resources. (3) Concentrating social capital has long been a fundamental strategy of power: witness the circles of privilege of aristocracies, 'old boy' networks, clubs, inner circles, secret societies, lodges, sects and crime networks. It has also been a strategy of subversion, insurgence, revolution, or conquest of state power: witness the Jacobins, Carbonari and the cells in international communism. Women's networks have cultivated sisterhood and autonomy. Features in common include boundary-establishing rituals of initiation that serve to concentrate social capital, create bonds of obligation, establish a circle of trust and a common frame of understanding. (4) Cooperation can also be a competition strategy. Examples range from alliances, non-aggression pacts or peace treaties to firm mergers, all of which seek to reduce risk.

As Coleman notes, 'most forms of social capital are created or destroyed as byproducts of other activities' (1988: 118). The question is what difference policy can make, in other words, can social capital or civic participatory culture in some fashion be nurtured, fostered, or harnessed as part of social development policies? In addition, to look for enabling features of social capital one must look not merely at internal relations within groups but at relations *among* groups. Under what conditions do we get widening circles of social capital?

On the premise that embeddedness involves inclusionary and exclusionary elements, the work on 'ethnic economies' may serve as an example (Light and Karageorgis 1994, Waldinger et al. 1990); the informal economy may also be a field of inquiry (e.g. Portes 1994). An interesting line of research would be not merely ethnic economies but *interethnic economies*, in other words the development or generation of trust across ethnic boundaries. For instance, the Chinese diaspora in the Pacific Rim countries involves not merely ethnic enclave economies but a wide range of collaboration with locals, such as joint ventures (Seagrave 1996).

What attitude governments take in relation to these forms of cooperation can make a huge difference. The New Order government of Suharto utilized the Chinese business community as a classic 'trading minority', 'the Jews of the East' – keeping them politically dependent, with limited political rights, while nurturing relations with a small coterie of tycoons (Irwan 1996); whereas the Malaysian new economic policy (1970-90) has been able to strike an interethnic deal.

It would follow that a policy of *democratization*, rather than polarization, of interethnic relations can contribute to economic achievement. This may be an instance with wider implications. Social development in this sense refers to policies promoting social trust among and across diverse communities – classes, status groups, minorities, etc. It may also refer to the creation of social infrastructure such as housing, schools, clinics, water supply; or asset development among low-income groups to encourage savings among the poor, which will foster social investments (Midgley 1995: 160). Government can play a facilitative role, in the form of managed pluralism. Synergies between regional, urban and local economic development are another relevant approach. The principle of cooperation also applies to relations among firms and between firms and subcontractors (see e.g. Dore 1992 on goodwill in Japan).

An extensive literature documents intersectoral cooperation and synergies in the context of community or local economic development (CED, LED). This approach may also have international, macro-regional and global implications (cf. Thrift and Amin 1997, Kuttner 1991, Gerschenkron 1992). The emerging theme of transnational social policy is worth considering (Deacon et al. 1998). A further proposition is that of a World Social Development Organization to effect economic and social policy jointly on a world scale (Petrella 1995: 22). Examining transnational social capital in the informal (Portes 1996) and the formal sector (Strange 1996) may enrich these propositions.

Conclusion

> Economic growth does not cause an increase in the quality of life, but increase in quality of life does lead to economic growth. (Mizanur Rahman Shelley, Center for the Study of the Global South 1994: 62)

Structural adjustment programmes and social safety nets make up a convenient combination, and so do the 'Washington consensus' and the Copenhagen summit. In this configuration, social development is a matter of tidying up after the market: a polarizing mode of economic growth, followed by social impact studies to assess its pauperizing impact and poverty alleviation measures to compensate for the immiserization effect. This is the repair or damage control mode of social development. Upon closer consideration it is not so much social development as social fixing and political risk management. Along the way, however, social inequality entails not merely a moral cost and political consequences: 'there is a point at which social injustice undermines economic efficiency' (Center for the Study of the Global South 1994: 15).

In development theory a distinction runs between development as planned change or engineering, and development as immanent change, a process from within (Cowen and Shenton 1996). Modernization theory followed a logic of development from above and outside. Structural adjustment follows in the same footsteps. Modernization policies in the past, and at present the application of liberal productivism to developing countries, first *destroy* existing social capital for the sake of achieving economic growth, and then by means of social policy seek to *rebuild* social tissue. Obviously along the way there is a lot of slippage, displacement, and realignment of power relations. Pursuing Darwinist economics and then sending Florence Nightingale after to tidy up the damage is a cumbersome and economically counterproductive approach to development.

The point of this chapter is to take social development beyond poverty alleviation toward a substantive and pro-active approach. The second objective is to go beyond the human capital approach of human development. A productivist approach to social development involves not merely investing in education, health, housing – the standard fare of human capital approaches – but also accommodating and investing in networking across communities and groups and designing enabling institutional environments – in other words, a social capital or participatory civic society approach. As a supply-side approach, i.e. enhancing productivity and output, rather than promoting consumption, this addresses the criticism of Keynesian demand stimulus policies on the part of the supply-siders of the 1980s. To address the problem of technological change and jobless growth requires a wider approach of investment-led growth (cf. Griffin 2000a).

On several grounds and in multiple fashions – human capital, social capital, democratization – social development can contribute to overall economic achievement. In the words of Amin and Thrift (1997: 160), 'the argument within socioeconomics that there can be a close connection between democracy and economic success is to be welcomed in our market-driven age'. If the market dominates it might as well serve socially useful purposes.

The neoclassical trickle-down argument cannot be made in generic terms because outcomes vary according to political and social circumstances; for the same reason, equity-growth or *trickle-up* arguments cannot be made in general terms either: as such they would have very limited purchase. A social productivist approach might require an interventionist, developmental state,[10] but this may be too heavy-handed. A more modest approach is managed pluralism (Midgley 1995). Intersectoral synergies between local government, NGOs and people's organizations and firms are another field of cooperation (Brown and Ashman 1999, Wignaraja 1992).

Managed pluralism involves political regulation. Merging social and market concerns also involves the development of collective bargaining systems. This may be difficult to achieve in segmented societies. Ethnic segmentation is a case in point; caste and class antagonism is another obstacle. A civic culture that strongly privileges individualism, as in North American free enterprise culture, may be more conducive to a casino mentality than to socially inclusive political settlements. Even so, one application of this kind of approach would be to review affirmative action policies in the United States and reservations policies in India. For these legacies need not to be taken as destinies. The point of the social development approach is not to provide a menu but to suggest a direction of analysis and policy.

Social development, redefined in a wide sense, can serve as an orientation for a new social contract and as such become a new assembly point for development.

Notes

1 In considering infant mortality rates, Drèze and Sen (1989) distinguish two patterns: growth-mediated security, in which the crucial factor in lowering infant mortality rates have been growth and employment (e.g. in Hong Kong, Singapore, South Korea) and support-led security in which infant mortality rates have come down although growth rates have been low (in Chile, Costa Rica, Jamaica, Cuba during the 1970s). The latter countries have since changed course or been overtaken by events: Chile embarked on a different course under the Pinochet regime; Costa Rica and Jamaica have implemented macroeconomic reforms since the 1980s; Cuba's economy is stagnant.

2 In view of the status of the Kerala model (Robin 1992), a little more information may be in order. 'The open unemployment rate is around three times the national average.... Kerala has earned the dubious distinction of being the only state in India whose real social expenditure has decreased during 1985-86/1991-92 period, compared to the decade 1974-75/1984-85' (Isaac and Tharakan 1995: 1996). Further discussions are Tharamangalam 1998 and 'The Kerala model of development: a debate' 1998.

3 This is a British usage, parallel to e.g. social anthropology.

4 For instance, Indonesia's report to the Copenhagen summit is entirely framed by the 'Presidential Instruction No. 5/1993 regarding the Intensification of Efforts to Alleviate Poverty', the so-called IDT Program (IDT Program Implementation Guide, Jakarta, National Development Planning Agency and Ministry of Home Affairs, 1994). A report such as *Social Dimensions in the Agenda of the IDB* (Inter-American Development Bank 1995) is also confined to an inclusionary social policy approach. By contrast, the parallel meeting organized by NGOs followed a different track. An example is the Philippine Rural Reconstruction Movement's *The Way of Power: Development in the Hands of the People* (Quezon City 1994) which develops a civil society and grassroots-centred Sustainable Rural District Programme, in other words, a social action and participatory policy approach. Several submissions combine social action and policy approaches, from below and above, such as Møller and Rasmussen (1995). UNRISD (1995) reviews various approaches, from poverty alleviation to participatory social policy and notions such as promoting global citizenship.

5 The components of the Adelman-Morris index of social development are: size of the traditional agricultural sector; extent of dualism; extent of urbanization; character of basic social organization; importance of indigenous middle class; extent of social mobility; extent of literacy; extent of mass communication; crude fertility rate; degree of modernization of outlook (in Temple and Johnson 1996: 10).

6 Cultural bias may be another limitation to HD. Griffin and McKinley (1994) seek to accommodate this by making HD responsive to cultural difference and disaggregating HDI according to ethnic groups within society. Griffin (2000b) takes this a step further by considering cultural difference as an engine of economic growth.

7 Paul Streeten (in ul Haq 1995: xi) mentions the conflict between human resource developers (who emphasize HD as a means to growth) and humanitarians (who view it as an end and are also concerned with the unproductive and unemployable).

8 I address this in a paper on the 'interaction of modernities' (Nederveen Pieterse 2000c).

9 This context only allows a brief engagement. There is now a broad stream of publications on social capital particularly in economics and political science.

10 Or, an 'intelligent' or educator state that is ahead of civil society, such as France and Singapore; a principle that is not part of the Anglo-American tradition, which leans towards the minimal state.

9

CRITICAL HOLISM
AND THE TAO
OF DEVELOPMENT

For Vincent Tucker

Life is poetic and harsh, momentary and evolutionary, personal and abstract, physical, emotional, mental and intuitive. Human experience is layered and multi-faceted, but social science, circumscribed by a Cartesian and Newtonian matrix of knowledge, captures only a narrow slice of experience. Disciplinary bound-aries further narrow and theories bend the range. Development processes likewise take place across dimensions – on a physical level, in an ecological framework, as shifts in social relations, changes in emotional landscapes, on a mental plane, in a political field, a historical context, on a moral plane and in a universe of meaning. Given the partial nature of development theories – which reflect disciplinary territories – and policy interventions – which, in addition, reflect political and institutional interests – the development field is carved up in many ways. How then to arrive at a comprehensive approach? Opting for a holistic approach may produce syntheses that are too quick and whose centre of gravity is located outside social science, for instance in ethics, so they yield commen-taries with outsider status. One can identify the world of development as 'a total-ity of fragments' and the world of capitalisms as one of 'difference within a structured totality' (Pred and Watts 1992: 11); yet that does not tell us very much. In fact the notion of 'fragments' implies some kind of pre-existing wholeness. Responding to this dilemma is the context of this chapter. This is a reflexive chapter that is concerned with questions of general methodology and philosophy of development.

Remedying Remedies

This treatment is inspired by Vincent Tucker's work on critical holism, which he developed in relation to sociology of health. He combines sociology of health with critical development studies. In criticizing the role of transnational pharma-ceutical industries and their commercialization of health he arrives at a new com-bination of concerns – holism and critical thinking, or holism with a bite, holism with an attitude. Part of this is an anthropological sensitivity to cultural dimen-sions of development (Tucker 1996b), a personal engagement with healing, which include following a holistic health course and taking a degree in holistic massage, and interests ranging from music to psychotherapy.

Tucker's starting point is modern medicine, or the biomedical approach: the 'clinical gaze', 'a pill for every ill' (1997: 37), 'a magical fix for all ailments' (30), and the idea that 'health = doctors + drugs' (1996a: 17); a hegemonic system sustained and propagated by medical professionals and pharmaceutical industries. All along his interest has been not only in the politics of dependence in the South and Ireland but also in the possibilities for dependency reversal (Tucker 1996c) and, likewise, in alternatives to conventional medicine. In this respect his approach differs from treatments of modern medicine which are primarily critical (e.g. Nandy 1995; Kothari and Mehta 1988). Modern medicine is contrasted to an emerging 'new holistic health paradigm' (1997: 32) which is considered at several levels. 'The emergence of the holistic paradigm will require not only a change in the practice of medicine and health care, but also in the knowledge system and the model of science on which it is based. It will also require changes in the institutional fabric of health care' (ibid.). At the same time his approach is concerned with extending holism itself: 'it also addresses weaknesses in holistic thinking and practice by incorporating into the model perspectives from more critical traditions of public health' (1996a: 1). For instance Fritjof Capra's work, 'like most approaches to holism, is less well developed when it comes to incorporating social, economic and cultural systems into the model' (1997: 42). Hence Tucker distinguishes between

> two versions or tendencies in holistic thinking. One focuses primarily on the individual organism. Most holistic health practice belongs to this tendency. It differs from biomedicine in that in its diagnostic techniques and therapies in takes into account a broader range of systems, which include the biological, the energetic, the psychic, the interpersonal and the spiritual. While it is more cognisant of the social and environmental factors which impact on the health of the individual, and takes these into account in its diagnosis, it does not provide ways of analysing or intervening in these macro systems. The second version of holism derives from the more sociological approach of Engels and Virchow... It also derives from the public health tradition. It encompasses economic and political systems as well as biological and environmental systems and is based on the notion that health and illness are not simply biological phenomena but are socially produced. This more sociologically informed holism has been further developed by Marxist political economy and radical development theory... (1997: 42)

Tucker then initiates a further move. While the sociological tradition 'adds a critical edge often missing in holistic health practice... it has little to contribute to our understanding of the personal and interpersonal dimensions of illness and well-being' (1997: 43). Finally: 'The critical combination of these two perspectives, which forms the basis of an expanded and more critical notion of holism, can provide a comprehensive alternative to the biomedical model' (ibid.).

Vincent Tucker's synthesis involves multiple movements: from biomedical reductionism to holism, from individual holism to sociological holism, from sociology and political economy to holism in personal, interpersonal and spiritual dimensions. The components of critical holism are spelled out in several places: 'a critical synthesis of holistic medicine, political economy, development theory, environmentalism and feminism... a theoretical synthesis of holistic theory,

Marxist political economy and culture critique' (1996a: 3); 'critical holism encompasses social, economic, political and environmental systems including world systems' (1996a: 41). In health practice this yields the following combination: 'A holistic perspective on health promotion, while not excluding biomedical interventions, may include public health practices, environmental campaigns, political action, educational activities and complementary forms of medicine. It will include not only changes in personal life style, but also collective action to challenge organisations and institutions... which act in ways detrimental to public health' (1997: 45).

This is a high-wire synthesis. While it is developed in relation to health it addresses gaps in our knowledge that are of general relevance. Its triple movement – providing remedies and remedying not only the original deficiencies but the shortcomings of the remedies as well – is welcome medicine in relation to development studies and social science generally. It involves a developed sense of balance. Thus, we all know, not only intellectually but viscerally, the limitations of modern medicine. We may acknowledge the merits of holism, while its weakness is also evident – no critical edge, no political economy. The reverse applies to political economy – materialist savvy and sociological finesse, but no emotional or spiritual depth. If in a combined movement all these are brought together, balancing the limitations of each with the strengths of others, we have a bridge of uncommon strength and sophistication. This has been Vincent Tucker's contribution. In passing, Tucker notes that his critical holism paradigm 'also provides a basis for elaborating a general theory of human development' (1996a: 1), so it is worth probing what would be the general ramifications of this synthesis. Generally, the limitations of a position or paradigm are often remedied by switching to another position while the limitations of *this* position are not addressed. People often move from one ideological fix to another. The result is the usual pendulum swing alternating between extremes – a common spectacle in everyday politics and theory, and an everlasting merry-go-round of limited options.

Critical holism is an uncommon synthesis. Criticism and holism refer to different modes of cognition. This makes it a welcome synthesis: without a critical edge, holism easily becomes totalizing, romantic, soggy. Without holism, criticism easily turns flat, sour. If we re-code these sensibilities, perhaps the synthesis becomes easier. To 'criticism' there are several strands: it refers to the exercise of analytical faculties; it means a repudiation of 'faith' and dogmatism in the Enlightenment tradition; it entails a commitment to class struggle in Marxism; an emancipatory knowledge interest in critical theory; and equality and social justice in dependency theory. Key elements of criticism then are analysis, anti-dogmatism and social justice. How does this tally with holism as a concern for the whole, the totality? If we take criticism in its affirmative sense it means acknowledging dimensions which have been *left out*. Through criticism an inclusive knowledge is to be achieved, which represents those elements which are outside or not acknowledged in the status quo. Accordingly, criticism is also an attempt at healing in the sense of restoring wholeness – by acknowledging and rendering visible that which has been ignored, left out. In a broad sense both criticism and holism then refer to modes of healing: from the point of view of completeness in a societal sense by way of emancipation and justice, and from the point of view of wholeness in a multidimensional sense.

Conventional therapies implicitly refer to 'wholeness' through the notion of deficiencies. Through 'additives' or supplements, food or vitamin deficiencies can be remedied. Only, here wholeness is confined to the physical sphere, which permits medicalization and 'fixing'. Modern medicine recognizes psychological dimensions of health, as in psychosomatic illness, but these are compartmentalized away in domains such as psychology, psychiatry, neurology. (Here the idea of multiple layers is well established – such as the id, ego and superego in psychoanalysis – but this hardly feeds back into conventional medicine.) The difference between holistic and conventional therapies is that the former acknowledge emotional, psychological, spiritual (and moral and social) levels of being as dimensions of health and well-being, and seek to integrate them into the healing process.

Wholeness, Holism

> Once the whole is divided, the parts need new names. (Lao Tsu, 6th century BC, 1973: 29)

According to a dictionary of word origins, '*Whole* is at the centre of a tightly knit family of English words descended from prehistoric Germanic *khailaz* "undamaged"' (Ayto 1990: 573). Other members of this family include *hail* 'salute', *hale, hallow, heal, health* and *holy*. 'Etymologically, *health* is the "state of being whole"…. The verb *heal* [OE] comes from the same source' (277). '*Holy* originated as a derivative of the prehistoric Germanic adjective which produced modern English *whole*, and so its etymological meaning is perhaps "unimpaired, inviolate"' (285). In Germanic languages there is a connection between health, healing, holiness and wholeness which also exists in other language groups, as in Latin *salvus* 'healthy', *salus* 'bliss, health', Irish *slan* 'healthy, whole', Greek *holos* 'whole', old Indian *sarva* 'undamaged, whole' (de Vries 1963: 257). 'Saviour' (Dutch heiland) means 'healer' and connects to the Greek *soter* (de Vries 96). The Dutch *genezen* (healing, healed) refers to Gothic *ganisan* 'saved, healthy, holy', which may be connected to Greek *neomai*, 'I come back, come home'. According to an etymologist (de Vries 82), this would give the meaning of 'coming home safely'.

Health, then, refers to a state of wholeness, and healing is restoring a person to wholeness. Viewed in this light 'holistic healing' becomes a tautology, for apparently all along health basically means wholeness and healing 'making whole'. This tautology makes sense only in distinction to conventional medicine. Holism, in this light, appears to be a cerebral attempt at *recovery* of interconnections lost in the course of analysis, in the process establishing different connections.

Holism is defined as 'the theory that whole entities, as fundamental and determining components of reality, have an existence other than as the mere sum of their parts' (*Random House Dictionary of the English Language*, quoted in Craig 1992: 4). 'Jan Christiaan Smuts gave the word currency in his 1926 book *Holism and Evolution*, where he advocated the exploration of matter, life, and mind in relation to each other, rather than as isolable realms of existence. Since then, *holistic* has been applied to approaches and attitudes, in the humanities and the social sciences as well as the sciences, that privilege the study of a system over analysis of its parts' (ibid.: 4-5). In Smuts' work wholeness and holism are used interchangeably. His book follows an essay of 1912, 'An inquiry into the whole'. *Holism and Evolution* is a high-minded work that was influenced by the Cambridge Platonists, Bergson's vitalism, and ideas of evolution from Darwin to de Vries (Meurs 1997). Holism in this work derives from Greek *holos* and stands for 'the activity of the Whole'. 'Holism that is the ultimate activity which prompts and pulsates through all other activities in the universe' (Smuts, quoted in Meurs 1997: 115). The first chapter deals with 'The holisation of the whole' which refers to assimilation and homogenization processes (Meurs 1997: 118).

Apparently there is slippage between wholeness and holism. As a notion wholeness is evocative and descriptive, whereas to holism there is a programmatic element. Now *systems* thinking comes into the picture, as part of the analysis recovery syndrome. Once the analytical mode has generated distinctions and separations, systems thinking is an attempt to piece together again that which has been taken apart. The attributes of system, however, are unlike the properties of wholeness. Holism may be a step forward in relation to the Enlightenment habit of taking everything apart but it's short of wholeness. Humpty Dumpty put together again is not the same Humpty Dumpty. *Esprit de système* is not the spirit of wholeness. More precisely, there are different notions of system. It derives from the Greek *synhistanai*, 'to place together', so to understand things systematically means to put them in a context and to establish the nature of their relationship. This relationship may be thought of as calculable and machine-like, as in mechanistic notions of system; or as approximate network relations, as in general systems theory (Capra 1996: 27f.). In social science the notion of system ranges from structural functionalism *à la* Parsons, and world-system theory, to the complex systems approach of Niklas Luhmann. In Luhmann's words: 'Sociology can only describe society in society.... It is a science of the social system and a social system of science. To make matters even more complex, as a science and, as a social system, sociology is also an internal observer of whatever system it participates in' (quoted in Lee 1997: 15). One problem of systems approaches is that they imply a closure of the field; they achieve understanding (and manipulability) by framing the field, and even reflexivity may not remedy this.

It makes sense then to distinguish between wholeness and holism as perspectives with related but separate lineages: wholeness refers to a comprehensive field which may be divided according to spiritual criteria (there are divisions also in mystical or magical universes); holism is the systemic or scientific recombination of fragments in a new totality. From a historical point of view, wholeness resonates with neolithic and older sensibilities, while holism brings to mind the technology and mindset of the industrial era. While there are continuities between wholeness and holism, 'This is not to say that the differences between modern holistic thinkers and earlier ones are easily reconcilable' (Dunn 1986: 3). Both are relevant angles, each with its range of applicability.

The slippage between wholeness and holism leaves room for a politics of holism. In combination with ideas of evolution, holism can apparently be taken in any political direction. Jan Smuts is a case in point. A Cambridge graduate, back in South Africa Jan Smuts became a general, minister of defence and mining in the new republic and Prime Minister from 1919 to 1924 and during the Second World War. A pro-British Boer and an empire builder in the tradition of Cecil Rhodes, he was part of the Milner Group, and as a member of the British Imperial War Cabinet he was a party to the Balfour Declaration which partitioned Palestine, and an active negotiator in the partition of Ireland (Quigley 1966, Sampson 1987, Nederveen Pieterse 1989). Smuts endorsed segregation and introduced pass laws. His views on the 'native question' in South Africa were much like those of Rhodes. Africans, 'if left to themselves and their own tribal routine... do not respond very well to the stimulus of progress'. Therefore, in white areas 'the system should only allow the residence of males for limited periods, and for purposes of employment among the whites' (quoted in Minter 1986: 43).[1]

To wholeness there are obviously many dimensions. Wholeness is evoked in mysticism, myth, religion. Faces of wholeness in the theatre of the gods are Pan, who gives us the word for 'all', Okeanos or the world stream and Varuna the encompasser. Wholeness carries intimations of the unity of being as in *unio mystica*, oceanic feeling, cosmic consciousness (Mehta 1989). Religion is replete with 'whole' metaphors such as the tree of life, wheel of life, dharma, 'Thou art That' and other references to the inner interconnectedness of phenomena. Paradise is a state of wholeness and the fall means the loss of wholeness. Paradise regained is wholeness regained. In Christian theology 'the whole of creation' envelops the non-human world. A conventional difference between mysticism and religion is that, in the former, wholeness may be a matter of experience, while in religion it becomes a point of doctrine, so that religion relates to mysticism as abstraction does to experience. While some religions superimpose a 'monotheistic consciousness', 'our psyches are "polytheistic" by nature' and contain an inner pantheon (Ahmed 1997: 33, 36). Wholeness is woven into personal experience – in life's transitions, in love, in experiences of pain and healing, in peak experiences. The paradox of wholeness is the powerful materiality of life and the immaterial nature of the full realization of life. Wholeness includes 'life beyond', but there is no life beyond without life within. The materiality of life makes transcendence possible and constrains it, casting a spell of material life that is shattered only at life's edges – in peak experiences or in the face of death.

It is not difficult to read philosophy from Plato to Aquinas, Hegel to Heidegger as elaborations, systematizations of sensibilities originally set forth in vision, revelation, religion, although to say so is of course sacrilege in reverse. At least, this is the argument of the *philosophia perennis* (à la Huxley 1946). Neo-Platonism, one of the strands in idealistic philosophy, connects Eastern religions with Western philosophy (Nederveen Pieterse 1994). What comes to mind is Hegel's view of world history as a rendezvous with the unfolding *Geist*. Richard Rorty is reproached for his 'undifferentiated, monotonous holism' (Bhaskar 1991: 100), which involves yet a different meaning and facet of holism.

So as a theme, wholeness functions like a kaleidoscope of sensibilities. Among lineages of holism Vincent Tucker mentions ecological thinking in biology which spread to social science. Related currents are Gestalt psychology, psychotherapy and Buddhist thought (1997: 41). In social science wholeness is thematized in several ways. Marxism represents a commitment to 'the whole' within a materialist ontology. Harrod's plea for 'a research for a lost completeness' refers to a return to critical political economy (1997: 108). Gestalt psychology led Ruth Benedict (1935) to a view on cultures as wholes or 'configurations' organized around core meanings. Talcott Parsons' social systems approach is centred on structural differentiation and functional integration. Louis Althusser viewed societies as structured wholes.

In the social sphere wholeness is often associated with romanticism and nostalgia, as in the idealization of 'tradition', communitarianism and the idealization of 'community'. In politics it can involve homogenizing projects of 'totality', as in some types of utopian politics, or nostalgia for a lost political 'unity'. In this light, a dose of difference can be quite a relief. A different and concrete angle on wholeness is the social exclusion approach (Bhalla and Lapeyre 1997). In liberation theology's 'preferential option for the poor' this sensibility is stated affirmatively. For the architect Robert Venturi, part of postmodern sensibilities is 'the obligation toward the difficult whole' (McHale 1992: 3).

Contradictions of Modernity

The question of modern medicine is a subset of a larger problem – the question of modernity and, in turn, the contradictions of modernity: in particular the contradiction between the 'two cultures', the scientific-technological and humanistic cultures, the worlds of science and art. The core of scientific culture is often traced back to Descartes and his project of 'certain knowledge' on the basis of mathematics as a universal scientific method, or 'the world according to mathematics'. The mathematical mind abstracts, generalizes, dichotomizes and is given to formalism (Davis and Hersh 1986, cf. Passmore 1978).[2] Critiques of Cartesianism, in the company of Bacon and Newton, go back a long way, among others to the Neapolitan philosopher Giambattista Vico: 'Mathematics is created in the self-alienation of the human spirit. The spirit cannot discover itself in mathematics. The human spirit lives in human institutions' (quoted in Davis and Hersh 1986: x; Pompa 1990). This general current of dissent is as old as 'the other West of William Blake and Paracelsus' (Nandy 1995: 60). A different twist to this kind of dispute is the argument between Habermas and Lyotard on the virtues of the Enlightenment and the debate on postmodernism.

There is something jarring about the way the tension within modernity is usually conceptualized and represented on either side of the argument. Viewing the relationship between scientific and humanistic cultures as a dichotomy itself follows a Cartesian paradigm. Representing this tension as a dualistic, polarized relationship gives either side the opportunity to profile its position and in the process exaggerate the issue. It is clearly a superficial representation from the outset. Viewing this relationship as a continuum of views that meet and diverge on multiple levels is much more adequate. In addition this involves a one-sided representation of the Enlightenment, which is a much more complex historical field than is granted in conventional views.[3] This is worth keeping in mind when considering the long-standing attempts to bridge these worlds and reintegrate the sciences and humanities. Siu's *Tao of Science* attempted such a reintegration in 1957, long before Capra's *Tao of Physics*. Generally elements of this fusion include the following:

❏ *Ecology*. Ecological knowledge as part of a general systems approach and deep ecology (as in Arne Naess, 1976).

❏ *History of science*. Joseph Needham's work on the history of Chinese science and technology and its influence on Western science is part of a wider body of work documenting the historical connections between 'Western knowledge and Eastern wisdom'. The Enlightenment also includes figures such as Leibniz and Goethe who bridged Western and Eastern sensibilities. Later Werner Heisenberg was influenced by Indian philosophy through conversations with Tagore, and Niels Bohr was inspired by his visit to China (Weber 1982: 218). On a conceptual level, Kuhn's work on scientific revolutions (1962) debunked the self-representation of progress in science, and through the notion of paradigm shifts introduced a meta level of analysis of scientific procedures and gatekeeping.

❏ *Physics*. Subatomic physics has generated a stream of findings that upset Descartes' certain knowledge, including Heisenberg's uncertainty principle, according to which the instrument of measurement affects the outcome, also known as the observer effect. In the 1920s Alfred North Whitehead developed an inclusive notion of reality beyond dualisms such as those of mind and matter: 'In a certain sense, everything is everywhere at all times. For every location involves an aspect of itself in every other location' (quoted in Siu 1957: 157). In quantum physics this has been taken further in David Bohm's work on the implicate order (1980). Several of these reorientations have been grouped together under the heading of the holographic paradigm (Wilber 1982), building on Dennis Gabor's work on holography.

❏ *New science*. This includes developments such as catastrophe theory, chaos theory, complexity theory, fuzzy logic, the theory of emergence, self-organizing systems (Prigogine and Stengers 1984) and new trends in biology and mind–brain research.

Some of these reorientations turn on a fusion or complementarity of 'Western knowledge and Eastern wisdom'. What is the status of this fusion? To what extent is the new science a marginal concern? It is not quite so marginal if we think of developments such as chaos theory, which has found wide application (Gleick 1988), including in business (Peters 1988) and social science (Eve et al. 1997, Anderla et al. 1997). The butterfly effect, or sensitive dependence on initial conditions, may be interpreted as an instance of the implicate order in action. Subatomic physics finds application in nano technology and advanced materials research. What several accounts suggest is that on the other side of science we come out at findings that intimate an interconnectedness of being that is similar to what has been intuited in mysticism – arguably, a complementarity between 'moonshine physics' and ground-floor mysticism.[4] In this view, the splitting process carried all the way through, to subatomic quantums and quarks, arrives at the ultimate unity of all being, or the universe as a 'sea of quarks' (Adachi 1996). At these deeper strata, contradictions such as those between the sciences and the humanities unravel. They turn out to be 'regional contradictions' that make sense within a certain limited context, but do not hold in the larger field. It is true, of course, that the world of everyday action is not a world of quantums or quarks, yet on the level of the foundational claims of science and epistemology it does matter that the Cartesian and Newtonian premises apply within a narrow range only. This argument cuts two ways. While to all human faculties and expressions there may be a 'territorial drive' and an urge toward functional autonomy, by this wide-angle logic, all are part of the whole and cannot be denied their potential to contribute to wholeness. This also holds for mathematics – in Plato's words, God ever geometrizes; and for computers – without computers the intricate calculations that led to chaos theory could not have been generated. In other words, 'both reductionism and holism are necessary' (Capra in Weber 1982: 241). New science does not replace but supplements Newtonian science.

> Typically, the new paradigm demonstrates that knowledge gained under the old paradigm is true *under specific boundary conditions*. Thus, the rules of motion put forth by Newton are not demolished by Einsteinian physics, but are shown to be a special case of a larger, more inclusive physics.... Chaos and complexity do not 'overthrow' former conceptions and scientific knowledge, but merely supplement them. (Eve 1997: 275)

Development and High Modernism

The contradictions of modernity are of profound relevance to development studies. Considering that development is applied modernity, all the contradictions of modernity are reproduced within development as dramatically unresolved tensions. Development theory is now being torn between paradigms – mainstream, alternative and post-development – or between internal and external critiques of development. What then is the relevance of these disputes over modernity for development studies and of attempts to reconceptualize or bridge these concerns? Arguably, the most fundamental question concerns the meaning of development, which in turn boils down to the question of what is evolution.

The social sciences have a long lineage, but as sciences they go back less than two hundred years. Development thinking goes back to nineteenth-century political economy, but modern development thinking is no more than fifty years old. In relation to the complexities of social life, at times development as applied social science gives the impression of navigating the ocean in a rowboat, or a Lego imitation of collective existence, in which mechanistic notions of social dynamics in tandem with political and hegemonic interests push and shove for the driver's seat. Really existing development has been an arena of ideological posturing or pragmatic reformism, either way involving brutal simplifications and crude interventions. At times in relation to the collective body, development interventions seem like performing surgery with a chainsaw. All the same, in some conditions surgery with heavy equipment beats no surgery at all, although even that depends on which side of the operation one is on.

Development knowledge is fragmented and characterized by discipline-centrism. 'The development process is compartmentalised by each discipline to suit its own areas of specialization, research methods, and theoretical frameworks' (Brohman 1995: 303). In this division of labour there has been a definite hierarchy. 'Development in its halcyon days was mainly economic development. Other disciplines entered the area apologetically or stealthily – as the supplementary knowledge of social structures facilitating or hindering economic growth, as insights into the psychological factors motivating or discouraging economic growth, as information about the political factors influencing economic decisions' (Nandy 1995: 146). Meanwhile divergent theories have often been applied in different policy spheres and economic sectors at the same time, making really existing development a patchwork of zigzag premises and policies.

Development thinking is steeped in mathematics – a world of numbers, indicators and statistics. Neoclassical economics is a formidable instance of applied Cartesianism. Part of this is a rendezvous with intellectual and managerial power – power to classify, administer and change the world. The theoretical and methodological characteristics of neoclassical economics – the assumptions of universal applicability, measurability, objectivity, formal modelling – make it a powerful instrument. Reductionism along with disciplinary fragmentation has made expert regimes and technocratic interventions possible, and has generously contributed to development policy failures. According to a former president of the American Economic Association, 'When you dig deep down, economists are scared to death of being sociologists. The one great thing [they] have going for [them] is the premise that individuals act rationally in trying to satisfy their preferences. This is an incredibly powerful tool because you can model it' (Charles Schultze in Brohman 1995: 302). Conventional development is a politics of measurement, a matter of 'fixing' within limited spheres, achieving desired change by manipulating indicators and modifying numerical relationships, such as the ratio of external debt to GDP, or debt to exports. The gap between economic development and social and cultural development, or the hard and soft dimensions of development, is reproduced in the institutional division between the Bretton Woods institutions and UN agencies, in which the former hold the purse strings. Indeed, this mathematical universe is inhabited in many different ways. For the sake of macroeconomic and financial management – by the IMF and Bank of International Settlements; with a view to economic growth in combination with sustainable development and poverty alleviation – by the World Bank; with a view to human development and the indicators of schooling, health, housing, sustainability – by the UNDP. What they share is a commitment to social engineering.

The American psychotherapist Thomas Moore proposes to add another ailment to psychology's list of disorders: 'I would want to include the diagnosis "psychological modernism", an uncritical acceptance of the values of the modern world. It includes blind faith in technology, inordinate attachment to the material gadgets and conveniences, uncritical acceptance of the march of scientific progress, devotion to the electronic media, and a life-style dictated by advertising. This orientation towards life also tends toward a mechanistic and rationalistic understanding of matters of the heart' (1992: 206). Modern development has suffered from a severe case of psychological modernism, has erected monuments to modernism, placing technological progress over human development. In Latin America the work of the *científicos* is not yet complete. In Asia 'laboratory states' have used science as an instrument of power and reason of state (Visvanathan 1988). Modernization and development, including critical Marxist development thinking, have been 'scientist' in temperament. 'Science became the integrating myth of industrial society' (Berman 1984: 187), so it became the guiding light of development policy. Rationalization was the key to modernization, so it became the master key to development. This is the familiar Enlightenment headache syndrome. We now turn to the countermoves.

Shortcuts and Other Remedies

> Do you think you can take over the universe and improve it? (Lao Tsu, 6th century BC, 1973: 29)

Rather than another round of diagnosis, what the situation calls for is a scrutiny of remedies. Often what is presented as the way ahead is no more than a shortcut – the ailment may be diagnosed correctly but the remedy is not examined. Some medicine turns a headache into a migraine, induces medicinal toxification, or provides only temporary or local relief. So in considering remedies for the culture of high modernism we may apply Vincent Tucker's recipe of remedying remedies. Some of the problems affecting the antidotes to high modernism are reproducing dichotomous thinking, skipping levels, and neolithic nostalgia, or framing contemporary dilemmas in anachronistic terms.

Positions and counterpositions in the development field often operate on the basis of simplistic dichotomies – such as modernization versus 'tradition', science versus indigenous knowledge, the impersonal versus the personal, the global versus the local. Also, critiques of development modernism often take the form of dualisms that in effect replicate the dichotomous thinking of modernism. Does it make sense to subject modernity to the same simplistic treatment to which the project of modernity has subjected social life? We need to distinguish between the *project* of modernity and *really existing modernities* (and the sociology of modernity), which are far more complex than blueprint modernity. Opposition to modernization has been part of modern experience and the dialectics of modernity include modernism, as a cultural politics that at times runs contrary to modernity, critical theory and reflexive modernity.

The world of post-development ranges from militant development agnosticism and rejectionism to the New Age development thinking of the Schumacher College, which offers courses on 'Systems thinking and learning for change' and 'Buddhist economics'. There is a beatific island effect to this project. It describes itself as 'A truly Green oasis, a centre for deep green values expressed beautifully by people from all over the world' (1997). At either end of the spectrum, adherents of post-development use statistics to make their case. 'For example, it has been estimated that a single edition of the *New York Times* eats up 150 acres of forest land' (Rahnema 1997: 379). According to Gustavo Esteva, 'if all countries "successfully" followed the industrial example, five or six planets would be needed to serve as mines and waste dumps' (1992: 2). In other words, post-development too inhabits a mathematical universe. The opponents of abstraction, generalization, dichotomization and formalism often apply abstraction, generalization, dichotomization and formalism in order to make their case, including in the development field. While presenting itself as an external critique, the post-development critique is external to (some of) the goals and not necessarily to the premises or the means of development. Some of the points of reference of post-development – opposition to reductionist science and modernity (Nandy 1988, Alvares 1992) – are unreflective and dichotomous in their logic. They exhibit a similar polarized and dualistic thinking to that of modernization theory, which dichotomizes 'tradition' and 'modernity', and thus tend to fall into the trap of modernization in reverse. The question, however, is how to overcome dichotomies, not merely to change the direction of the current.

Majid Rahnema criticizes 'compulsory actomania' and the 'mask of love' in development aid. In his view what lies behind solidarity or 'charity' is 'the great fear we have of becoming fully aware of our powerlessness in situations when nothing can be done' (1997: 392, 393). Who are we to intervene in other people's lives? He recalls the Chinese notion *wu-wei*, which is variously translated as 'non-intervention' or 'action through non-action' (397). What is odd in Rahnema's treatment is that he proceeds to explain this Taoist notion by setting forth the Confucian 'arts of governance' and 'aesthetic order', as if unaware of the tensions between Taoism and Confucianism, which run as deep as those between mysticism and official religion, and of Confucianism's comeback as an ideological prop for authoritarian regimes. It may be argued that 'non-intervention' is a superficial translation of *wu-wei*. A relevant passage in the *Tao te Ching* is: 'Tao abides in non-action, / Yet nothing is left undone' (Lao Tsu 1973: 37). 'Nothing is left undone' is not the same as doing nothing. Again, what is offered as the road ahead is a shortcut, a rapid and easy synthesis that does not do justice to the multiple dimensions of existence, each of which involves tensions which require engagement in their own right and appropriate to the level at which they are experienced. This is holism without sufficient critical edge.

A polemical polarization that is similar in structure is taking shape in relation to globalization. Some who identify globalization with corporate, market-driven transnationalism opt, in reaction to globalization, for localization and, in reaction to free trade, for 'new protectionism'. An example is the volume *The Case against the Global Economy and for a Turn toward the Local* (Mander and Goldsmith 1996). This position reduces globalization to economic globalization, confuses opposition to neoliberalism with opposition to globalization, and thus mixes up the current form of globalization with the underlying trend of globalization. This involves setting up a false dichotomy between the global and the local. The global and the local require and sustain one another in many ways. Examples of interpenetration are 'glocalization' and 'insiderism', or the thesis according to which transnational corporations can enter foreign markets effectively only if they become insiders; the argument according to which flexible specialization leads towards the relocalization of operations so as to be close to consumers, suppliers, competitors and high-skilled labour; the dialectics of globalization which show, for instance, that transnational corporations may well end up as active promoters of localism (Miller 1997); and a host of cultural studies which show that the global and the local are embedded in one another. A further argument is that the local itself is a construction, a performative stance that owes its meaning and dynamics to its relationship to wider units, including the global (Boon 1990). So on several counts the contrast between the global and the local does not work as a clear-cut distinction or as a dichotomy, because for either to function it requires the other.

'Identifying with the whole' is a formidable challenge and taking shortcuts is tempting. Part of the remedy for modernism is to recover lost sensibilities, a 'resurrection of subjugated knowledges'; or, 'rediscovering traditional knowledge' (Fals-Borda 1985). This may involve reconnecting with spiritual sources sidelined and bulldozed by the incursions of colonialism and modernization, for instance reinvoking the shaman (Nandy 1989). Max Weber already pointed to charisma as a way out of the 'disenchantment of the world'. However, the problem with charisma is that it makes no distinction between Hitler and Gandhi. The shaman stands in contrast to the scientist and the priest, but that is only half the story; the other half includes the different types of shamans, for example distinguishing between the *brujo* or wizard and the *curandero* or healer. A recourse to cults is another option, with obvious limitations: 'cults can have either a tranquilizing or a liberating effect on people, depending, among others, on the leadership's inspiration and the social context' (Huizer and Lava 1989: 15). Morris Berman made a point about the 'flip side of Cartesianism' which, even if he overstates his case, is still valid:

> Why not abandon Cartesianism and embrace an outlook that is avowedly mystical and quasi-religious, that preserves the superior monistic insight that Cartesianism lacks? Why not deliberately return to alchemy, or animism, or number mysticism? ... The problem with these mystical or occult philosophies is that they share ... the key problem of all nondiscursive thought systems: they wind up dispensing with thought altogether. To say this is not, however, to deny their wisdom.... My point is that once the insight is obtained, then what? These systems are, like dreams, a royal road to the unconscious, and that is fine; but what of nature, and our relation to it? What of society, and our relationship to each other? ... In fact, it is but the flip side of Cartesianism; whereas the latter ignores value, the former dispenses with fact. (1984: 188)

'The commitment toward the difficult whole' is ill served by binarisms. What is needed is a combination of wholeness and difference, as in Vincent Tucker's synthesis. Shortcut holism may just produce neolithic nostalgia – revisiting Arcadia, which yields only temporary comfort, island paradises that provide merely local relief, politics of ecstasy that produces a hangover. Recovering the wisdom of ages is needed, but not as a shortcut. What is needed, rather than simply flipping over to another extreme, is a new sense of balance, between science and art, fact and value, analysis and meaning. Nowadays this means bridging the development gap and crossing sensibilities ranging all the way from neolithic to postindustrial settings. It involves recognizing multiple dimensions of existence and, accordingly, multiple modes of cognition, which need to coexist rather than compete. The assumption that only a single mode of cognition should prevail implies skipping levels.

Towards the Tao of Development

Vincent Tucker's critical holism cannot be readily translated into a general theory of development because, unlike in health, there is no holistic practice in development. Alternative development practices tend to be local and short of a holistic approach. While there is a mysticism of the human body, a theory and a practice (holistic medicine), there is no equivalent holism of the social field. This is the missing element. There are, so to speak, 'a thousand points of light', but they are scattered about, like 'ten thousand things' – local alternatives, cultural and spiritual alternatives, rival theories, counterpoints and countercurrents,[5] but there is no unifying, overarching paradigm as there is, up to a point, in relation to health. The appeal of critical holism is that it places holistic theorizing and practice in relation to collective existence on the agenda and thus renders it imaginable: at least steps can be taken in its general direction.

Since in its epistemology social science has been a follower of natural science, would it not be logical for it also to follow new developments in science, including new science? It would be, except that the extent of specialization has narrowed the nexus between the two. The present situation in social sciences and development studies is an uneven combination of trends – towards polemical antagonisms, partial recombinations and occasional syntheses.

Criticisms of Cartesian science also have deep roots in the South. Both science and critique of science movements have played a role in development activism and popular movements (Zachariah and Sooryamoorthy 1994). One trend is to view science as a religion,[6] and as power. Suspicion of Enlightenment science is also a leitmotif in radical ecological thinking (e.g. Shiva 1988a). Science here stands for Cartesianism, Newtonian mechanism, positivism, an instrument to achieve mastery over nature. At times this presents a caricature of science that ignores ongoing developments in science and new science. Why should critique of science and of science-as-power mean being anti-science? This would be a Luddite view and at times 'anti-development' comes across as twentieth-century Luddism. Meanwhile science, of course, is a major instrument of ecological monitoring. The 'Limits to Growth' takes the form of a mathematical argument. 'Green accounting' uses scientific measures to arrive at realistic costing and pricing. Critique of science is part of reflexive modernity. What this means is the integration of multiple knowledges within a larger framework.[7]

Positivism is no longer the dominant temperament in social science except in economics and number-crunching sociology. Increasingly the lead paradigm in social science is constructivism. In development studies, one-sided disciplinary perspectives are gradually in retreat and being relegated to the status of partial knowledge. A development economist can no longer afford to ignore politics, sociology, gender, ecology, culture; nor can a political scientist or sociologist afford to ignore economics. Most problems now faced in development require a combined approach, such as structural adjustment, currency instability, corruption, the environment, gender, poverty, conflict prevention, complex emergencies, post-conflict reconstruction. Many policies that are now initiated involve partnerships of different parties, joint efforts of government agencies, social organizations and firms. Clearly the 'partnership' gospel itself prompts new forms of critical engagement; but even so the field is changing profoundly. To make synergies possible in policy they must become part of development thinking. Also, now that participation and empowerment have become part of the mainstream, even if primarily in rhetoric, the bottom-up, ground-up sensibilities and local culture that were the domain of grassroots, activist and anthropological approaches need to be integrated into mainstream discourse. Many new concepts that are current in development talk imply a combination of disciplines: good governance, accountability, human development, institutional development. New theoretical perspectives are likewise interdisciplinary, such as new institutional economics and public action. We witness both a return to and renewal of political economy and new combinations such as ecological economics (which is more than simply resource economics) and sociology of economics. Economic sociology shows, for instance, that markets are socially embedded and politically constituted and vary culturally, and yields novel notions such as social systems of production (Hollingsworth and Boyer 1997). At the same time these reorientations tend to be *ad hoc* and only dimly reflected in general theoretical reorientations or in everyday research, which remains empiricist. Disciplinary knowledge still ranks as foundational knowledge. Interdisciplinary research is more widely applauded than it is practised. A multidisciplinary approach refers to a combination and an interdisciplinary approach to an interaction of disciplines; a holistic approach is a step further. Holistic means integrated from the outset, which implies a revisioning of each discipline (a new view of economics,[8] etc.) and not just an adding up.

An example of holistic science is Gregory Bateson's synthesis, which Berman refers to as 'a non-Cartesian mode of *scientific* reasoning ... a methodology that merges fact with value and erodes the barrier between science and art' (1984: 232). For Berman this represents a general point of reference: 'I see our immediate future in a post-Cartesian paradigm, not in a premodern one' (271). The difference between Bateson's holism and the archaic tradition, according to Berman, is its 'self-conscious character' (272). Berman's *Reenchantment of the World* likewise is a self-conscious re enchantment.[9]

Considering that one of the problems of conventional development thinking is linearity, a relevant option is the application of chaos theory to development. In social science, chaos theory can be used as the basis of a non-modern social theory (Lee 1997) and with a view to public policy (Elliott and Kiel 1997; Anderla et al. 1997). A preliminary point is that there is no ready translation of chaos theory from natural to social systems (Elliott and Kiel 1997: 72). Chaos does not mean randomness or the absence of order; it refers to the unpredictability of the outcome of processes because of small differences in initial conditions. The butterfly effect, or sensitive dependence on initial conditions, has its place in folklore:

For want of a nail, the shoe was lost;
For want of a shoe, the horse was lost;
For want of a horse, the rider was lost;
For want of a rider, the battle was lost;
For want of a battle, the kingdom was lost! (traditional, quoted in Gleick 1988: 23)

Chaos theory suggests distinguishing between different spheres of collective existence: those in which Newtonian dynamics prevail, and where robust policy interventions may be effective; and those in which non-linear dynamics predominate and where 'gentle action' is appropriate. In addition chaos theory suggests an ecological perspective: 'If chaos theory is right, a myriad of interactions in the nonhuman world is required to support and sustain the human world. Perhaps the Gaia hypothesis is undergirded by the mathematics of chaos to a degree even its originator might be surprised to learn of' (Eve 1997: 279-80).

Thus, some spheres would lend themselves to intervention: 'In those cases where a stable and predictable response is known, related policy is eminently sensible. In areas such as tax expenditures where consumers and corporations do behave as Newtonian machines in response to interest rates or tax abatements, public policy is quite effective in altering behavior' (Elliott and Kiel 1997: 77). Whether this would apply in countries in the South with 'soft states' is an open question. Neoclassical economics with its assumption of atomistic individuals exercising rational choice proceeds as *if this* sphere is the only sphere. In reality the sphere in which this applies is quite circumscribed. Complexity is by far the more common condition, North and South. In the North this has led to an awareness of the limited effectiveness of social engineering and of the malleability of society as a fiction. 'As societies become more complex, even the most arduous efforts to change social dynamics provide only minimal benefit' (ibid.: 76). This insight has barely penetrated development thinking. Modernization efforts remain surgery with a chainsaw. Poverty alleviation remains a matter of advanced arithmetic. Now chaos theory confirms what anthropologists have known all along: that 'Complex adaptive systems often exist on the edge of chaos' (Eve 1997: 280; an example given is the irrigation system in Bali). Many so-called traditional ways of life involve a sophisticated, time-tested social and ecological balance. That outside interventions can do more damage than good is confirmed by the harvest of several development decades.

Where non-linear dynamics prevail, the counsel for policy is 'gentle action' (Elliott and Kiel 1997: 73). This may be a more faithful approximation of *wu-wei* than 'non-intervention'. Thus, chaos theory yields a complex range of action orientations. Consideration for the ramifications of small differences can be translated in several ways – as sensitivity to local conditions and cultural differences, and as an antidote to abstract models that gloss over local conditions and the actual implementation of development interventions. This is the point of the cultural turn in development, the return of anthropology to development. It also suggests regard for the organizational and managerial dimensions of development on the ground and points to institutional analysis. A related consideration concerns the reflexivity of development as a form of applied cybernetics. Reflexivity here has two meanings – the self-referential character of development thinking, which in effect represents layer upon layer of reflexive moves, each a reaction to and negotiation of previous development interventions, as an ongoing trial and error motion. And also the importance of subjectivities in the development process, the reactions of people on the ground to development plans, projects, outcomes, or people's reflexivity, which should be built into the development process. Steps in this direction include popular development (Brohman 1996) and public action theory.

The contributions of chaos theory to social science are preliminary and schematic. The distinction between linear and non-linear dynamics is of some use but too sketchy to be of much use. Already at times development processes are regarded as curvilinear, rather than linear.[10] Development refers both to a *process* (as in a society develops) and an *intervention* (as in developing a society). For Cowen and Shenton, this produces an intrinsic tension: 'Development defies definition... because of the difficulty of making the intent to develop consistent with immanent development' (1996: 438).

Considering this kind of difficulty, would it make sense to think of the Tao of development? While the Tao of physics refers to a combination of physics and mysticism, the Tao of development is a more difficult combination because development is not merely a science or analytics (development theory) but also a politics. Taoism evokes an association of inaction, quietism. It is not clear whether this really applies to Tao, but there is no historical example of existing Taoism that disputes this and historically there is a dialectic between Taoism and Confucianism.[11] Still this does not simply close the issue. For instance, by analogy, although existing socialism has not met expectations, Marxism continues to be relevant as a method.

One of the core problems of development is its pretentiousness, the insurmountable arrogance of intervening in other people's lives. This may be balanced by an equally pretentious notion, but an entirely different kind of pretension – the Tao of development. Setting a high goal for development may be better than setting no goal at all, or declaring development over and done with – as in postdevelopment approaches – while, in the meantime, development business-as-usual goes on. Setting an elusive goal for development may be better than carrying on with development as a positivist politics of measurement; although when it comes to, for instance, poverty alleviation there will obviously be different opinions on this. The Tao of development means acknowledging paradox as part of development realities: such as the antinomies between measurement and meaning, between intervention and autonomy, or the tension between the local and the global. These antinomies are part of the perplexities of the human condition. Development participates in these perplexities and is not in some fashion outside or beyond them. Some will regard this acknowledgement of complexity as a gain, and others – who are fighting a different kind of battle – as a loss. The Tao of development is asymptotic – never entirely approachable, like an ever-receding horizon. What it involves is a subtle and sophisticated sense of balance across different dimensions of collective existence.

Balanced development in a conventional sense refers to a balance between economic growth and redistribution, and between growth across different sectors. Critical holism as a balancing act involves balance in a wider and more fundamental sense, across dimensions of collective existence, from the epistemological to the practical, which may take several forms.

❑ A *multidimensional* approach, or a balance between the horizontal and vertical dimensions of collective existence. The horizontal refers to the worldly and social spheres; the vertical refers to the inner dimension of subjectivities and meanings, to the depth of the social field, its layered character, which Anouar Abdel-Malek referred to as the 'depth of the historical field'.

❑ A *multifaceted* approach or a diamond social science, which reflects or shines light upon relations and dynamics across sectors (economy, politics, social, cultural) and levels (local, microregional, national, macroregional, global) and achieves a balance between them.[12] This might be termed Gestalt sociology.

❑ A *chiaroscuro* social science which abandons the assumption of full transparency of society. The assumption of transparency is what lent the Enlightenment its totalitarian bend, as in Bentham's panopticism and in socialist state ideology (Laclau 1990). This is a matter of modesty, a sense of the contingency of knowledge, or self-limiting rationality (Kaviraj 1992).[13] *Clair–obscur*, originally a term to describe the play of light and shadow in oil paintings, here refers to a sense of balance and interplay between that which is known and unknown, conscious and unconscious, the day and night sides of life.

❑ A distinction between and combination of objective and subjective dimensions of development. Development thinking is now increasingly anchored in people's subjectivities rather than merely in overarching institutions – the state or international institutions. While development thinking has become more participatory and insider-oriented, as in the actor-oriented approach (Long 1994), development practice has not been democratized, particularly when it comes to macroeconomic management, so there is a growing friction between development thinking and practice.

❑ A trend in local and increasingly also in large-scale development is towards partnerships across sectors, or synergies between different development actors – government, civic associations and firms. This is a marked departure from times when development was seen as either state-led, or market-led, or civil society-led (cf. Chapter 6). This might be considered a holistic approach;[14] but not a critical approach because talk of partnership in unequal relations of power is clearly apolitical (cf. Tvedt 1998: 224).

❑ Since development is concerned with the measurement of desirable change over time, it is chronocentric. For a more complex awareness what is needed is combining multiple time frames and a balance between 'slow knowledge' and the 'fast knowledge' of instant problem solving. 'Slow knowledge is knowledge shaped and calibrated to fit a particular ecological context' (Orr 1996: 31). The conventional time horizon of development policy – the mid-term time span of a generation, or shorter, down to five years or so, in the case of planning, development projects and project-based lending – has changed with sustainable development and the implied notions of intergenerational equity and 'coevolutionary development'. It is changing also as a consequence of the duration of the development era and the failures of 'development decades', which gradually brings to the fore the *longue durée* of development. Evolution, a long-time silent partner of development, is coming to the foreground.

On the whole, this sense of balance is better achieved in social science than in development studies; it is comparatively more developed in relation to situations

that are geographically and socially near than those which are distant (as a function of insider knowledge); and more developed in relation to the past and in
history (where hindsight makes it easier to acknowledge complexity of motive,
action and result) than in relation to the present or future. In forecasting and
future projects, one-dimensional science and technology treatments, or the flat
earth extended in time, are almost the norm, except in science fiction.

There is an affinity between spatially wide and temporally long approaches, or
between globalization and evolution. Both are forms of holism, spatial and tem-
poral. With evolution coming back to the foreground, ideas such as those of
Teilhard de Chardin are making a comeback (e.g. Arruda 1996). Terhal has compared Teilhard de Chardin's ideas of 'evolutionary convergence', the noosphere
and the dawn of collective reflection, with Kuznets and Wallerstein's perspectives on world development.[15] He finds that Teilhard underestimates social stratification and inequality in human evolution (1987: 228) and that there are
elements of Eurocentrism to his work (266-7), which makes it another instance
of shortcut holism.

In Skolimowski's perspective too evolution is taking a reflexive turn: 'we are
evolution conscious of itself' (1994: 92). For Skolimowski, 'The feast of life is
participation' (157). For Stuart Todd, what follows from this kind of perspective
is that the clue for development is to 'align with life processes' (1997: 36). But
this is too generic a recipe, like an all-purpose elixir, or like Bergson's vitalism,
for what are 'life processes'? Are not development and its contradictions themselves manifestations of 'life processes'? This introduces 'life processes' in a normative, discriminating sense, without providing the terms of distinction.
Goonatilake (1991) introduces the notion of 'merged evolution' to characterize
the situation in which through biogenetic engineering the strand of cultural
evolution – which hitherto has run a separate course – merges with and impacts
on biological evolution. This perspective distinguishes *and* combines: rather than
positing a shortcut 'evolutionary convergence' it confronts the dilemmas of really
existing convergence.

As to globalization, critical holism calls for a perspective on world history and
globalization beyond conventional disciplinary methodologies (e.g. Mazlish and
Buultjens 1993). There is no doubt that the future lies with visions of cooperative
globalization (as in Arruda 1996), in contrast to competitive globalization,
although these cannot be neatly separated, because competition and cooperation
are also two sides of the same coin. However, shortcut holism – which ignores or
underrates inequality and difference – falls short as a remedy.

This sense of balance means treating development as a tightrope act. The
source of critical holism is the field of health and healing, in which individual and
collective concerns typically come together. Feminism is another approach in
which personal and social concerns are combined by rethinking the boundaries
between the private and the public, the personal and the political. These combinations, along with the idea of Gestalt sociology or social science, raise a further
option: viewing social science not merely as explanation or as critique, the standard assignments of social science, but as healing, as socio-therapy. As there is
therapy in relation to the individual body and psyche, can there be healing of the

collective body? In popular culture the idea is not uncommon, as in Sinéad O'Connor's lyrics about Ireland: 'And if there ever is going to be healing, there must be remembering, and then grieving, so that then there can be forgiving' ('Famine', O'Connor 1994). In development work this is not such an uncommon idea either – after all, what else is post-conflict rehabilitation and conflict prevention? Both notions have emerged in relation to complex emergencies and ethnic conflict. Yet if the notion of development as healing sounds novel, it is presumably because it makes explicit that which has been implicit, and in doing so combines sensibilities which are usually kept neatly apart in separate boxes. These then are elements of the Tao of development: a holistic approach, a sense of balance across dimensions, a notion of collective healing. Critical holism in combining holism and difference merges these sensibilities in a balancing act.

Wholeness then should not be expected from a shortcut towards an undivided whole in a divided world but should be sought in a new balance. The counsel for development studies and social science is to distinguish between multiple spheres and levels, each of which requires engagement on its own terms, and not merely to contrast but to combine knowledges. As to implications for action and policy, this involves a case-by-case, contextual assessment of whether linear or non-linear dynamics prevail and whether robust or gentle action is appropriate. It also exceeds local alternatives. Critical holistic development includes macroeconomic management, global democratization and planetary ethics. Identifying with the whole means that development can no longer be simply geared to material aims and achievements but includes non-material dimensions, as in cultural development. It means that development can no longer be anthropocentric but encompasses the planetary ecology. Stretching the meaning of development to its fullest, it may be summed up as a collective learning process of human self-management according to the most comprehensive standards conceivable and practicable.

Notes

1 Note the reference to 'system' in this quotation. As Minter notes (1986: 42), several biographies try to whitewash Smuts' reputation as a humanitarian philosopher-statesman. An example is Meurs 1997 who presents him as an obstacle in the way of the architects of apartheid.

2 'The computerization of the world represents an advanced stage of Cartesianism. Within that stage, programs become autonomous. We have even been given intimations of automated concept formulation and of action instigated as a consequence of such automation' (Davis and Hersh 1986: 303). Current developments in global currency trading are an example of automated action: triggers built into trading programmes set in motion series of financial operations whose ripple effects can upset financial systems. For a more developed argument, see Yurick 1985.

3 A standard omission in representations of the Enlightenment is that it was not only an epoch of rationalism, but also of romanticism, and that these occurred in combination. For instance, what is one to say of these statements of Diderot: 'what makes me angry is that the passions are never regarded from any but the critical angle. People think they do reason an injury if they say a word in favor of its rivals. Yet it is only the passions, and the great passions, that can raise the soul to great things... The language of the heart is a thousand times more varied than that of the mind, and it is impossible to lay down the rules of its dialectics' (quoted in Gay 1977: 188, 189).

4 The complementarity between new physics and mysticism is disputed by, among others, Wilber, who deems it a false complementarity and at most concedes that new physics *accords* with mysticism

(1982: 166-79). While mysticism addresses all levels – physical, biological, mental, subtle, causal and ultimate – physics pertains only to a single level (159).

5 Besides alternative development literature (Chapter 6) see e.g. Henderson 1996a, Whitmyer 1995, Roszak 1976.

6 'Positivism is just a crank religion' (Chris Mann in Dunn 1986: 2).

7 Capra gives another example of this integration of multiple knowledges: 'From the very beginning it was clear to me that there was no reason to abandon the biomedical model. It could still play a useful role for a limited range of health problems within a large, holistic framework, as Newtonian mechanics was never abandoned but remains useful for a limited range of phenomena within the larger framework of quantum-relativistic physics' (1988: 171; cf. Abraham et al. 1992).

8 According to Hazel Henderson (1996b), economics is not a science but politics in disguise.

9 This is not as clear with Toulmin, who advocates not the abandonment of modernity or a return to pre-modernity, but *humanizing modernity* and a return to the oral, the particular, the local, the timely (1990: 180f.).

10 E.g. Cowen and Shenton about Hegel's views on development: 'Unlike the linear image that the idea of progress evoked, the course of development was curvilinear or spiral-like, always impeded or arrested within its own logical structure' (1996: 130).

11 As to Taoism: 'It is inconceivable to a Taoist that Tao should be actualized in this world by human efforts because the core of Taoist doctrine is to teach its followers to transcend merely human affairs and psychologically dwell in "nothingness" (*wu*) so as to be in line with the "nonaction" (*wu-wei*) of the great Tao' (Wei-ming 1979: 10-11). Generally, while there have been episodes of a working balance between mysticism and official or state religion – between Buddhism and governance, Qabbala and Judaism, Christian mysticism and Christendom, Sufism and Islam, etc. – such episodes are not well known or readily accessible, so that they could act as sustainable examples.

12 Several of the significant books in social science achieve this in different ways. It applies to the oeuvre of Max Weber, Gramsci and Braudel and to books such as Wertheim's *Evolution and Revolution* (1974), Stavrianos' *Global Rift* (1981), Worsley's *The Three Worlds* (1984), David Harvey's *The Condition of Postmodernity* (1989).

13 'I plead not for the suppression of reason, but an appreciation of its inherent limits' (Gandhi in Parekh 1997: 68).

14 This is the theme of a report in the *Irish Times* on social partnerships, particularly in disadvantaged areas. The partnerships include 'business, trade unions, farming organizations, schools, health boards, state agencies ... and representatives from the local community' (Catherine Foley, 'The holistic way of solving problems', *Education & Living* supplement, 17 February 1998, pp. 2-3).

15 For instance, according to Teilhard de Chardin, 'Although mounting demographic pressure causes quite a number of evils at one level of human interaction', in principle it leads to 'social unification and a higher level of collective consciousness' (quoted in Terhal 1987: 176).

10

FUTURES OF DEVELOPMENT

Whither development is an old question. Considering future trends in development by way of trend extrapolation, even if it is a limited exercise, provides an opportunity to uncover background questions. Clearly there will not be a single future trend. Secondly, complexity is a factor of growing importance in development, and this raises the question of whether complexity is enabling or disabling. For some time the dominant mood in the development field has been scepticism bordering on pessimism – can't work, can't do. From a shortcut to utopia, development has become a dystopia.

This closing chapter seeks to problematize and open up futures of development. This is taken up first through an overview of futures of development thinking, by taking a stroll through the current preoccupations of the major development theories and, by way of extrapolation, their likely future problematics. In bird's-eye fashion this also recapitulates key themes of the book. The second section signals major changes in the development field and argues that these add up to a growing awareness of the complexity of development, which is taken further under the heading of reflexivity. Considering that the career of development follows from and parallels that of modernity, reflexivity is taken up first in relation to modernity and next as it relates to development. Reflexive development and politics brings us to forward options in relation to philosophies of change and politics of change. This involves redefining development, no longer as 'improvement', but as collective learning. The final section focuses on reconstructions of development and submits that a reform platform in development thinking is in the making that may add up to a coherent alternative to neoliberalism.

Futures of Development Thinking

To start with, let me make a general note on development theory. 'Development theory' is a limited notion. It would be more adequate to say 'perspective' or 'analysis', and thus make the point that theories are important as ways of seeing and analytics. Many 'development theories' are not development theories properly speaking; they are derived from other social sciences and are being applied to the development terrain. The singular in 'development theory' is distracting, considering that development issues generally require a combination of analytical perspectives. Development is multidimensional and hence issues are not simply settled at one level. The terrain is complex also from a theoretical point of view because there are multiple dimensions to development thinking – of explanation, methodology, epistemology, interest articulation, imagination and policy agenda (Chapter 1).

The current array of perspectives in the development field represents a dispersal in stakeholders and interest positions (Chapter 1) that is likely to be sustained. This means that for each of the current development perspectives there is a set of options in facing changes and challenges. Accordingly, futures of development are being viewed through multiple analytical lenses and each shows different options. Several options are prefigured in current debates and others are hypothetical or can be inferred by logic. The starting point in this section is the existing set of development perspectives, each of which, as a framework or sensibility, continues to attract adherents and renew itself. This is a sketch rather than an exhaustive treatment. Addressed are the major development perspectives: modernization theory, dependency, neoclassical economics, alternative development, human development and post-development.

Modernization Theory

Current themes in relation to modernization theory include neo-modernization theory, which involves a complex understanding of modernity and a revaluation of 'tradition', no longer as obstacle but as resource (So 1990). This revaluation matches more profound and less schematic understandings of modernity in the West (e.g. Tiryakian 1996), yielding options such as the 'modernization of tradition'. A practical application of this kind of outlook is cooperation between development agencies such as NGOs, and 'traditional' social organizations, which has been under way in several places. The current emphasis on good governance recalls the concern with political modernization and nation building in modernization thinking.

A current theme that will likely become a future trend is to view *modernities* in the plural. This means that developing countries no longer view themselves merely as consumers of modernity (Lee 1994) but also as producers of modernity, 'reworking modernity' (Pred and Watts 1992), generating new and different modernities. Voices in the majority world are now not merely critical of Western modernity, or argue for some kind of fusion, but assert alternative modernities (e.g. Ibrahim 1996, Mahathir and Ishihara 1995). Another trend is a serious engagement with postmodernism, not merely as a condition (flexible specialization, post-Fordism, urban and social complexity) or a target of criticism, but also as a sensibility, a style and philosophical disposition (e.g. Giri 1998). Postcolonial studies and its destabilizing of modernist assumptions is part of this outlook.

Dependency Theory

In reworking dependency theory, a well-established trend is the analysis and critique of NICs. Rethinking dependency theory includes the renewal of structuralist analysis (Kay 1998) and innovative historical revisions (e.g. Frank 1996, 1998). Approaches that involve a renewal of dependency thinking in a broad sense are new political economy and international political economy. In the 1990s, key problems revisited from a dependency point of view were neoliberalism and uneven global development (e.g. Cardoso 1993, Boyer and Drache 1996). This takes the form of a general critique of uneven globalization (e.g. Amin 1997, Hoogvelt 1997, Chossudovsky 1997). A crucial distinction that is rarely clearly drawn runs between globalization as a *process* and as a specific *project*, or between globalization as a historical trend and recent global neoliberal policies.[1] Analyses of globalization projects focus, for instance, on the World Trade Organization and multinational corporations, but globalization involves more than specific projects.

Neoclassical Economics

In the 1980s Deepak Lal argued that 'The demise of development economics is likely to be conducive to the health of both the economics and the economies of developing countries' (1983: 109). How does the 'counterrevolution in development' shape up in the twenty-first century? Now structural adjustment no longer appears as the end of development, as was believed some years ago, but rather as an intermezzo. The adjustment of structural adjustment policies has been a major concern for some time. Earlier adjustments sought to give structural adjustment a 'human face' in combination with safety nets and poverty alleviation; another concern is to make structural adjustment policies country-specific and more user-friendly. Good governance and state effectiveness represent further adjustments (World Bank 1997, Kiely 1998). In the 1990s, the World Bank returned to its 1970s position in favour of equitable growth. This reorientation involved a growing tension between neoliberalism and the politics of the 'Wall Street-Treasury-IMF complex' (Wade and Veneroso 1998), and the social or populist liberalism of the World Bank. Obviously, the 'Washington consensus' is not what it used to be (discussed below).

Alternative Development

Elements of alternative development, such as participation, have increasingly been coopted in mainstream approaches. The strength of alternative development is its regard for local development and social agency, from grassroots groups and social movements to NGOs. With local development comes a concern with project failure, cultural diversity and endogenous development (e.g. Carmen 1996). The disaffection with the state in alternative development resonates with neoliberal misgivings about state failure and this odd conjuncture has contributed to the great wave of 'NGO-ization' since the 1980s. The trend of NGO professionalization runs the risk of depoliticization and managerialism, along with the erosion of state capabilities and 'alternative dependency' on donor support and agendas. The current trend of 'strengthening civil society' by supporting NGOs is deeply apolitical, ignores contradictions within civil society, overrates NGOs and weakens state capabilities (cf. Tvedt 1998: 170ff.). On the other hand, the blurring of the line separating alternative and human development approaches, or society and state-oriented perspectives, opens the way to synergies between civic organizations, local government and firms, which *may* contribute to supply-side social development (Chapter 8).

Alternative development thinking used to be strong on critique and weak on alternatives beyond local empowerment and decentralization politics. For some time the attention also turns to global-scale alternatives 'beyond Bretton Woods', or 'alternative globalization' (e.g. Korten 1990, Arruda 1996).

It may be argued that now that it is no longer simply 'alternative', alternative development is not an appropriate heading and a more distinctive terminology would be welcome. Besides, alternative development is tainted by the discourse of strengthening 'civil society'. Alternative terminologies could be grassroots or 'popular development' (Brohman 1996); but such headings gloss over the trend of NGO professionalization and alternatives beyond the local level (meso, macro, global alternatives) slip out of the picture. Another option is 'participatory development', but participation is too vague to serve as a centrepiece. It may be possible to redefine core components of alternative development (such as empowerment, emancipation) more sharply and critically to distinguish participatory from mainstream approaches, but to suggest a different heading is more difficult.

Human Development

The human development approach now extends to gender (as in the Gender Development Index), political rights (as in the Freedom Development Index) (UNDP 1997) and environmental concerns (sustainable human development). Through regional human development reports, it extends to different regions and countries (e.g. ul Haq and Haq 1998). In combination with participatory development, new fusions arise such as 'just development' (Banuri et al. 1997). The theme of human security refers to a new combination, at the conjunction of conflict and development (e.g. Naqvi 1996). This finds expression in the problematic of humanitarian action and 'linking relief and development' (e.g. Nederveen Pieterse 1998a).

What may be a substantive growth area for the human development approach is to examine the relationship between human capital (its starting point) and social and cultural capital. Bourdieu (1976, 1988) has argued all along that the different forms of capital are interrelated and interchangeable. For Bourdieu, this served as an analysis of 'modes of domination'. What is on the agenda now is the significance of these interrelations from an analytical and a policy-oriented view. This ties in with new institutional economics (Harriss et al. 1995) and socioeconomics, with the cultural turn in development and social capital (Fine 1999). Social capital now figures in social and economic geography: 'institutional densities' and civic political culture emerge as significant variables in explaining regional economic success or failure (Chapter 8). Thus, what underlies the success of micro-credit schemes may be the fact that they build on people's social capital. Part of the cultural turn in development is regard for local cultural capital, for instance in the form of indigenous knowledge. Cultural diversity and the mingling of different cultural flows (diasporas, migrants, travellers) are found to be potent ingredients in economic innovation and growth (Griffin 2000a).

The human development approach has all along been concerned with global reform, from the role of the UN system in relation to the Bretton Woods institutions and the World Trade Organization (Singer and Jolly 1995) to macroeconomic regulation and global taxes (Cleveland et al. 1995, ul Haq et al. 1996). Global reform (discussed below) is likely to remain a major preoccupation.

Anti-development

Anti-development has all along been concerned with local autonomy, at times advocating local delinking. A constructive turn is the nexus with ecological liberation movements (Peet and Watts 1996). Another major concern is 'resistance to globalization' such that anti-development and anti-globalization are becoming synonyms: economic globalization is viewed as the main form of developmentalism at the turn of the millennium (Korten 1995, Mander and Goldsmith 1996). The local orientation risks overlooking wider dimensions. Thus in this view, the Zapatista rebellion in Chiapas is concerned with local autonomy and land rights; but the Zapatistas also organize with a view to political reform in Mexico and global alliances of resistance (Castells 1997). The major limitation of the post-development approach is that beyond local autonomy it offers no significant future perspectives, so that the most likely future of post-development is localism.

Table 10.1 gives a telegram-style précis using key words of (column 1) understandings of development according to the major development perspectives, (2) ongoing revisions and (3) future options.

We stand on the shoulders of these perspectives, they make up the terms of our analytics and, as if through a kaleidoscope of multiple angles, we perceive the field of development through them, for they have been the guiding lights through several development decades. But these optics are also coloured by old polemics, as strategic simplifications that make sense in particular contexts that, by and large, are no more. Each of these paradigms is swarmed by a growing number of 'exceptions' that cannot be accommodated. Often they are no longer in the centre of our vision but at the periphery, so we no longer see simply through but also past them. They are but one way of looking at development, only part of the toolbox.

Development and Complexity

This section takes up general analytical and methodological features of the development field and then considers changes that have taken place at an institutional level and general policy directions, recapitulating points made in previous chapters.

Development involves different stakeholders and actors, who typically hold different perspectives and policy preferences. Yet these agents and their preferences should not be essentialized. Seen up close each position itself is a cluster of positions and an arena of different views and arguments. In Table 10.2 these internal differences are briefly summed up in key words signalling salient bones of contention. For example, in relation to structural adjustment there are conflicts within and between the Bretton Woods institutions, within and between the World Bank and IMF, also involving the scope of poverty alleviation. Obviously all these characterizations are shorthand and meant only as illustrations of the present situation.

Table 10.1   *Development perspectives and future options*

Theories and definitions of development	Current themes	Future options
Modernization Development is state-led growth. Keynotes: industrialization, Western model, foreign aid, linear progress, convergence	Revaluation of 'tradition'. Neomodernization. Triumphalism, 'end of history'	Modernities plural. Postmodernism
Dependencia Development is underdevelopment (or dependent development) by comprador bourgeoisie; or state-led autocentric development (associated dependent development) by national bourgeoisie	Critique of NICs, new international division of labour, social exclusion. New political economy: brings the state back in. International political economy: power and economics. Uneven global development	Critique of uneven globalization
Neoclassical economics, neoliberalism Development is market-led growth. Keynotes: overcome state failure through structural reform (deregulation, privatization, liberalization) and get prices right	Market failure, safety net, human capital, infrastructure, good governance, sustainability. Debt reduction. New institutional economics: institutional analysis	Regulation of finance. Civic economy
Alternative development Development should be society-led, equitable, participatory and sustainable	Adopted in mainstream. Decentralization. Professionalization. Alternative globalization.	Social economy, social development. Global reform
Human development Capacitation or human resource development is the means and end of development, measured in Human Development Index	Gender DI, Freedom DI, human security, global reform	Social and cultural capital. Social development. Global reform
Anti-development Development is destructive, immiserizing, authoritarian, past. Keynotes: discourse analysis, critique of science and modernity	Local delinking. Connection with ecological movements. Resistance to globalization	Localism

Development unfolds in diverse contexts of relations of power, cultural values, social practices, ecological conditions and historical itineraries. Development is intrinsically contextual. However, these contexts are not sealed off from one another. Thus, while cultural differences matter, they are not rigid boundaries; they are crossroads, traffic circles and junctions where different kinds of traffic meet. Development is an intercultural transaction (Chapter 5). This refers to the meanings of development as well as to implementation. Hence conventional modernization = Westernization views, on the one hand, and endogenous or indigenous development views on the other, are both too simple. They are based on binary oppositions and by privileging either end of the continuum of perspectives, ignore the fact that actual development involves continuous traffic back and forth across the spectrum.

While profound changes have taken place in the development field, assessing change is itself a complex operation, polycentric in meaning and significance. So

Table 10.2   *Another outline of the development field*

Agents	Perspectives	Policies	Conflict areas
IMF and World Bank	Neoliberalism, monetarism, social liberalism	Structural reform, structural adjustment (SA)	Adjust SA. World Bank vs. IMF. Poverty alleviation
WTO	Free trade	Multilateral agreement on investment, trade-related intellectual property rights	With regions, states, trade unions, INGOs
UN system	Human development	Capacity building, human resource development, safety net, human security	Conflicts in UN system and between UN and international financial institutions, OECD. 20:20 compact
States	Modernization, human development, neoclassical economics, monetarism	SA, capacity building, security, human development, innovation, competitiveness	SA, corporations, globalization, regionalism, decentralization, donors, social cohesion, poverty alleviation
(I)NGOs	Human and alternative development	Empowerment, humanitarian assistance, lobbying, poverty eradication	Revise SA. Conflict with GOs, among and within NGOs. Tension between relief and development
Local actors	Alternative development and/or post-development	Autonomous development, democratization	Conflicts among locals about participation, autonomy, values

it is not easy to indicate a general direction in which changes in development thinking and policy point, and even less to rank them in importance. With this proviso, let's signal some of the most significant changes, focusing on the post-war period.

The first change concerns the understanding of the nature of development. Early development efforts concentrated on the hardware of development, such as infrastructure, capital inputs and technology. The recent trend is to pay equal attention to the software of development, to institutions, processes and management (e.g. World Bank 1997), education and knowledge (World Bank 1998). Or indeed to argue that development is essentially human software development, as in the human development approach and the World Bank's aspiration to become a 'knowledge bank'. The emphasis on knowledge parallels the shift in the North towards the knowledge-intensity of production. It implies a major reorientation, from a general preoccupation with the external dimensions and façade of development (infrastructure, capital inputs) to its 'inner' conditions: from a one-dimensional to a multidimensional understanding of development. This includes environmental management as a learning process. 'Sustainable development' is now part of any approach to development, which presents the option of 'anthropocentrism with a human face' (Ariansen 1998).

Another major change is that the unit of development has become multi-scalar. This in turn affects the agency of development. If early on this was the state, now it includes international and regional institutions and regimes, urban and local government, civic associations (operating at multiple scales) and households. Development actors have become polycentric. Grassroots interests count more than previously (for instance Dalits in India who have become politically active). It follows that development is no longer simply a mathematics of power and reshuffling the status quo.

If previously the West dominated development thinking, in recent decades perspectives from the South and Japan have become increasingly important.[2] While this happens at a policy level, it ties in with profound revisionings of history (e.g. Frank 1998). At the same time, development is no longer simply confined to the South. Since the former Eastern Bloc countries have become 'transition' countries (in transition toward market economies and democracies) development policies are relevant also here. Changes taking place in the advanced economies – regionalization, deindustrialization, flexibilization, migration, urban problems – also lead to what are in effect development policies, albeit at different economic and institutional levels. Accordingly the line between 'developing' and 'developed' worlds has been blurring. The North faces questions of social exclusion (Judt 1997, Gaventa 1998, Young 1999), empowerment (as in urban empowerment zones and in management-speak), good governance (crony capitalism in the North also requires transparency; Warde 1998) and the renewal of democracy. Learning from South–North links takes place for instance in microfinance (Rogaly and Roche 1998).

A related trend is towards the convergence of advanced countries and NICs. In light of technological change and globalization, NICs are presently developing much like advanced countries, though starting from a lower base, with less stable institutions and less diversified economies. If we compare the forward policy profiles of the United States with those of e.g. Korea and Brazil, we find broadly similar agendas. In both, much emphasis is on innovation-driven growth, human capital, technopoles, industrial districts, research & development and knowledge intensity (e.g. Connors 1997). This is a new form of 'betting on the strong', driven by the imperatives of global competitiveness and efficiency. The crises in Mexico, Asia and Latin America show the frailty of the emerging markets. While the net figures in terms of productivity and exports may line up with those of advanced countries, the institutional settings are much more vulnerable. At the same time, while the gap between advanced countries and NICs is in some respects narrowing, the gap between both of these and the least developed countries is widening.

The sprawling delta of development actors and concerns raises the question of *policy coherence*: what understanding of purpose and process conceivably unites all these diverse actors? In international cooperation, this is the issue of consistency – between bilateral and multilateral policies, between trade, finance and security policies and international development policies. This would imply a trend towards a broad collaborative understanding of development efforts. 'Participatory development' in this context signals an undercurrent of deep-seated change. Development action is dialogical, involving the concerted efforts of actors in different settings and at many levels. In development thinking this reorientation is in evidence in social choice theory, public action and new institutional economics. At a policy level, it comes across in the concern with interactive decision-making, public–private partnership, empowerment, social inclusion, migration and managing urban problems.

However, the trend towards the democratization of development coincides with the simultaneous extension of transnational power structures and regimes. These twin trends are in contradiction. The democratization of development runs into the hurdle of power structures, from local landlords all the way to international financial institutions. This is not a simple opposition or contradiction that can be settled through conventional politics of resistance and conflict (e.g. Chin and Mittelman 2000). Democratization also requires institutionalization (deinstitutionalization and reinstitutionalization).

In a brief time span, there have been profound changes in the Gestalt of development. The changes do not all point in the same direction. There is a growing awareness of development as an asymptotic rendezvous, an undertaking that like the horizon recedes and changes as we approach. Development by this understanding is intrinsically uncertain and contested: coherence is a moving target; concertation is never fully achieved; dialogue is ever imperfect; software is never complete; learning never ends. In addition, development is not simply progress but the trial-and-error clarification, redefinition and management of progress. It concerns the translation of growing human capabilities into hardware and the translation of hardware into software, including collective reflection and institutions of collective management.

Complexity Politics

These considerations affect the understanding and definition of development. It may be argued that in the absence of a simple yardstick, the conventional understanding of development as some form of *improvement* is no longer tenable. Over time improvement has meant economic growth, modernization, nation building, industrialization, betterment of life opportunities, enlarging people's choices, enhancement of capacities, rollback of the state, good governance, state effectiveness, sustainability, poverty alleviation, poverty eradication, social inclusion, etc. It follows from the different meanings of development over time (Chapter 1) that improvement is a historically contingent notion. It follows from the plurality of development actors that development is polycentric in its meaning, objectives, agency and methods of implementation, and therefore what constitutes improvement in development is intrinsically contested. 'Development' is a moving target situated somewhere in between underdevelopment and post-development, to take two extremes on the continuum of development perspectives (and one might add over-development). Actual development thinking and action is about finding a balance or accommodation between different actors, perspectives, interests and dimensions within specific historical, political and ecological settings, and thus requires a holistic approach (Chapter 9).

It remains attractive to understand development as improvement, but which improvement and how? Understanding development as improvement virtually inevitably invites a one-dimensional perspective, privileging one or other dimension, and a managerial approach, while actually what constitutes improvement never is and never can really be settled. Consequently, development unfolds in a peculiar 'as if' mode: while everybody knows that development-as-improvement in any form is open to question, it seems necessary to proceed as if there is a consensus. Wouldn't it be more appropriate to make this contingency part of the understanding of development? It would mean redefining development as a collective learning experience. This includes learning about different understandings of improvement, as a collective inquiry into what constitutes the good life and sensible ways of getting there. Learning is open-ended. This also makes sense as a point about development methodology, in action and inquiry.

Learning is a theme of growing salience. Collective learning figures in organization studies and the 'learning organization' (Senge 1990, Cooperrider and Dutton 1999), local economic development and industrial districts (Lawson and Lorenz 1999), planning and sustainability (Meppem and Gill 1998), risk analysis and disaster management (Comfort 1999). Collective learning is a way of looking at social action (Foley 1999) and public action and social choice theories centre on collective learning and feedback processes. In this view, local policy formulation and implementation is a 'social experiment requiring flexibility, experimentation and social learning with the people' (Olowu 1988: 17). Collective learning as the point of development places development policy discussions on a different footing: the focus shifts to the role of complexity in development.

The diagnosis of complexity is often the endpoint of analysis or critique. An approach or policy is scrutinized and then criticized because it ignores certain elements and the conclusion is the diagnosis of complexity. The usual coda is to call for further research. Matters are complex and therefore.... This kind of weary note has been a standard conclusion in public administration. Matters are complex; therefore, nothing or not much can be done, which in effect celebrates the comforts of the status quo. This weariness informs the classic definition of public administration as the science of 'muddling through' (Lindblom 1959).[3] Thus, complexity *per se* is easily a cul-de-sac. So if we have established the complexity of development, the next question to ask is whether complexity is disabling or enabling.

Emery Roe in *Taking Complexity Seriously* argues for 'triangulation' or the 'use of multiple methods, procedures and/or theories to converge on what should or can be done for the complex issue in question' (1998: 5). Part of this approach is recourse to perspectives that involve a theory of uncertainty and theories that defamiliarize the problem, considering that 'more conventional analytical frameworks, such as microeconomic analysis, are often part of the problem being analyzed' (1998: 23). One of the issues is management: 'The more managers (want to) manage, the more they (have to) confront the unmanageable. But it is equally true that the more unmanageable things are, the greater the pressure to manage them' (1998: 96). Following critical theory in the version of the journal *Telos*, Roe draws a distinction between 'organic negativity', or resistance at a popular level, and 'artificial negativity', in the sense of disputes within the 'new class' of managers. The question that follows from this kind of approach is, whom does triangulation serve? Is complexity analysis an instrument of managers, or does or can it contribute to popular self-organization? This becomes a key issue in deciding whether complexity is disabling (leave it to experts) or enabling (creating an opportunity and necessity for democratization). A detour via the theme of reflexivity may yield further insight.

Modernity has resurfaced as a central theme in social science and has been reproblematized from various angles, as in notions such as high, late, advanced, neo, critical, reflexive, radical, post modernities. A strand that runs through these lines of questioning is that modernity has become its own problem. Ulrich Beck (1992) contrasts simple modernity concerned with 'mastering nature' with *reflexive modernity*, the condition in which the moderns are increasingly concerned with managing the problems created by modernity. Reflexivity figures in relation to the self, social theory, cultural studies, political economy, financial markets, organization studies and research methodology. New social movements are said to be reflexive in the sense of information oriented, present oriented and concerned with feedback (Melucci 1989).

Beck refers to the 'new modernity' as risk society, emerging in conditions in which scarcity is no longer the dominant theme because of the growth of productive capacities. Risk distribution society, which in Germany emerged in the early 1970s, is contrasted to scarcity society, which predominates in the South where the primary concern is with modernization through techno-scientific development. All the same, scarcity societies and risk societies interact and overlap in various ways. One, they interact through the globalization of risk: through generalized effects such as the erosion of the ozone layer; through the commonality of anxiety; and boomerang effects of crisis in developing countries on developed countries (as in Susan George's argument of the *Debt Boomerang*) and vice versa. Stagnation in the advanced economies also affects the developing economies. Two, they interact through the export of risk to scarcity society. The relocation of traditional industries in the South is affected by different trade-offs between accumulation and risk in scarcity societies (witness the Bhopal disaster). Countries in the South may serve as an ecological waste dump also because of rural naivety in relation to industrial risk. Extreme poverty and extreme risk attract one another. Third, there is a North–South transfer of risk awareness, among others as mobilization arguments for social movements. Critique of science and of corporate practices and public relations, for instance oil companies and pharmaceuticals, is increasingly being transnationalized (as in campaigns on Nestlé baby formula or Shell in Ogoniland in Nigeria). This is addressed in political ecology (Peet and Watts 1996). Environmental movements in the South also inspire collective action in the North (Martinez-Alier 2000).

These interactions are reflected in ongoing debates. Can we understand these debates better in light of the notion of reflexive development? Is there an emerging pattern of reflexive development? In the course of several development decades, development thinking and policy have become increasingly aware of failures and crises of development. Development also entails the 'production of errors'. Evaluation and impact studies have become a major industry alongside development programmes. New policies are increasingly concerned with managing the hazards, unintended consequences and side-effects brought about by development. In development theory this questioning is reflected in the rejection of developmentalism and linear progress. Critiques of the role of science and techno-scientific development lead to revaluation of indigenous technical and local knowledge, which is a logical turn in view of the crisis of 'Western' models.

This section develops four arguments: (1) Development thinking *is* reflexive. That is, almost invariably, development theory stems from a reaction to and thus also a reflection on the limitations of a preceding development policy or theory. (2) One way of looking at development thinking over time is as a *layer* of reflexivities, i.e. reflection upon reflection upon reflection. (3) Development thinking increasingly participates in the general trend towards reflexivity in and in relation to modernity. (4) Development thinking is not consistently and sufficiently reflexive; it should be more reflexive and its reflexivity should be thematized.

Arguably, there is both a historical and an emerging pattern of reflexive development. Critiques of development follow from and lead to critiques of modernity and its consequences, and from the crisis of development policies. A feedback pattern is emerging in which development policy becomes increasingly concerned with the management of development itself. A similar process took place in modernity, and as offspring of modernity, development participates in its dialectics.

Risk society, according to Beck, is a 'catastrophic society', replete with dystopias and subject to apocalyptic mood swings. In countries in the South, extremes of pessimism are frequent – on account of negative growth, the failure of trickle-down and the consequences of development, populist swings in politics or the paralysis of politics, and double dealing on the part of Western institutions. The perplexities of progress are shared North and South. The modern crisis of techno-scientific progress translates into a crisis of development. 'Progress is a blank check to be honoured beyond consent and legitimation' (Beck 1992: 203) and now there is a breakdown of faith that technical progress = social progress. It is no longer taken for granted either that the negative effects of technical progress can be treated separately, as mere social consequences of technological change. A parallel questioning in development is whether growth = development and economic growth = social development. Progress as a paradox is an established theme (e.g. Stent 1978, Ashton and Laura 1999). Ashis Nandy's definition of progress as 'the growing awareness of oppression' (1989) is insightful, but serves more as a warning signal than a guiding light. Probing the meaning of progress in the light of North–South differences goes back some time (e.g. Banuri et al. 1993) and 'redefining progress' has become a major preoccupation North (Halstead and Cobb 1996) and South.

Thus, 'anti-development' thinking parallels critiques of progress, and post-development resembles the aprogrammatic, directionless, radical scepticism prevalent in postmodernism. The core problem posed in post-development is the question of modernity. However, to be 'for' or 'against' modernity is, either way, too simple a position. Post-development, as an uneven combination of post-modern methodologies and neo-traditionalist sensibilities, articulates profound sensibilities but is not policy-oriented and does not have a future programme. Reflexive development, as a corollary to reflexive modernity, may be more

enabling as a perspective (Chapters 1 and 6). There are different stages and kinds
of modernity and, short of rejection, reflexive development offers a critical negotiation of modernity and development.

The deeper argument here is that *development has been reflexive all along.*
According to the conventional interpretation, development thinking was an extension of 'progress', but Cowen and Shenton (1996) document that the origins of
development thinking lie in the critique of progress. Classical political economy
was a reaction to the social problems and dislocations brought about by industrialization, and thus the origins of development thinking lie in reflexivity in relation to
industrialization and not simply in catching-up policies. In this light we can reread
the seesaw history of economics and development policy as a series of reactions to
and reflections on policy dilemmas caused by previous policies and conditions.
Viewed in this way, the neomercantilism of the late industrializers (Germany,
France, etc.) was a reaction to Britain's dominant position as the workshop of the
world. Central planning and building 'socialism in one country' were variations
along the same route. In Britain in the 1870s, neoclassical economists resumed
the Manchester School legacy in order to capitalize on Britain's leading position.
In the 1890s bankers adopted monetarism and attempted to control inflation in reaction to the depression and the boom-and-bust cycle. During the 1930s Depression,
Keynesian demand management sought to mitigate the business cycle and Fordism
was founded on Keynesian principles. Neoliberalism in the 1980s was a reaction to
the limitations of Keynesian demand management under conditions of stagflation
in the 1970s in conjunction with technological and political changes. If the keynote
of neoliberalism was state failure, the recent preoccupation is market failure. The
'Third Way' is an attempt at a new political balance and synthesis.

In the development field, modern development theory while rejecting the universal applicability of neoclassical economics resumed the legacy of classical
political economy (which had been a reaction to the social dislocation and instability brought about by industrialization). Its first orthodoxy was modernization
and growth theory. Structuralism, dependency theory (resuming the legacies of
Keynesianism and neomercantilism) and alternative development (resuming the
legacy of populism) arose out of the failure of modernization policies. The
neoliberal counterrevolution (resuming the tradition of liberalism) was a rejection
of orthodox development economics and state intervention. Post-development
involves a rejection of conventional development *in toto*. Human development
builds on East Asian education-centred policies, resumes the 'growth and equity'
approach of the 1970s along with Rawlsian social liberalism, and rejects neoliberalism. The preoccupation with safety nets and structural adjustment 'with a
human face', human security and poverty alleviation is a reaction to the limitations of neoliberal reform. This zigzag history is usually interpreted in terms of
the pendulum swing of state–market predominance (with different emphases
reflecting the changing status of various development actors).[4] However, these
historical processes also show a pattern and layering of reflexivities, represented
in institutional changes and policy measures and accompanying shifting indices.

A disadvantage of redefining development as collective learning is that it
suggests an evolutionary bias and a linear process of accumulative knowledge.

This can be remedied by considering learning as a non-linear process. Another disadvantage is that it is apolitical, because where is struggle in this framework? Do landlords, multinational corporations or governments yield their positions of privilege and power on account of learning and reflexivity? They do so only under pressure of collective action. Thus, reflexivity must have a political edge and refer to collective feedback loops that generate and inform collective action challenging existing power relations. It must refer explicitly to reflexive politics that translates collective learning into forward analytics and politics.

One layer of reflexivity arises from methodological and philosophical reflection on development, but reflexivity is not a purely intellectual process: it concerns ongoing political changes. Reflexivity is taken here not as an academic exercise but as *collective reflexivity*:[5] a collective awareness that unfolds as part of a historical process of changing norms, ideologies and institutions, which crumble and then regroup under different headings. Collective reflexivity takes shape through changing institutions and policies, changing expectations and agendas. There is distortion along the way when reflexivity arising from particular circumstances is institutionalized or abstracted as an ideology or theory and then applied out of context; this is the problem of institutional lag, generalization and orthodoxy. Since theory implies generalization, this effect is inherent in economic and development theory. Specificity, diversity, contingency have only recently been adopted as principles of methodology and policy, and current development policies seek to strike a balance between specificity and generality.

Reconstructions

Like all social change, development unfolds in parallel universes. It unfolds as philosophies of change and politics of change, as structural and conjunctural changes, as local politics and as transnational regimes generated in faraway places.

The challenge facing development is to retrieve hope from the collapse of progress. The collapse of progress is not just an occasional episode of collective moodiness but the onset of a different awareness. The Enlightenment has cast a long shadow. Through most of its career development has been steeped in authoritarian high modernism (Scott 1998), which is part of the failure of three development decades. But all along, as argued above, it has also been a series of reactions to and negotiations of the crises of progress. The dilemmas of development parallel the dilemmas of modernity on one question at least: what of a politics of hope? In one view, the current situation is a retreat of intellectuals (Petras 1990), but is the recovery of old positions an option? Presently the development field is bifurcating into a managerial stream – managing development as part of development bureaucracies – and an interpretative stream whose major concern is to deconstruct development, to unpack its claims and discourses, and once that is done, to deconstruct the deconstruction, for deconstruction is a never-ending task. This is the interpretative turn in development studies. In the career of modernity, in the wake of the routinization and bureaucratization of modern institutions, intellectuals from legislators became administrators or interpreters (according to Bauman 1992), and for some time, development intellectuals have been facing similar career options.

According to Rorty (1997), what good politics needs are not principles but 'stories'. The reflexive turn is disabling if it leads to a cul-de-sac of pessimism. What matters is not just the methodology but the intention; what matters is not just deconstruction but why deconstruction. If the intention is to tell a story of the uselessness of stories, it will end up a thin story; if the intention is to tell a story of the significance of stories, it's a different story. Reflexivity is enabling if it is taken as the achievement of a new level of awareness, awareness of the meanings of trying as well as of failure.

Among the reconstructions discussed in the course of this work the widest and most general forward reorientation is critical holism (Chapter 9). More specific is development as intercultural transaction (Chapter 5). Participatory development (Chapter 6) and supply-side social development (Chapter 8) go together as alternative politics and alternative economics of development. These two are now considered in relation to neoliberalism, asking the question whether there is scope for a coherent policy alternative to neoliberalism. The discussion on critical globalism (Chapter 3) is resumed in concluding observations on global transformations.

The development field is a field of hegemonic compromise that papers over the differences between the dominant stakeholders. These can be characterized as different modernities or different capitalisms: Anglo-American free enterprise capitalism, West European welfare capitalism (Rhineland capitalism), East Asian capitalism, the NICs, market socialism in China, transitional countries, the *rentier* capitalism of the oil-producing countries, etc. The differences among them reflect geographical locations, historical itineraries, the timing of development, levels of technology, cultural capital, institutional differences and resource endowments.[6] Typically, in line with their own historical experiences, these different capitalisms take diverse approaches to development; but development is also a transnational undertaking. The first synthesis in modern development was the state-centred Keynesian consensus, which reflected the experiences of European capitalisms (and East European socialism). The current successor to this approach is human development, which is close to the experiences of East Asian capitalism. The market-centred neoclassical approach as represented by the Washington consensus reflects the interests of Anglo-American capitalism. The third major synthesis, society-centred participatory development, is now being coopted by the other two approaches, which both embrace 'participation'.

The diverse approaches to development are being papered over in the hegemonic language of development. Who can reasonably object to 'good governance', 'democracy', 'civil society', 'transparency'? Of course, each of these can be unpacked. Thus, embedded in 'good governance' is the contentious idea that the free market and democracy go together (cf. Attali 1997). Seen from this angle, development discourse appears as a large-scale spin-doctoring operation, in which the Washington consensus is dressed up as a Trilateral consensus and next, as a global consensus. Against the backdrop of the long hegemony of Anglo-American capitalism, the Washington agenda is now being transmitted globally through the international financial institutions, the WTO, the G8 and G22, in part by default, in the absence of an alternative policy consensus. The Washington consensus 'maintains that economic growth is best furthered by more open trade, export-led growth, greater deregulation, and more liberalized financial markets' (Palley 1999: 49).

Neoclassical economics and monetarism represent (a) good house-holding (don't spend more than you earn), (b) technical expertise, (c) a theoretical legacy, (d) an ideological mindset and (e) an interest coalition. These dimensions cannot be neatly separated. The technical skills of economic and financial monitoring and planning are steeped in analytical and ideological assumptions, mental frameworks and institutional paths, such as competitiveness indexes, international credit ratings and banking policies. They tend to assume Anglo-American capitalism as the 'norm' of capitalism, and in the process represent the perspectives and interests of major financial institutions such as the Wall Street-Treasury-IMF complex. This approach faces several problems: growing inequality, financial instability and crisis management.

We inhabit a global theatre of the absurd, a winner-takes-all world in which the wealthiest billionaires own as much as approximately half the world population. The statistics are familiar.[7] If trickle-down does not hold in national economies it is even less valid at a global level. There is no global trickle-down. Global inequality, refracted in local inequality, goes together with environmental imbalances. Development and environment are the two central world problems. Such is the world fashioned by Anglo-American capitalism and the Washington consensus is part of the problem. The problems of the Washington consensus have been widely discussed.[8] For decades, criticism of and protest against the Washington consensus have been plentiful, but no *coherent* alternative has emerged, as if confirming that 'there is no alternative'. But in recent times, several streams have gradually been coming together. International civic organizations have long argued for an alternative to Bretton Woods (e.g. Niva 1999, Griesgraber and Gunter 1996b). Now there is a growing reform consensus in international development (e.g. Edwards 1999) which includes reorientations in the World Bank and OECD. In addition, the Washington consensus has been cracking itself. Criticisms of the IMF's handling of financial crises show a rift within the Washington consensus: within the IMF (Camdessus 1998) and World Bank (Stiglitz 1998), and among free market advocates such as Jeffrey Sachs who have come back on their endorsement. Dissident voices in Wall Street (Soros 1998) also plead for reform. These are signs of and responses to the growing difficulty of the neoliberal regime in reproducing itself. What used to be the Washington consensus has now been reduced to a Washington agenda. Financial instability poses risks even for the winners. Reform proposals converge on calls for financial re-regulation, in particular change in the international financial architecture to control the flows of 'hot money' (Akyuz 2000). In the wake of the Mexican, Asian, Latin American and Russian crises, the IMF (and the US Treasury, which finances the bailouts) has been pondering the scope for re-regulation. The regulation of international finance has temporarily made place for a concern with transparency, which refers to the world-wide alignment and standardization of accounting systems. If double bookkeeping was essential to the rise of modern capitalism, the standardization of accounting systems is part of the globalization of capitalism.

The other approaches also have their problems, in part as a function of Washington hegemony. Participatory development is an indication of a larger change that is imperceptibly taking place in political systems and cultures. It reflects a relative disempowerment of states and political systems in relation to development and technological change, that takes the form of depoliticization and technocracy, and repoliticization through the emergence of subpolitics, manifesting in special interests, lobbying, social movements and localization, ethnic mobilization and religious resurgence. As both cause and effect of democratization, civil actors seek empowerment and the boundaries between political and non-political, public and private spheres have become increasingly fluid. Informalization and liberalization involve a transfer of responsibilities from government to NGOs and the emergence of parallel structures, for instance in welfare and public health. Thus in several countries in sub-Saharan Africa, much of the health care and welfare sector has been subcontracted to foreign-funded NGOs. But what are not being replaced are the procedures of accountability, inadequate as they were. Hence, the new democratic culture of which participatory development is part also has new democratic deficits. The problems of participatory development are in part a function of the Washington hegemony. While 'participation' has become the leading development talk since the 1990s, it is a highly elastic term.[9] The alternative platform matches the Washington consensus in the common theme of state failure, the trend toward privatization and informalization, i.e. a greater role for firms or NGOs; and the discourse of civil society and democracy. The new policy agenda of civil society building and 'NGO-ization', community development and self-reliance matches the new right agenda of government rollback and decentralization. Another problem is alternative dependency through foreign-funded NGOs. Accordingly, in the words of Michael Woost, 'we are still riding in a top-down vehicle of development whose wheels are greased with a vocabulary of bottom-up discourse' (1997: 249).

In view of these problems, should we go back to the Keynesian consensus? Structural conditions are now different. If we look at the difficulties of welfare states in the North, could they survive in the South under much more difficult circumstances? The human development approach is state-centred at a time when government influence is being curtailed. The capabilities approach that underlies human development does not challenge power relations. There is no going back to governmentalism as it used to be; there is no going back to daddy state because of changes in technology, organization, production, markets and consumption. The conjunction of the Washington consensus and the alternative platform is too significant to be merely a matter of ideological manipulation. The point then is to find a narrow path in which participatory approaches retain their meaning, the role of the state is reinvented through public sector reform, and the Washington agenda itself is reconsidered. This task is common to North and South. The general concern with public–private partnership and corporate citizenship is part of this change.

Participatory development (articulating social interests) and human development (articulating perspectives of states and international institutions) form a strategic combination of development perspectives, for together they represent social, state and institutional perspectives. The major rift in the development field now runs between these approaches and the Washington agenda. Underlying this rift is the central question of finding a way for the world of banking and finance, their abstract indicators and narrow agendas, to communicate meaningfully with the real world of social questions, work, poverty and human security. The core of the Washington agenda, 'free markets and sound money', is the ratio of the world of banking and finance as viewed through the lens of Anglo-American capitalism. Viewed from a global perspective, the Washington agenda is a minority concern and development, per definition, is a majority concern. A major principle for reform in the development field is that the accommodation between different capitalisms should take place according to majority and not according to hegemonic interests. Against this backdrop, the contours of a coherent alternative to neo-liberalism may gradually be taking shape. This involves a new convergence in development thinking and a consensus that, though short of a global consensus, is broad and growing. With apologies for offering another list, the outlines of this reform platform include the following components:

❑ Investment-led growth (Griffin 2000b) and domestic demand-led growth. 'This is a strategy that lifts all boats, because demand growth in one country pulls in exports from others, so that all grow together' (Palley 1999: 50).
❑ Human rights, core labour standards and independent unionism. Domestic demand-led growth requires rising wages and this entails evening the balance between capital and labour.
❑ Political reform and active democracy to counteract economic cronyism.
❑ Controls on short-term capital movements to require investors to commit for a minimum period.[10]
❑ Taxes on buying and selling of currencies to curb financial speculation.
❑ Measures to prevent tax competition.
❑ Debt reduction for low-income countries (as in Jubilee 2000).
❑ Reform of the IMF and World Bank to make them more accountable.
❑ A review of global trade and investment institutions and policies.

These measures would contribute to evening the balance between capital and labour. A growing ensemble of social forces and political institutions shares this approach. In the South, this broadly matches the politics of reforming governments. It matches the *Alternativo Latinoamericana* (Conger 1998). It matches the forward proposals by critics of liberalization in South Asia (Bhaduri and Nayyar 1996: Ch 6). In the North, Third Way politics is a significant departure, not so much in terms of principles but in terms of establishing a centre-left political momentum. In terms of principles, the Third Way is too vague (Giddens 1998); in practice, it has been driven by electoral opportunism, and in delivery it has been too weak (Faux 1999, Ryan 1999). Labour, civic organizations, reform and Green parties might be able to carry the Third Way beyond electoral opportunism. In the United States, a coalition of left Democrats and labour adds up to a 'Mainstreet Alternative' (Palley 1999). In the UK, there are significant perspectives and political forces beyond New Labour (e.g. Hutton 1995) and similar conditions exist presently in most countries in the North.

Internationally the principles of a reform alternative to neoliberalism are broadly shared in the UN system and other international institutions. The World Bank's comprehensive development framework endorses pro-poor growth (e.g. Sen and Wolfensohn 1999). The IMF has begun to accommodate social and human dimensions of development. In international development cooperation, where criticism of policy incoherence has been rife (Smillie 1997), reform initiatives are now being widely shared, including by the OECD (Bernard et al. 1998). Labour internationalism and the ILO are significant forces. International NGOs and civic organizations have contributed significantly to changing public discourse and promoting public and private accountability.

Features of this reform platform are that it bridges concerns North and South, avoids old left orthodoxy and populism as well as right sloganeering and market worship, and combines national reform with global reform. It's not a matter of going back to conventional Marxism or Keynesianism. Several components of the Washington agenda – public sector reform to achieve effective government, good governance, accountability and transparency – are part of the reform agenda. A difference is that if accountability in the Washington formula refers primarily to international monitoring institutions and overseas investors through the standardization of accounting systems, in the reform agenda it refers primarily to accountability to the electorate.

Part of the reform platform is the awareness that no matter how ingeniously development is reinvented, it cannot be settled without global reform. Virtually all development approaches now engage the global level. In dependency thinking, this takes the form of criticizing uneven globalization. Neoliberalism involves the project of neoliberal globalization. Alternative development envisages alternative globalization and human development seeks global reform, while anti-development converges on anti-globalization. The global horizon is a compelling rendezvous, a prism in which all angles on development are refracted. This illustrates the dramatic salience of globalization as well as the diversity in development thinking. Since we have entered the era of global capitalism, while national settlements are important, global engagement is essential. Globalization requires political adjustments for all development actors, while development actors seek political adjustment of globalization. The crossroads of globalization may be summed up as either neoliberal globalization or taking a developmental approach to globalization (Pronk 2000). A Keynesian approach to a global new deal could take the form of global neo-Keynesianism (e.g. Lipietz 1992). Straddling society-centred and state-centred approaches to global reform are proposals for global social contracts (Group of Lisbon 1995) and transnational social policy (Deacon et al. 1998). The challenge for a global development approach is to bring separate and opposing interests and constituencies together as part of a world-wide bargaining and process approach. Together with proposals for reform of the UN system and strengthening the international legal order, this adds up to a global reform platform.[11] At this point, development becomes world development, a horizon radically different from the original Gestalt of development.

Notes

1 Global neoliberal projects are widely discussed, among others by McMichael 1996 and Dessouki 1993. The distinction between globalization as process and as project is discussed in Nederveen Pieterse 2000b.

2 A case in point is the role of Japan in representing the 'East Asian Miracle', discussed in Wade 1996.

3 For forty years, this has been the most quoted source in public administration.

4 This is a summary treatment; a more extensive discussion is in Chapter 3.

5 Several perspectives concentrate on reflexivity of the self (Taylor 1989, Habermas 1990, Giddens 1991) while others (e.g. Beck 1992, Soros 1998, Foley 1999) use reflexivity in a collective sense, including reflexive institutions (Fischer 1993). Self-reflexivity and collective reflexivity are combined in approaches that bring together the personal and the political, such as feminism and new social movement research (Melucci 1989). A new approach to NGOs combines commitments to social justice with attentiveness to interpersonal relations and psychological states (Edwards and Sen 1999). In discussing the work of Aurobindo, Pande and Habermas, Giri also probes the relationship between self-reflexivity and collective reflexivity (1998: Ch. 11). A critical discussion of reflexivity is Lynch 2000.

6 Different capitalisms and different modernities are twin-track descriptions. Cf. Eisenstadt 2000, Nederveen Pieterse 2000c.

7 Since the 1980s the gap between rich and poor countries has been widening dramatically. The poorest 20 per cent of the world population accounts for 1.3 per cent of total private consumption expenditure, while the highest 20 per cent, i.e. those living in the highest-income countries, account for 86 per cent (UNDP 1998: 2).

8 E.g. Bienefeld 1994, Gills and Philip 1996, Cypher 1998. For instance, 'One country's exports are another country's imports, and this means that all cannot rely on export-led growth' (Palley 1999: 50). Export-led growth may lead to competitive devaluation and global deflation or global shortage of demand (Greider 1997).

9 Also the World Bank publishes a *Participation Sourcebook* (1996). Arguably, it should not be 'community participation in development', but state and international agencies participating in community affairs. Cf. Stiefel and Wolfe 1994.

10 Proposed by Soros 1998 and shared by Stiglitz and others (cf. Conger 1998: 383).

11 Global reform is addressed in Nederveen Pieterse 2000a.

REFERENCES

Abdel-Malek, A. (1963) 'Orientalism in crisis', *Diogenes*, 44: 109-42.

Abdel-Malek, A. (ed.) (1980/1983) *Contemporary Arab political thought*. London: Zed.

Abraham, R., T. McKenna and R. Sheldrake (1992) *Trialogues at the edge of the West*. Santa Fe, NM: Bear.

Abu-Lughod, L. (1990) 'The romance of resistance: tracing transformation of power through Bedouin women', *American Ethnologist*, 17 (1): 41-55.

Adachi, I. (1996) *The law of undulation*. Tokyo: EVHA.

Addo, H., S. Amin, G. Aseniero, A.G. Frank, M. Friberg, F. Fröbel, J. Heinrichs, B. Hettne, O. Kreye, H. Seki (1985) *Development as social transformation*. London: Hodder and Stoughton.

Adelman, I. and C.T. Morris (1967) *Society, politics and economic development*. Baltimore: Johns Hopkins University Press.

Adelman, I. and S. Robinson (1978) *Income distribution policy in developing countries*. Oxford and Washington, DC: Oxford University Press and World Bank.

African Rights (1994) *Humanitarianism unbound?* Discussion Paper 5. London: African Rights.

Agrawal, A. (1995a) 'Dismantling the divide between indigenous and scientific knowledge', *Development and Change*, 26 (3): 413-40.

Agrawal, A. (1995b) 'Indigenous and scientific knowledge: some critical comments', *Indigenous Knowledge and Development Monitor*, 3 (3): 3-6.

Ahmed, D.S. (1997) 'Women and religion: problems and prospects', in *Women and religion: debates on a search*. Lahore: Heinrich Böll Foundation, pp. 23-58.

Ake, C. (1979) *Social science as imperialism: the theory of political development*. Ibadan: University of Ibadan Press.

Akiwowo, A. (1988) 'Universalism and indigenization in sociological theory: introduction', *International Sociology*, 3 (2): 155-61.

Akiwowo, A. (1999) 'Indigenous sociologies: extending the scope of the argument', special issue *International Sociology*, 14 (2).

Akyuz, Y. (2000) 'The debate on the international financial architecture: reforming the reformers', *UNCTAD Discussion Paper* 148.

Alavi, H. (1973) 'The state in postcolonial societies: Pakistan and Bangladesh', in K. Gough and H.P. Sharma (eds) *Imperialism and revolution in South Asia*. New York: Monthly Review Press, pp. 145-73.

Albert, M. (1993) *Capitalism against capitalism*. London: Whurr.

Almond, G.A. (1964) 'Comparative political systems', in R.C. Macridis and B.E. Brown (eds), *Comparative politics*, revised ed. Homewood, IL: Dorsey, pp. 50-64.

Alvares, C. (1979) *Homo faber*. Bombay: Allied Publishers.

Alvares, C. (1992) *Science, development and violence: the revolt against modernity*. Delhi: Oxford University Press.

Alvesson, M. and K. Skjöldberg (1999) *Reflexive methodology*. London: Sage.

Amin, A. (ed.) (1994a) *Post-Fordism: a reader*. Oxford: Blackwell.

Amin, A. (1994b) 'Post-Fordism: models, fantasies and phantoms of transition', in Amin (ed.), pp. 1-39.

Amin, A. (1997) 'Beyond associative democracy', *New Political Economy*, (1) 3: 309-33.

Amin, A. and N. Thrift (1993) 'Globalization, institutional thickness and local prospects', *Revue d'économie régionale et urbaine*, 3: 405-27.

Amin, A. and N. Thrift (1997) 'Globalisation, socioeconomics, territoriality', in R. Lee and J. Willis (eds), *Society, place, economy*. London: Arnold, pp. 151-61.

Amin, S. (1976) *Unequal development*. Brighton: Harvester Press.

Amin, S. (1980) *Class and nation, historically and in the current crisis*. New York: Monthly Review Press (orig. French edn 1979).

Amin, S. (1982) 'Crisis, nationalism, and socialism', in S. Amin, G. Arrighi, A.G. Frank and I. Wallerstein, *Dynamics of global crisis*. New York: Monthly Review Press, pp. 167-231.

Amin, S. (1989) *Eurocentrism*. London: Zed (orig. French edn 1988).

Amin, S. (1990a) *Delinking: towards a polycentric world*. London: Zed (orig. French edn 1985).

Amin, S. (1990b) 'Black Athena: la fabrication de la Grèce antique', *Ifda Dossier*, 77: 93-4.

Amin, S. (1990c) *Maldevelopment: anatomy of a global failure*. London: Zed.

Amin, S. (1992) 'The perils of utopia', interview by Monty Narsoo, *Work in Progress*, December: 28-30.

Amin, S. (1997) *Capitalism in the age of globalization*. London: Zed.

Amin, S. (1999) *Spectres of capitalism: a critique of current intellectual fashions*. London: Zed.

Amin, S., D. Chitala and I. Mandaza (eds) (1987) *SADCC: prospects for disengagement and development in Southern Africa*. Tokyo, United Nations University Press.

Anderla, G., A. Dunning and S. Forge (1997) *Chaotics: an agenda for business and society for the 21ˢᵗ century*. London: Adamantine Press.

Antweiler, C. (1993) 'Entwicklungsethnologie und Entwicklungssoziologie', *Entwicklungsethnologie*, 2 (1): 40-60.

Apffel-Marglin, F. and S. Marglin (eds) (1990) *Dominating knowledge: development, culture and resistance*. Oxford: Clarendon Press.

Apffel-Marglin, F. and S. Marglin (cds) (1996) *Decolonizing knowledge: from development to dialogue*. Oxford: Clarendon Press.

Appadurai, A. (ed.) (1986) *The social life of things*. Cambridge: Cambridge University Press.

Apter, D.E. (1987) *Rethinking development: modernization, dependency, and postmodern politics*. London: Sage.

Apthorpe, R. and D. Gasper (eds) (1996) *Arguing development policy: frames and discourses*. London: Frank Cass.

Ariansen, P. (1998) 'Anthropocentrism with a human face', *Ecological Economics*, 24 (2-3): 153-62.

Aronowitz, S. (1989) *Science as power: discourse and ideology in modern society*. London: Macmillan.

Arrelano-Lopez, S. and J.F. Petras (1994) 'Non-governmental organizations and poverty alleviation in Bolivia', *Development and Change*, 25 (3): 555-68.

Arruda, M. (1994) 'A creative approach to structural adjustment: towards a people-centred development', in Cavanagh et al. (eds), pp. 132-44.

Arruda, M. (1996) Globalization and civil society: rethinking cooperativism in the context of active citizenship. Rio de Janeiro: PACS (Alternative Policies for the Southern Cone).

Ashton, J. and R. Laura (1999) *The perils of progress*. London: Zed.

Attali, J. (1997) 'The crash of Western civilization: the limits of the market and democracy', *Foreign Policy*, 107: 54-64.

Ayto, J. (1990) *Bloomsbury dictionary of word origins*. London: Bloomsbury.

Badie, B. (1989) 'Comparative analysis in political science: requiem or resurrection?' *Political Studies*, 37 (3): 340-52.

Balasubramaniam, A. (1987) *Participatory Action Research*. Singapore: Friedrich Naumann Stiftung.

Banuri, T. (1990) 'Modernization and its discontents: a cultural perspective on the theories of development', in Apffel-Marglin and Marglin (eds)

Banuri, T. et al. (1993) 'A North-South debate: the meaning of progress', *UNESCO Courier*, 46, December.

Banuri, T., S. Rafi Khan and M. Mahmood (eds) (1997) *Just development: beyond adjustment with a human face*. Karachi: Oxford University Press.

Bauman, Z. (1992) *Intimations of postmodernity*. London: Routledge.

Bazin, M. (1987) 'Tales of underdevelopment', *Race & Class*, 28 (3): 1-12.

Beck, U. (1992) *Risk society: towards a new modernity*. London: Sage.

Bell, D. (1978) *The cultural contradictions of capitalism*. New York: Basic Books.

Benedict, R. (1935) *Patterns of culture*. London: Routledge and Kegan Paul.

Berger, P. and T. Luckmann (1967) *The social construction of reality*. London: Allen Lane.

Berman, Marshall (1988) *All that is solid melts into air*. New York: Penguin.

Berman, Morris (1984) *The reenchantment of the world*. New York: Bantam.

Bernal, M. (1987) *Black Athena: Afroasiatic roots of classical civilization: the fabrication of Ancient Greece* 1785-1985. London: Free Association Press.

Bernard, A., H. Helmich and P.B. Lehning (eds) (1998) *Civil society and international cooperation.* Paris: OECD.

Bhabha, H.K. (1994) *The location of culture.* London: Routledge.

Bhaduri, A. and D. Nayyar (1996) *The intelligent person's guide to liberalization.* New Delhi: Penguin.

Bhalla, A. and F. Lapeyre (1997) 'Social exclusion: towards an analytical and operational framework', *Development and Change*, 28 (3): 413-34.

Bharadwaj, K. and S. Kaviraj (1989) 'Introduction', in Bharadwaj and Kaviraj (eds), *Perspectives on capitalism.* New Delhi: Sage, pp. 9-19.

Bhaskar, R. (1991) *Philosophy and the idea of freedom.* Oxford: Blackwell.

Bienefeld, M. (1994) 'The New World Order: echoes of a new imperialism', *Third World Quarterly*, 15 (1): 31-48.

Black, M. (1992) *A cause for our times: Oxfam the first fifty years.* Oxford: Oxford University Press.

Bohm, D. (1980) *Wholeness and the implicate order.* London: Routledge and Kegan Paul.

Boon, J.A. (1990) *Affinities and extremes.* Chicago: University of Chicago Press.

Booth, D. (1993) 'Development research: from impasse to a new agenda', in Schuurman (ed.), pp. 49-76.

Booth, D. (ed.) (1994a) *Rethinking social development.* Harlow: Longman.

Booth, D. (1994b) 'How far beyond the impasse?', in Booth (ed.), pp. 298-311.

Bourdieu, P. (1976) 'Les modes de domination', *Actes de la recherche en sciences sociales*, 2 (2-3): 122-32.

Bourdieu, P. (1988) *Homo academicus.* Stanford, CA: Stanford University Press.

Bourdieu, P. and J.-C. Passeron (1990) *Reproduction in education, society and culture*, 2nd edn. London: Sage.

Bourdieu, P. and L. Wacquant (1992) *An invitation to reflexive sociology.* Chicago: University of Chicago Press.

Boyer, R. and D. Drache (eds) (1996) *States against markets: the limits of globalization.* London: Routledge.

Broad, R. and C. Melhorn Landi (1996) 'Whither the North-South gap?, *Third World Quarterly*, 17 (1): 7-17.

Brohman, J. (1995) 'Economism and critical silences in development studies: a theoretical critique of neoliberalism', *Third World Quarterly*, 16 (2): 297-318.

Brohman, J. (1996) *Popular development: rethinking the theory and practice of development.* Oxford: Blackwell.

Brokensha, D., D. Warren and O. Werner (eds) (1980) *Indigenous knowledge systems and development.* Lanham, MD: University Press of America.

Brookfield, H. (1975) *Interdependent development.* London: Methuen.

Brown, D.L. and D. Ashman (1996) 'Participation, social capital, and intersectoral problem-solving: African and Asian cases'. Boston: Institute for Development Research Report 12 (2).

Brown, D.L. and D. Ashman (1999) 'Social capital, mutual influence, and social learning in intersectoral problem solving in Africa and Asia', in Cooperrider and Dutton (eds), pp. 139-67.

Burkey, S. (1992) *People first: a guide to self-reliant participatory rural development.* London: Zed.

Burne, S. (ed.) (1995) *Let the dawn come: social development, looking behind the clichés.* London: Panos.

Buvini, M., C. Gwyn and L.M. Bates (1996) *Investing in women: progress and prospects for the World Bank.* Washington, DC: Overseas Development Council.

Camdessus, M. (1998) 'Camdessus discusses new global architecture', *IMF Survey*, 27 (10): 157, 161-3.

Capra, F. (1988) *Uncommon wisdom.* London: Century Hutchinson.

Capra, F. (1996) *The web of life.* New York: Doubleday.

Cardoso, F.H. (1993) 'North-South relations in the present context: a new dependency?', in Carnoy et al., pp. 149-60.

Carmen, R. (1996) *Autonomous development: humanizing the landscape.* London: Zed.

Carnoy, M. (1993) 'Multinationals in a changing world economy: whither the nation state?' in Carnoy et al., pp. 45-96.

Carnoy, M., M. Castells, S.S. Cohen and F.H. Cardoso (1993) *The new global economy in the information age*. University Park, PA: Pennsylvania State University Press.

Carr, B. (1999) 'Globalization from below: labour internationalism under NAFTA', *International Social Science Journal*, 159: 49-59.

Castells, M. (1993) 'The informational economy and the new international division of labor', in Carnoy et al., pp. 15-43.

Castells, M. (1996) *The information age*, Vol. 1, *The rise of the network society*. Oxford: Blackwell.

Castells, M. (1997) *The information age*, Vol. 2, *The power of identity*. Oxford: Blackwell.

Cavanagh, J., D. Wysham and M. Arruda (eds) (1994) *Beyond Bretton Woods: alternatives to the global economic order*. London: Pluto.

Center for the Study of the Global South (1994) *Social summit, Copenhagen: expectations of the global South*. Washington, DC: American University.

Chambers, R. (1983) *Rural development: putting the last first*. London: Longman.

Chatterjee, P. (1986) *Nationalist thought and the colonial world*. London: Tokyo: Zed.

Chenery, H. et al. (1974) *Redistribution with growth*. Oxford: Oxford University Press.

Chiejina, T.O. (1993) 'A tale of two Rajni Kotharis', The Hague, Institute of Social Studies, unpublished paper.

Chin, C.B.N. and J.H. Mittelman (2000) 'Conceptualising resistance to globalisation', in B.K. Gills (ed.), *Globalization and the politics of resistance*. London: Macmillan, pp. 29-45.

Chirot, D. (1977) *Social change in the twentieth century*. New York: Harcourt Brace Jovanovich.

Chossudovsky, M. (1997) *The globalization of poverty: impacts of IMF and World Bank reforms*. London: Zed.

Christopherson, S. (1994) 'The fortress city: privatized spaces, consumer citizenship', in Amin (1994a), pp. 409-27.

Clark, J. (1991) *Democratizing development: the role of voluntary organizations*. London: Earthscan.

Clarke, G. (1998) 'Non-governmental organizations and politics in the developing world', *Political Studies*, 46: 36-52.

Cleveland, H., H. Henderson and I. Kaul (eds) (1995) *The United Nations: policy and financing alternatives*. New York: Apex Press.

Clifford, J. (1988) *The predicament of culture*. Cambridge, MA: Harvard University Press.

Clifford, J. (1992) 'Travelling cultures', in L. Grossberg, C. Nelson and P. Treichler (eds), *Cultural studies*. London: Routledge, pp. 96-116.

Coetzee, J.K. (ed.) (1989) *Development is for people*. Halfway House, South Africa: Southern Book Publishers.

Coleman, J.S. (1988) 'Social capital in the creation of human capital', *American Journal of Sociology*, 94: 95-120.

Collingsworth, T., J.W. Goold and P.J. Harvey (1994) 'Time for a global new deal', *Foreign Affairs*, 73 (1): 8-13.

Colman, D. and F. Nixson (1994) 'Alternative views of development: underdevelopment and dependence', in idem, *Economics of change in less developed countries*, 3rd edn. London: Harvester Wheatsheaf, pp. 48-67.

Comfort, L.K. (1999) *Shared risk: complex systems in seismic response*. Amsterdam: Pergamon.

Commission on Global Governance (1995) *Our global neighbourhood* (report). New York: Oxford University Press.

Conger, L. (1998) 'A fourth way? The Latin American alternative to neoliberalism', *Current History*, November: 380-4.

Connors, M. (1997) *The race to the intelligent state: charting the global information economy in the 21st century*. Oxford: Capstone.

Constantino, R. (1985) *Synthetic culture and development*. Quezon City, Philippines: Foundation for Nationalist Studies.

Cooperrider, D.L. and J.E. Dutton (eds) (1999) *Organizational dimensions of global change: no limits to cooperation*. London: Sage.

Corbridge, S. (1994) 'Post-marxism and post-colonialism: the needs and rights of distant strangers', in Booth (1994a), pp. 90-117.

Corbridge, S. (ed.) (1995) *Development studies: a reader*. London: Edward Arnold.

Corbridge, S. (1998) '"Beneath the pavement only soil": the poverty of post-development', *Journal of Development Studies*, 34 (6): 138-48.

Cowen, M.P. and R.W. Shenton (1996) *Doctrines of development*. London: Routledge.

Cox, R.W. (1991) 'Gramsci, hegemony and international relations: an essay in method', *Millennium*, 12 (2): 162-75.

Craig, B.J. (1992) *Laying the ladder down: the emergence of cultural holism*. Amherst, MA: University of Massachusetts Press.

Crehan, K. (1991) 'Structures of meaning and structures of interest: peasants and planners in north-western Zambia', in Kaarsholm (ed.), pp. 185-208.

Crocker, D.A. (1991) 'Insiders and outsiders in international development', *Ethics & International Affairs*, 5: 149-73.

Crush, J. (ed.) (1996a) *The power of development*. London: Routledge.

Crush, J. (1996b) 'Introduction: imagining development', in idem (ed.), pp. 1-23.

Cypher, J.M. (1998) 'The slow death of the Washington Consensus on Latin America', *Latin American Perspectives*, 25 (6): 47-51.

Dag Hammarskjöld Foundation (1975) 'What now? Another development', *Development Dialogue*, 1-2.

Dallmayr, F. (1996) 'Global development? Alternative voices from Delhi', *Alternatives*, 21 (2): 259-82.

Daly, H.E. and J.B. Cobb Jr. (1994) *For the common good*, 2nd edn. Boston: Beacon Press.

Dasgupta, P. (1988) 'Trust as a commodity', in D. Gambetta (ed.), *Trust: making and breaking cooperative relations*. Oxford: Blackwell, pp. 49-72.

Dasgupta, S. (1985) *Towards a post development era*. London: Mittal.

Davis, A. (1991) 'Hazardous lives – social work in the 1980s: a view from the left', in M. Loney et al. (eds), *The state or the market: politics and welfare in contemporary Britain*, 2nd edn. London: Sage, pp. 83-93.

Davis, M. (1990) *City of Quartz*. London: Verso.

Davis, P.J. and R. Hersh (1986) *Descartes' dream: the world according to mathematics*. Boston: Houghton Mifflin.

Deacon, B., M. Hulse and P. Stubbs (1998) *Global social policy*. London: Sage.

Desai, A.R. (ed.) (1971) *Essays on modernization of underdeveloped societies*, 2 vols. Bombay: Thacker.

Dessouki, A.E.H. (1993) 'Globalization and the two spheres of security', *Washington Quarterly*, 16 (4): 109-17.

Development and social diversity – development in practice readers (1996) Oxford: Oxfam.

Doornbos, M.R. (1989) 'The African state in academic debate', The Hague: Institute of Social Studies.

Dore, R. (1992) 'Goodwill and the spirit of market capitalism', in Granovetter and Swedberg (eds), pp. 159-80.

Drabek, A.G. (ed.) (1987) *Development alternatives: the challenge for NGOs* in *World Development*, 15, Supplement: 1-261.

Drèze, J. and A. Sen (1989) *Hunger and public action*. Oxford: Clarendon Press.

DSE (1994) *Social security in Africa: old age, accident and unemployment*. Berlin: Deutsche Stiftung für Internationale Entwicklung.

DuBois, M. (1991) 'The governance of the Third World: a Foucauldian perspective on power relations in development', *Alternatives*, 16: 1-30.

Duffield, M. (1996) 'The globalisation of public policy: managing the systemic crisis in the South', Birmingham, School of Public Policy, unpublished paper.

Dumont, R. (1965) *Lands alive*. New York: Monthly Review Press.

Dumont, R. (1974) *Utopia or else...* London: André Deutsch.

Dunn, D. (1986) 'Synchronisms: toward a phenomenological science', *International Synergy Journal*, 1: 2-8.

Edwards, M. (1999) *Future positive: international cooperation in the 21st century*. London: Earthscan.

Edwards, M. and D. Hulme (eds) (1992) *Making a difference: NGOs and development in a changing world*. London: Earthscan.

Edwards, M. and G. Sen (1999) 'NGOs, social change and the transformation of human relationships: a 21st century civic agenda', unpublished paper.

Eisenstadt, S.N. (1966) *Modernization: protest and change*. Englewood Cliffs, NJ: Prentice-Hall.

Eisenstadt, S.N. (2000) 'Multiple modernities', *Daedalus*, 129 (1), special issue: 1-30.

Ekins, P. (1992) *A new world order: grassroots movements for global change*. London: Routledge.

Elliott, E. and D. Kiel (1997) 'Nonlinear dynamics, complexity and public policy', in Eve et al. (eds), pp. 64-78.

Elson, D. (1993) 'Gender-aware analysis and development economics', *Journal of International Development*, 5 (2): 237-47.

Enloe, C. (1990) *Bananas, beaches and bases*. Berkeley, CA: University of California Press.

Escobar, A. (1985) 'Discourse and power in development: Michel Foucault and the relevance of his work to the Third World', *Alternatives*, 10: 377-400.

Escobar, A. (1992a) 'Planning', in Sachs (1992a), pp. 132-45.

Escobar, A. (1992b) 'Reflections on "Development": grassroots approaches and alternative politics in the Third World', *Futures*, June: 411-36.

Escobar, A. (1995) *Encountering development: the making and unmaking of the Third World*. Princeton, NJ: Princeton University Press.

Escobar, A. (1996) 'Imagining a post-development era', in Crush (1996a), pp. 211-27.

Esman, M.J. and N.T. Upton (1984) *Local organizations: intermediaries in rural development*. Ithaca, NY: Cornell University Press.

Esping-Andersen, G. (1994) 'Welfare states and the economy', in Smelser and Swedberg (eds), pp. 711-31.

Esposito, J.L. (1992) *The Islamic threat: myth or reality?* New York: Oxford University Press.

Esteva, G. (1985) 'Beware of participation' and 'Development: metaphor, myth, threat', *Development: Seeds of Change*, 3: 77 and 78-79.

Esteva, G. (1992) 'Development', in Sachs (ed.), pp. 6-25.

Esteva, G. and M.S. Prakash (1998) *Hope at the margins: beyond human rights and development*. London: Zed.

Eve, R.A. (1997) 'Afterword', in Eve et al. (eds), pp. 269-80.

Eve, R.A., S. Horsfall and M.E. Lee (eds) (1997) *Chaos, complexity and sociology*. London: Sage.

Fabian, J. (1983) *Time and the other: how anthropology makes its objects*. New York: Columbia University Press.

Fagan, G.H. (1999) 'Cultural politics and (post) development paradigm(s)', in Munck and O'Hearn (eds), pp. 178-95.

Falk, R. (1994) *On humane governance: towards a new global politics*. Cambridge: Polity.

Fals-Borda, O. (1985) Wisdom as power, *Development: Seeds of Change*, 3: 65-7.

Fanon, F. (1967) *The wretched of the earth*. Harmondsworth: Penguin.

Faux, J. (1999) 'Lost on the Third Way', *Dissent*, 46 (2): 67-76.

Fei, J., G. Ranis and S. Kuo (1979) *Growth with equity: the Taiwan case*. Oxford: Oxford University Press.

Femia, J.V. (1981) *Gramsci's political thought*. Oxford: Oxford University Press.

Ferguson, J. (1990) *The anti-politics machine: 'development', depoliticisation and bureaucratic power in Lesotho*. Cambridge: Cambridge University Press.

Fernandes, R.C. (1993) 'Looking for alternatives after the cold war', *Cultures and Development: Quid Pro Quo*, 15: 6-14.

Feyerabend, P. (1975) *Against method*. London: New Left Books.

Fine, B. (1999) 'The developmental state is dead – long live social capital?', *Development and Change*, 30 (1): 1-20.

Fischer, F.G. (1993) 'Emergence of a circumspect society: introducing reflexive institutions', *Futures*, 25 (10): 1077-82.

FitzGerald, E.V.K. (1991) 'Kurt Mandelbaum and the classical tradition in development theory' in K. Martin (ed.), *Strategies of economic development*. London: Macmillan, pp. 3-26.

Foley, G. (1999) *Learning in social action*. London: Zed.

Foucault, M. (1980) *Power/knowledge*. C. Gordon (ed.) New York: Pantheon.

Foucault, M. (1984) 'Nietzsche, genealogy, history', in P. Rabinow (ed.), *The Foucault reader*. New York: Pantheon, pp. 76-100.

Frank, A.G. (1969) *Latin America: underdevelopment or revolution*. New York: Monthly Review Press.

Frank, A.G. (1971) *Sociology of development and underdevelopment of sociology*. London: Pluto.

Frank, A.G. (1981) *Crisis: in the Third World*. New York and London: Holmes and Meyer.

Frank, A.G. (1996) 'The underdevelopment of development', in S. Chew and R. Denemark (eds) *The underdevelopment of development*. London: Sage, pp. 17-55.

Frank, A.G. (1998) *Re Orient: global economy in the Asian age*. Berkeley, CA: University of California Press.

Friberg, M. and B. Hettne (1985) 'The greening of the world – towards a nondeterministic model of global process', in Addo et al., pp. 204-70.

Friedman, E. (ed.) (1982) *Ascent and decline in the world-system*. London: Sage.

Friedmann, J. (1992) *Empowerment: the politics of alternative development*. Oxford: Blackwell.

Fukuyama, F. (1995) 'Social capital and the global economy', *Foreign Affairs*, 74 (5): 89-103.

Fukuyama, F. (1996) *Trust: social virtues and the creation of prosperity*. London: Penguin.

Galbraith, J.K. (1996) *The good society*. Boston: Houghton Mifflin.

Gao, Z. (1995) 'Market economy and social development', Beijing and Copenhagen: World Summit for Social Development.

García Canclini, N. (1992) 'Culture and power: the state of research', in P. Scannell, P. Schlesinger and C. Sparks (eds), *Culture and power*. London: Sage.

Gasper, D. (1996) Review of B. Hettne, *Development theory and the three worlds, European Journal of Development Research*, 8 (2): 200-3.

Gasper, D. (1997) 'Sen's capability approach and Nussbaum's capabilities ethic', *Journal of International Development*, 9 (2): 281-302.

Gaventa, J. (1998) 'Poverty, participation and social exclusion in North and South', *IDS Bulletin*, 29 (1): 50-7.

Gay, P. (1977) *The Enlightenment: an interpretation*. New York: Norton.

Gbotokuma, Z. (1992) 'Cultural identity and under-development in Sub-Saharan Africa', special issue on culture and development, *Voices from Africa* (Geneva, UNNGLS), 4.

George, S. (1992) *The debt boomerang*. London: Pluto.

Gerschenkron, A. (1992) 'Economic backwardness in historical perspective' (1952), in Granovetter and Swedberg (eds), pp. 111-30.

Gibson-Graham, J.K. (1992) 'Waiting for the revolution or, How to smash capitalism while working at home in your spare time', unpublished paper.

Giddens, A. (1984) *The constitution of society: outline of the theory of structuration*. Cambridge: Polity.

Giddens, A. (1991) *Modernity and self-identity: self and society in the late modern age*. Cambridge: Polity.

Giddens, A. (1998) *The Third Way*. Cambridge: Polity.

Gill, S. and J.H. Mittelman (eds) (1997) *Innovation and transformation in international studies*. Cambridge: Cambridge University Press.

Gilligan, C. (1982) *In a different voice*. Cambridge, MA: Harvard University Press.

Gills, B. and G. Philip (1996) 'Editorial: towards a convergence in development policy?' *Third World Quarterly*, 17 (4): 585-91.

Giri, A.K. (1998) *Global transformations: postmodernity and beyond*. Jaipur: Rawat Publications.

Gledhill, J. (1994) *Power and its disguises: anthropological perspectives on politics*. London: Pluto.

Gleick, J. (1988) *Chaos: making a new science*. London: Heinemann.

Goetz, E.G. and S.E. Clarke (1993) *The new localism: comparative urban politics in a global era*. Newbury Park, CA: Sage.

Gomez, E.T. (1994) *Political business: corporate involvement of Malaysian political parties*. Townsville: James Cook University of North Queensland.

Goonatilake, S. (1991) *The evolution of information: lineages in gene, culture and artefact*. London: Pinter.

Goonatilake, S. (1999) *Toward a global science*. Bloomington: Indiana University Press.

Gordon, D. (1991) 'Inside and outside the long swing: the endogeneity/exogeneity debate and the social structures of accumulation approach', *Review*, 12 (2): 263-312.

Goulet, D. (1992) 'Development: creator and destroyer of values', *World Development*, 20 (3): 467-75.

Gow, D.D. (1991) 'Collaboration in development consulting: stooges, hired guns, or musketeers?' *Human Organization*, 50 (1).

Granovetter, M. (1992) 'Economic institutions as social constructions', *Acta Sociologica*, 35: 3-11.

Granovetter, M. and R. Swedberg (eds) (1992) *The sociology of economic life*. Boulder, CO: Westview.

Gray, H.P. (1993) 'Globalization versus nationhood: is economic integration a useful compromise?' *Development and International Cooperation*, 9 (16): 35-49.

Green, R. (1995) 'Reflections on attainable trajectories: reforming global economic institutions', in Griesgraber and Gunter (1996a), pp. 38-81.

Greider, W. (1997) *One world, ready or not: the manic logic of global capitalism*. New York: Simon and Schuster.

Griesgraber, M.J. and B.G. Gunter (eds) (1995) *Promoting development: effective global institutions for the 21st century*. London: Pluto.

Griesgraber, M.J. and B.G. Gunter (eds) (1996a) *Development: new paradigms and principles for the 21st century*. London: Pluto.

Griesgraber, M.J. and B.G. Gunter (eds) (1996b) *The World Bank: lending on a global scale*. London: Pluto.

Griffin, K. (1996) 'Culture, human development and economic growth', University of California, Riverside: Working Paper in Economics 96-17.

Griffin, K. (2000a) 'Culture and economic growth: the state and globalization', in Nederveen Pieterse (2000a), pp. 189-202.

Griffin, K. (2000b) *Studies in development strategy and systemic transformation*. London: Macmillan.

Griffin, K. and A. Rahman Khan (1992) *Globalization and the developing world*. Geneva: UNRISD.

Griffin, K. and T. McKinley (1994) *Implementing a human development strategy*. London: Macmillan.

Grillo, R.D. and R.L. Stirrat (eds) (1997) *Discourses of development*. Oxford: Berg.

Group of Lisbon (1995) *Limits to competition*. Cambridge, MA: MIT Press.

Guha, A. and F. Vivekenanda (1985) *Development Alternative*. Stockholm: Bethany Books.

Gupta, A. and J. Ferguson (1992) 'Beyond culture: space, identity, and the politics of difference', *Cultural Anthropology*, 7: 6-23.

Habermas, J. (1990) *Moral consciousness and communicative action*. Cambridge: Polity.

Halstead, T. and C. Cobb (1996) 'The need for new measurements of progress', in Mander and Goldsmith (eds), pp. 197-206.

Hamilton, G.G. and N. Woolsey Biggart (1992) 'Market, culture and authority: a comparative analysis of management and organization in the Far East', in Granovetter and Swedberg (eds), pp. 181-223.

Hampdon-Turner, C. and F. Trompenaars (1993) *Seven cultures of capitalism*. New York: Doubleday.

Hanloe, M., C.G. Pickvance and J. Urry (eds) (1990) *Place, policy and politics: do localities matter?* London: Unwin Hyman.

Hanlon, J. (1991) *Mozambique: who calls the shots?* London: James Currey.

Harris, N. (1986) *The end of the Third World*. Harmondsworth: Penguin.

Harrison, B. (1992) 'Industrial districts: old wine in new bottles?' *Regional Studies*, 26 (5): 469-83.

Harriss, J., J. Hunter and C.M. Lewis (eds) (1995) *The new institutional economics and Third World development*. London: Routledge.

Harrod, J. (1997) 'Social forces and international political economy: joining the two IRs', in Gill and Mittelman (eds), pp. 105-14.

Harvey, D. (1989) *The condition of postmodernity*. Oxford: Blackwell.

Harvey, D. (1993) 'From space to place and back again: reflections on the condition of post-modernity', in J. Bird, B. Curtis, T. Putnam, G. Robertson and L. Tickner (eds), *Mapping the futures: local cultures, global change*. London: Routledge, pp. 3-29.

Häusler, S. (1994) 'Alternative development', in R. Braidotti et al., *Women, the environment and sustainable development*. London: Zed, pp. 107-22.

Havel, V. (1985) 'The power of the powerless', in J. Keane (ed.), *The power of the powerless: citizens against the state in Central-Eastern Europe*. London: Hutchinson.

Hearn, J. (1998) 'The 'NGO-isation' of Kenyan society: USAID and the restructuring of health care', *Review of African Political Economy*, 75: 89-100,

Helleiner, G.K. (1992) 'Conventional foolishness and overall ignorance: current approaches to global transformation and development', in Wilber and Jameson (eds) *The political economy of development and underdevelopment*, 5th edn. New York: McGraw-Hill, pp. 36-54.

Henderson, H. (1991) *Paradigms in progress*. Indianapolis, IN: Knowledge Systems.

Henderson, H. (1993) 'Social innovation and citizen movements', Futures, 25 (4): 322-38.

Henderson, H. (1996a) *Building a win-win world*. San Francisco: Berrett-Koehler.

Henderson, H. (1996b) 'Changing paradigms and indicators: implementing equitable, sustainable and participatory development', in Griesgraber and Gunter (1996a), pp. 103-36.

Henwood, D. (1993) 'Global economic integration: the missing Middle East', *Middle East Report*, 184.

Hettne, B. (1990) *Development theory and the three worlds*. London: Longman.

Hettne, B. (1992) 'New trends in development theory', The Hague, Institute of Social Studies, unpublished paper.

Hettne, B. (1995) *Development theory and the three worlds*, 2nd edn. London: Longman.

Hewitt de Alcántara, C. (ed.) (1996) *Social futures, global visions*, special issue of *Development and Change*, 27 (2).

Hill, M. and L. Kwen Fee (1995) *The politics of nation building and citizenship in Singapore*. London: Routledge.

Hirschman, A.O. (1981) *Essays in trespassing*. Cambridge: Cambridge University Press.

Hirst, P.Q. (1993) *Associative democracy*. Cambridge: Polity.

Hirst, P.Q. and G. Thompson (1996) *Globalization in question*. Cambridge: Polity.

Hirst, P.Q. and J. Zeitlin (1991) 'Flexible specialisation versus post-Fordism: theory, evidence and policy implications', *Economy and Society*, 20 (1): 1-56.

Hirtz, F. (1995) *Managing insecurity: state social policy and family networks in the rural Philippines*. Saarbrücken: Verlag für Entwicklungspolitik.

Hobart, M. (ed.) (1993) *An anthropological critique of development: the growth of ignorance?* London: Routledge.

Hobsbawm, E.J. and T. Ranger (eds) (1983) *The invention of tradition*. Cambridge: Cambridge University Press.

Hodgen, M.T. (1964) *Early anthropology in the sixteenth and seventeenth centuries*. Philadelphia: University of Pennsylvania Press.

Holcombe, S. (1995) *Managing to empower: the Grameen Bank's experience of poverty alleviation*. London: Zed.

Hollingsworth, J.R. and R. Boyer (eds) (1997) *Contemporary capitalism: the embeddedness of institutions*. New York: Cambridge University Press.

Holton, R.J. and B.S. Turner (1986) *Talcott Parsons on economy and society*. London: Routledge.

Hoogvelt, A. (1997) *Globalisation and the postcolonial world: the new political economy of development*. London: Macmillan.

Hountondji, P.J. (1991) 'African philosophy: myth and reality', in T. Serequeberhan (ed.), *African philosophy*. New York: Paragon, pp. 111-31.

Hoy, D.C. (1986) 'Power, repression, progress: Foucault, Lukes, and the Frankfurt School', in Hoy (ed.), *Foucault: a critical reader*. Oxford: Blackwell, pp. 123-47.

Huizer, G. (1993) 'Development anthropology in global perspective', *Entwicklungsethnologie*, 2 (1): 66-82.

Huizer, G. and J. Lava (1989) *Explorations in folk religion and healing*. Manila: Asian Social Institute.

Huntington, S.P. (1976) 'The change to change: modernization, development, and politics', in C.E. Black (ed.) *Comparative modernization*. New York: Free Press.

Huntington, S.P. (1996) *The clash of civilizations and the remaking of world order*. New York: Simon and Schuster

Hutton, W. (1995) *The state we're in*. London: Jonathan Cape.

Huxley, A. (1946) *The perennial philosophy*. London: Chatto and Windus.

Ibrahim, A. (1996) *The Asian Renaissance*. Singapore: Times Books.

Inter-American Development Bank (1995) *Social dimensions in the agenda of the IDB*. Copenhagen.

Irwan, A. (1996) 'Rent and ethnic Chinese regional business networks: Indonesia's puzzling high economic growth', Kuala Lumpur, unpublished paper.

Isaac, T.M., Thomas and Tharakan, P.K., Michael (1995) 'Kerala: towards a new agenda', *Economic and Political Weekly*, 5-12 August: 1993-2004.

Iwasaki, T., T. Mori and H. Yamaguchi (eds) (1992) *Development strategies for the 21ˢᵗ century*. Tokyo: Institute of Developing Economies.

Jalibi, J. (1984) *Pakistan: The identity of culture*. Karachi: Royal Book Company.

Jessop, B. (1994) 'Post-Fordism and the state', in Amin (1994a), pp. 251-79.

Johnson, C. (1982) *MITI and the Japanese miracle*. Stanford, CA: Stanford University Press.

Johnston, D. (1991) 'The deconstruction of development', in C. Murphy (ed.), *The new international political economy*. Basingstoke: Macmillan.

Jolly, R. (1986) 'Adjustment with a human face', in K Haq and U Kidar (eds), *Human development: the neglected dimension*. Islamabad: North South Roundtable, pp. 386-400.

Jolly, R. (ed.) (1996) *Revitalizing African development: an agenda for 21ˢᵗ century reform*, special issue, *Development*, 2.

Jomo, K.S. (ed.) (1995) *Privatizing Malaysia: rents, rhetoric, realities*. Boulder, CO: Westview.

Jones, R.F. (1961) *Ancients and Moderns*. New York: Dover.

Judt, T. (1997) 'The social question redivivus', *Foreign Affairs*, 76 (5): 95-117.

Junejo, A.J. and M.Q. Bughio (eds) (1988) *Cultural heritage of Sind*. Jamshoro and Hyderabad, Sindh: Sindhi Adabi Board.

Just World Trust (1995) *Dominance of the West over the rest*. Penang: JUST.

Kaarsholm, P. (ed.) (1991) *Cultural struggle and development in Southern Africa*. Harare, London and Portsmouth: Baobab, James Currey and Heinemann.

Kabeer, N. (1994) *Reversed realities: gender hierarchies in development thought*. London: Verso.

Kandiyoti, D. (1991) 'Identity and its discontents: women and the nation', *Millennium*, 20 (3): 429-44.

Kang, Y.A. (1985) 'Rationality and development in Korea', in C.A. van Peursen and M.C. Doeser (eds), *Development and its rationalities*. Amsterdam: Free University Press, pp. 75-90.

Kaplinsky, R. (1994) *Easternisation: the spread of Japanese management techniques to developing countries*. London: Frank Cass.

Kaviraj, S. (1992) 'Marxism and the darkness of history', in J. Nederveen Pieterse (ed.), *Emancipations, modern and postmodern*. London: Sage, pp. 79-102.

Kay, C. (1993) 'For a renewal of development studies: Latin American theories and neoliberalism in the era of structural adjustment', *Third World Quarterly*, 14 (4): 691-702.

Kay, C. (1998) Relevance of structuralist and dependency theories in the neoliberal period: a Latin American perspective, The Hague: Institute of Social Studies, Working Paper 281.

Keesing, R.M. (1987) 'Anthropology as interpretive quest', *Current Anthropology*, 28 (2): 161-76.

Keohane, R.O. (1984) *After hegemony*. Princeton, NJ: Princeton University Press.

'The Kerala Model of Development: A Debate', *Bulletin of Concerned Asian Scholars*, 30 (3): 25-36.

Khor, M. (1997) 'Effects of globalisation on sustainable development after UNCED', *Third World Resurgence*, 81-82: 5-11.

Kiely, R. (1998) 'Neo liberalism revised? A critical account of World Bank concepts of good governance and market friendly intervention', *Capital & Class*, 64: 63-88.

Kiely, R. (1999) 'The last refuge of the noble savage? A critical account of post-development', *European Journal of Development Research*, 11 (1): 30-55.

Kishimoto, H. (1963) 'Modernization versus westernization in the East', *Cahiers d'histoire mondiale*, 7.

Kissinger, H. (1970) 'The white revolutionary: reflections on Bismarck', in D.A. Rustow (ed.), *Philosophers and kings: studies in leadership*. New York: Braziller, pp. 317-53.

Klauss, R. and D.C. Korten (1984) *People centered development: contributions toward theory and planning frameworks*. West Hartford, CT: Kumarian Press.

Konrád, G. (1984) *Antipolitics*. London: Quartet Books.

Korten, D.C. (1990) *Getting to the 21ˢᵗ century: voluntary action and the global agenda*. West Hartford, CT: Kumarian Press.

Korten, D.C. (1995) *When corporations rule the world*. London: Earthscan.

Kothari, M.L. and L.A. Mehta (1988) 'Violence in modern medicine', in Nandy (ed.), pp. 167-210.
Kothari, R. (1988) *Rethinking development: in search of humane alternatives*. Delhi: Ajanta.
Kothari, R. (1993a) *Poverty: human consciousness and the amnesia of development*. London: Zed.
Kothari, R. (1993b) 'The yawning vacuum: a world without alternatives', *Alternatives*, 18: 119-39.
Kothari, S. (1994) 'Global economic institutions and democracy: a view from India', in Cavanagh et al., pp. 39-55.
Kottak, C.P. (1985) 'Dimensions of culture in development', in G.C. Uhlenbeck (ed.), *The cultural dimension of development*. The Hague: Netherlands National Commission for UNESCO, pp. 38-48.
Kuhn, T.S. (1962) *The structure of scientific revolutions*. Chicago: University of Chicago Press.
Kuttner, R. (1991) *The end of laissez-faire: national purpose and the global economy after the Cold War*. New York: Alfred Knopf.
Laclau, E. (1990) *New reflections on the revolution of our time*. London: Verso.
Laclau, E. and C. Mouffe (1985) *Hegemony and socialist strategy*. London: Verso.
Lal, D. (1983) *The poverty of 'development economics'*. London: Institute of Economic Affairs.
Lal, D. (1995) 'The misconceptions of "development economics"', in Corbridge (ed.), pp. 56-63.
Lao Tsu (1973) *Tao te Ching*, trans. by Gia-fu Feng and J. English. London: Wildwood House.
Lash, S. and J. Urry (1994) *Economies of signs and space*. London: Sage.
Latouche, S. (1993) *In the wake of the affluent society: an exploration of post-development*. London: Zed (orig. French edn 1991).
Latour, B. (1993) *We have never been modern*. London: Harvester Wheatsheaf.
Lawson, C. and E. Lorenz (1999) 'Collective learning, tacit knowledge and regional innovative capacity', *Regional Studies*, 33 (4): 305-17.
Lee, M.E. (1997) 'From Enlightenment to chaos: toward nonmodern social theory', in Eve et al. (eds), pp. 15-29.
Lee, R.L.M. (1994) 'Modernization, postmodernism and the Third World', *Current Sociology*, 42 (2).
Leiken, R. (1996) 'Controlling the global corruption epidemic', *Foreign Policy*, 105: 55-73.
Leipziger, D.M. and V. Thomas (1995) *The lessons of East Asia: an overview of country experience*. Washington, DC: World Bank.
Levi, M. (1996) 'Social and unsocial capital: a review essay of Robert Putnam's Making Democracy Work', *Politics and Society*, 24 (1): 45-54.
Leys, C. (1996) *The rise and fall of development theory*. London and Nairobi: James Currey and EAEP.
Li Lulu (1989) 'Theoretical theses on "social modernization"', *International Sociology*, 4 (4): 365-77.
Light, I. and S. Karageorgis (1994) 'The ethnic economy', in Smelser and Swedberg (eds), pp. 647-71.
Lim, Y. (1995) 'Industrial policy, technological learning and productivity gains theory and evidence from South Korea', The Hague: Institute of Social Studies Industrialization Seminar.
Lindblom, C. (1959) 'The science of "muddling through"', *Public Administration Review*, 19 (2).
Lipietz, A. (1992) *Towards a new economic order: Postfordism, ecology and democracy*. Cambridge: Polity.
Lipietz, A. (1995) *Green hopes: the future of political ecology*. Cambridge: Polity.
Lipton, M. (1977) *Why poor people stay poor: a study of urban bias in world development*. London: Maurice Temple Smith.
Litonjua, M.D. (1994) 'Outside the den of dragons: the Philippines and the NICs of Asia', *Studies in Comparative International Development*, 28 (4): 3-30.
Lively, J. (1981) 'The Europe of the Enlightenment', *History of European Ideas*, 1 (2).
Long, N. (1994) 'From paradigm lost to paradigm regained? The case for an actor-oriented sociology of development', in Long and Long (eds), pp. 16-46.
Long, N. and A. Long (eds) (1994) *Battlefields of knowledge*. London: Routledge.
Long, N. and M. Villarreal (1993) 'Exploring development interfaces: from the transfer of knowledge to the transformation of meaning', in Schuurman (ed.), pp. 140-68.
Lummis, D. (1991) 'Development against democracy', *Alternatives*, 16: 31-66.
Lummis, D. (1994) 'The end of development', *AMPO*, 25 (3): 36-40.
Lynch, M. (2000) 'Against reflexivity as an academic virtue and source of privileged knowledge', *Theory, Culture & Society*, 17 (3): 26-54.
Macridis, R.C. and B.E. Brown (eds) (1964) *Comparative politics*. Homewood, IL: Dorsey Press.
Mahathir Mohamad and S. Ishihara (1995) *The voice of Asia*. Tokyo: Kodansha International.

Mair, L. (1965) *An introduction to social anthropology*. Oxford: Clarendon Press.

Mander, J. and E. Goldsmith (eds) (1996) *The case against the global economy and for a turn toward the local*. San Francisco: Sierra Club.

Mann, M. (1986) *The sources of social power*. Cambridge: Cambridge University Press.

Maquet, J. (1972) *Africanity: the cultural unity of Black Africa*. London: Oxford University Press.

Marcus, G.E. and M.J. Fischer (1986) *Anthropology as cultural critique*. Chicago: University of Chicago Press.

Marglin, F.A. and S. Marglin (eds) (1990) *Dominating knowledge: Development, culture and resistance*. Oxford: Clarendon Press.

Martin, K. (1991) 'Modern development theory', in idem (ed.), *Strategies of economic development*. London: Macmillan, pp. 27-74.

Martinez-Alier, J. (2000) 'Environmental justice as a force for sustainability', in Nederveen Pieterse (2000a), pp. 148-74.

Martinussen, J. (1997) *Society, state and market: a guide to competing theories of development*. London: Zed.

Massey, D. (1993) 'Power-geometry and a progressive sense of place', in J. Bird, B. Curtis, T. Putnam, G. Robertson and L. Tickner (eds), *Mapping the futures: local cultures, global change*. London: Routledge, pp. 59-69.

Max-Neef, M.A. (1982) *Experiences in barefoot economics*. Stockholm: Dag Hammarskjöld Foundation.

Max-Neef, M.A. (1991) *Human scale development*. New York: Apex Press.

Mazlish, B. and R. Buultjens (eds) (1993) *Conceptualizing global history*. Boulder, CO: Westview.

McEvilley, T. (1995) 'Here comes everybody', *Africus: Johannesburg Biennale*. Johannesburg: Exhibition Catalogue, pp. 53-7.

McHale, B. (1992) *Constructing postmodernism*. London: Routledge.

McLaren, P. (1995) *Critical pedagogy and predatory culture*. New York: Routledge.

McMichael, P. (1996) *Development and social change: a global perspective*. Thousand Oaks, CA: Pine Forge Press.

Meadows, D.L. and D.H. Meadows et al. (1972) *The limits to growth* (report to the Club of Rome). New York: Universe Books.

Mehmet, O. (1995) *Westernizing the Third World: the Eurocentricity of economic development theories*. London: Routledge.

Mehta, P.D. (1989) *Holistic consciousness*. Longmead, Shaftesbury: Element Books.

Melucci, A. (1988) 'Social movements and the democratization of everyday life', in J. Keane (ed.) *Civil society and the state: new European perspectives*. London: Verso.

Melucci, A. (1989) *Nomads of the present*. Ed by J. Keane and P. Mier. London: Hutchinson Radius.

Meppem, T. and R. Gill (1998) 'Planning for sustainability as a learning concept', *Ecological Economics*, 26 (2): 121-38.

Meurs, M. van (1997) J.C. *Smuts: staatsman, holist, generaal*. Amsterdam: Suid-Afrikaanse Instituut.

Mhlaba, L. (1991) 'Local cultures and development in Zimbabwe: the case of Matabeleland', in Kaarsholm (ed.), pp. 209-26.

Midgley, J. (1995) *Social development: the developmental perspective in social welfare*. London: Sage.

Mies, M. (1986) *Patriarchy and accumulation on a world scale: women in the international division of labour*. London: Zed.

Migdal, J.S. (1988) *Strong societies and weak states: state-society relations and state capabilities in the Third World*. Princeton, NJ: Princeton University Press.

Miller, C.L. (1990) *Theories of Africans: francophone literature and anthropology in Africa*. Chicago: University of Chicago Press.

Miller, D. (1997) *Capitalism: an ethnographic approach*. Oxford: Berg.

Ministry of Foreign Affairs (1991) *A world of difference*. The Hague: SDU.

Minter, W. (1986) *King Solomon's mines revisited*. New York: Basic Books.

Mishra, R. (1996) 'The welfare of nations', in Boyer and Drache (eds), pp. 316-33.

Mitchell, T. (1988) *Colonising Egypt*. Cambridge: Cambridge University Press.

Mittelman, J.H. (ed.) (1996) *Globalization: critical reflections*. Boulder, CO: Lynne Rienner Publishers.

Mohanty, M. (1989) 'Changing terms of discourse. A poser', *Economic and Political Weekly*, 16 September.

Moll, P., N. Nattrass and L. Loots (eds) (1991) *Redistribution: how can it work in South Africa?* Cape Town: David Philip.

Møller, K. and E. Rasmussen (eds) (1995) *Partnership for new social development: UN World Summit for Social Development*. Copenhagen: Mandag Morgen Strategisk Forum.

Moore Jr, B. (1969) *Social origins of dictatorship and democracy*. Harmondsworth: Penguin.

Moore, T. (1992) *Care of the soul*. London: Judy Piatkus.

Moser, C.O.N. (1991) 'Gender planning in the Third World: meeting practical and strategic needs', in R. Grant and K. Newland (eds), *Gender and international relations*. Buckingham: Open University, pp. 83-121.

Mosley, P., J. Harrington and J. Toye (1991) *Aid and power: the World Bank and policy-based lending*. London: Routledge.

Mouzelis, N. (1988) 'Sociology of development: reflections on the present crisis', *Sociology*, 22 (1): 23-44.

Mulgan, G. (1994) *Politics in an antipolitical age*. Cambridge: Polity.

Munck, R. and D. O'Hearn (eds) (1999) *Critical development theory: contributions to a new paradigm*. London: Zed.

Myrdal, G. (1968) *Asian drama: an inquiry into the poverty of nations*. New York: Twentieth Century Fund.

Mytelka, L.K. (1993) 'Rethinking development: a role for innovation networking in the "other two-thirds"', *Futures* 25 (6): 694-712.

Naess, A. (1976) *Ecology, community and lifestyle*. Cambridge: Cambridge University Press (1989).

Nandy, A. (ed.) (1988) *Science, hegemony and violence: a requiem for modernity*. New Delhi: Oxford University Press.

Nandy, A. (1989) 'Shamans, savages and the wilderness: on the audibility of dissent and the future of civilizations', *Alternatives*, 14: 263-77.

Nandy, A. (1995) *The savage Freud*. New Delhi: Oxford University Press.

Naqvi, N. (ed.) (1996) *Rethinking security, rethinking development*. Islamabad: Sustainable Development Policy Institute.

Nederveen Pieterse, J. (1989) *Empire and emancipation: power and liberation on a world scale*. New York: Praeger.

Nederveen Pieterse, J. (1992a) *White on black: images of Africa and blacks in Western popular culture*. New Haven and London: Yale University Press.

Nederveen Pieterse, J. (1992b) 'Emancipations, modern and postmodern', in idem (ed.) *Emancipations, modern and postmodern*. London: Sage, pp. 5-43.

Nederveen Pieterse, J. (1994) 'Unpacking the West: how European is Europe?' in A. Rattansi and S. Westwood (eds) *Racism, modernity, identity*. Cambridge: Polity, pp. 129-49.

Nederveen Pieterse, J. (1995) 'Globalization as hybridization', in M. Featherstone, S. Lash, R. Robertson (eds), *Global Modernities*. London: Sage, pp. 45-68.

Nederveen Pieterse, J. (1996) 'Varieties of ethnic experience and ethnicity discourse', in E.N. Wilmsen and P. McAllister (eds) *The politics of difference: ethnic premises in a world of power*. Chicago: University of Chicago Press, pp. 25-44.

Nederveen Pieterse, J. (1998a) 'Humanitarian intervention and beyond', in idem (ed.) *World orders in the making: humanitarian intervention and beyond*. London and New York: Macmillan and St Martin's Press, pp. 1-22.

Nederveen Pieterse, J. (1998b) 'Hybrid modernities: mélange modernities in Asia', *Sociological Analysis*, 1 (3): 75-86.

Nederveen Pieterse, J. (ed.) (2000a) *Global Futures: shaping globalization*. London: Zed.

Nederveen Pieterse, J. (2000b) 'Collective action and globalization', in H. Lustiger-Thaler, P. Hamel, J. Nederveen Pieterse and S. Roseneil (eds), *Globalization and collective action*. London and New York: Macmillan and St Martin's Press.

Nederveen Pieterse, J. (2000c) 'Globalization North and South: representations of uneven development and the interaction of modernities', *Theory, Culture & Society*, 17 (1): 129-37.

Nederveen Pieterse, J. and B. Parekh (eds) (1995) *The decolonization of imagination*. London: Zed.

Needham, J. (1981) 'Attitudes toward time and change as compared with Europe', in *Science in traditional China*. Cambridge, MA: Harvard University Press, pp. 107-32.

Nerfin, M. (ed.) (1977) *Another development: approaches and strategies*. Uppsala: Dag Hammarskjöld Foundation.

Nietzsche, F.W. (1976) *Twilight of the idols*, in *The portable Nietzsche*, trans. W. Kaufman. Harmondsworth: Penguin.

Nieuwenhuijze, C.A.O. van (1983) *Culture and development: the prospects of an afterthought*. The Hague: Institute of Social Studies.

Nisbet, R.A. (1969) *Social change and history*. Oxford: Oxford University Press.

Nisbet, R.A. (1980) *History of the idea of progress*. New York: Basic Books.

Niva, S. (1999) 'Alternatives to neoliberalism', *Middle East Report*, 29 (1): 16.

Norberg-Hodge, H. (1995) 'The development hoax', in Just World Trust, pp. 110-23.

O'Connor, S. (1994) *Universal mother*. London: Ensign Records.

Ohmae, K. (1992) *The borderless world: power and strategy in the global marketplace*. London: Collins.

Ohno, I. (1996) *Beyond the 'East Asian Miracle': an Asian view*. New York: UNDP, Office of Development Studies.

Okita, S. (1993) 'Many paths to development', in The South Centre (ed.), pp. 272-81.

Okun, A. (1975) *Equality and efficiency: the big trade-off*. Washington, DC: Brookings Institution.

Olowu, B. (1988) *African local governments as instruments of social development*. The Hague, International Union of Local Authorities.

Oman, C. (1993) 'Globalization and regionalization in the 1980s and 1990s', *Development and International Cooperation*, 9 (16): 51-69.

Oman, C. (1994) *Globalisation and regionalisation: the challenge for developing countries*. Paris: OECD.

Oman, P. and G. Wignaraja (1991) *The postwar evolution of development thinking*. London: Macmillan.

Oommen, T.K. (1998) 'Changing paradigms of development: the evolving participatory society', *Journal of Social and Economic Development*, 1: 35-45.

Orr, D. (1996) 'Slow knowledge', *Resurgence*, 179: 30-2.

Ottati, G. dei (1994) 'Trust, interlinking transactions and credit in the industrial district', *Cambridge Journal of Economics*, 18 (6): 529-46.

Palley, T.I. (1999) 'Toward a new international economic order', *Dissent*, 46 (2): 48-53.

Parekh, B. (1997) *Gandhi*. Oxford: Oxford University Press.

Park, D.H. (1985) 'Paradigms of rationality', in C.A. van Peursen and M.C. Doeser (eds), *Development and its rationalities*. Amsterdam: Free University Press, pp. 35-50.

Parker, I. (ed.) (1998) *Social constructionism, discourse and realism*. London: Sage.

Passmore, J. (1978) *Science and its critics*. London: Duckworth.

Peet, R. (with E. Hartwick) (1999) *Theories of development*. New York: Guilford Press.

Peet, R. and M.J. Watts (eds) (1996) *Liberation ecologies: environment, development, social movements*. London: Routledge.

Perkins, P.E. (1998) 'The potential of community-based alternatives to globalization', *Development*, 41 (3): 61-7.

Peters, T. (1988) *Thriving on chaos*. New York: Knopf.

Petras, J. (1990) 'Retreat of the intellectuals', *Economic and Political Weekly*, 25 (38): 2143-56.

Petras, J. and H. Brill (1985) 'The tyranny of globalism', *Journal of Contemporary Asia*, 15 (4): 403-20.

Petrella, R. (1995) 'Europe between competitive innovation and a new social contract', *International Social Science Journal*, 47 (1/ 143): 11-23.

Pitt, D.C. (ed.) (1976) *Development from below: anthropologists and development situations*. The Hague: Mouton.

Pletsch, C.E. (1981) 'The three worlds, or the division of social scientific labor, circa 1950-1975', *Comparative Studies in Society and History*, 23: 565-90.

Pompa, L. (1990) *Vico: a study of the 'New Science'*, 2nd edn. Cambridge: Cambridge University Press.

Porter, D. (1996) 'Scenes from childhood: the homesickness of development discourses', in Crush (ed.), pp. 63-86.

Portes, A. (1994) 'The informal economy and its paradoxes', in Smelser and Swedberg (eds), pp. 426-50.

Portes, A. (1996) 'Transnational communities: their emergence and significance in the contemporary world-system', in R.P. Korzeniewicz and W.C. Smith (eds), *Latin America in the world economy* Westport, CT: Greenwood Press, pp. 151-68.

Posey, D.A. (1994) 'Traditional resource rights: de facto self determination for indigenous peoples', in L. van der Vlist (ed.), *Voices of the earth: indigenous peoples, new partners and the right to self-determination in practice.* Amsterdam: Netherlands Centre for Indigenous Peoples, pp. 217-35.

Pradervand, P. (1989) *Listening to Africa: developing Africa from the grassroots.* New York: Praeger.

Pred, A. and M.J. Watts (1992) *Reworking modernity: capitalisms and symbolic discontent.* New Brunswick, NJ: Rutgers University Press.

Preston, P.W. (1996) *Development theory: an introduction.* Oxford: Blackwell.

Prigogine, I. and I. Stengers (1984) *Order out of chaos.* New York: Bantam Books.

Pronk, J. (1990) 'Two worlds in one', in *Solidarity against poverty.* Amsterdam: Evert Vermeer Foundation, pp. 29-42.

Pronk, J. (2000) 'Globalization: a developmental approach', in Nederveen Pieterse (2000a), pp. 40-52.

Putnam, R.D. (1993) *Making democracy work: civic traditions in modern Italy.* Princeton, NJ: Princeton University Press.

Quigley, C. (1966) *Tragedy and hope: a history of the world in our time.* New York: Macmillan.

Rahman, M.A. (1993) *People's self-development: perspectives on Participatory Action Research.* London and Dhaka: Zed and Dhaka University Press.

Rahnema, M. (1992) 'Poverty', in Sachs (1992a), pp. 158-76.

Rahnema, M. (1997) 'Towards post-development: searching for signposts, a new language and new paradigm', in Rahnema and Bawtree (eds), pp. 377-404.

Rahnema, M. and V. Bawtree (eds) (1997) *The post-development reader.* London: Zed.

Reich, R.B. (1983) *The next American frontier.* Harmondsworth: Penguin.

Rew, A. (1993) 'The coordination and integration of anthropology and investment project planning', unpublished paper.

Rew, A. (1997) 'The donors' discourse: official social development knowledge in the 1980s', in Grillo and Stirrat (eds), pp. 81-106.

Rist, G. (1990a) 'Development as the new religion of the West', *Quid Pro Quo*, 1 (2): 5-8.

Rist, G. (1990b) '"Development" as part of the modern myth: the western socio-economic dimension of "development"', *European Journal of Development Alternatives*, 2 (1): 10.

Rist, G. (1997) *The history of development: from Western origins to global faith.* London: Zed.

Rist, G., M. Rahnema and G. Esteva (1992) *Le Nord perdu: repères pour l'après-développement.* Lausanne: Editions d'en bas.

Robertson, R. (1992) *Globalization.* London: Sage.

Robertson, R. and F. Lechner (1985) 'Modernization, globalization and the problem of culture in world-systems theory', *Theory, Culture & Society*, 2 (3): 103-17.

Robin, J. (1992) *Women and wellbeing: how Kerala became a model.* Basingstoke: Macmillan.

Rodan, G. (1989) *The political economy of Singapore's industrialization.* Kuala Lumpur: Forum.

Roe, E. (1995) 'Critical theory, sustainable development and populism', *Telos*, 103: 149-62.

Roe, E. (1998) *Taking complexity seriously: policy analysis, triangulation and sustainable development.* Boston: Kluwer.

Rogaly, B. and C. Roche (1998) *Learning from South-North links in microfinance.* Oxford: Oxfam working paper.

Rorty, R. (1991) *Objectivity, relativism, and truth.* Cambridge: Cambridge University Press.

Rorty, R. (1997) *Achieving our country: leftist thought in 20th century America.* Cambridge, MA: Harvard University Press.

Rosenau, P. (1992) *Postmodernism and the social sciences.* Princeton, NJ: Princeton University Press.

Rostow, W.W. (1960) *The stages of economic growth.* Cambridge: Cambridge University Press.

Rostow, W.W. (1971) *Politics and the stages of growth.* Cambridge: Cambridge University Press.

Roszak, T. (1973) *Where the wasteland ends.* New York: Doubleday.

Roszak, T. (1976) *Unfinished animal.* London: Faber and Faber.

Rowe, W. and V. Schelling (1991) *Memory and modernity: popular culture in Latin America*. London: Verso.

Ryan, A. (1999) 'Britain: recycling the Third Way', *Dissent*, 46 (2): 77-80.

Sabetti, F. (1996) 'Path dependency and civic culture: some lessons from Italy about interpreting social experiments', *Politics and Society*, 24 (1).

Sachs, I. (1972) 'The logic of development', *International Social Science Journal*, 24 (1) (reprinted 1998, 157: 361-5).

Sachs, W. (ed.) (1992a) *The development dictionary: a guide to knowledge as power*. London: Zed.

Sachs, W. (1992b) 'Introduction', *The development dictionary*. London: Zed, pp. 1-5.

Sachs, W. (1999) *Planet dialectics: explorations in environment and development*. London: Zed.

Said, E.W. (1981) *Covering Islam*. New York: Pantheon.

Said, E.W. (1985) *Orientalism*. Harmondsworth: Penguin (orig. edn 1978).

Said, E.W. (1986) 'Foucault and the imagination of power', in Hoy (ed.), pp. 149-56.

Said, E.W. (1993) *Culture and imperialism*. New York: Alfred Knopf.

Salmen, L. (1987) *Listen to the people: participant observation evaluation of development projects*. New York: Oxford University Press.

Salmond, A. (1982) 'Theoretical landscapes: on cross-cultural conceptions of knowledge', in D. Parkin (ed.) *Semantic anthropology*. London and New York: Academic Press.

Sampson, A. (1987) *Black and gold: tycoons, revolutionaries and Apartheid*. New York: Pantheon.

Sanyal, B. (1994) 'Ideas and institutions: why the alternative development paradigm withered away', *Regional Development Dialogue*, 15 (1): 23-35.

Sato, T. and W.E. Smith (1996) 'The new development paradigm: organizing for implementation', in Griesgraber and Gunter (eds) (1996a), pp. 89-102.

Scholte, J.A. (1993) *International relations of social change*. Buckingham: Open University Press.

Scholte, J.A. (1998) The International Monetary Fund and civil society: an underdeveloped dialogue. The Hague, Institute of Social Studies, Working Paper 272.

Schudson, M. (1994) 'Culture and the integration of national societies', *Social Science Journal*, 139: 63-82.

Schumacher College (1997) *Course programme 1997-1998*, Dartington, Devon.

Schuurman, F. (ed.) (1993) *Beyond the impasse: new directions in development theory*. London: Zed.

Schutz, A. (1972) *The phenomenology of the social world*. London: Heinemann (orig. edn 1932).

Scott, J.C. (1985) *The weapons of the weak*. New Haven: Yale University Press.

Scott, J.C. (1991) *Domination and the arts of resistance*. New Haven: Yale University Press.

Scott, J.C. (1998) *Seeing like a state: how certain schemes to improve the human condition have failed*. New Haven: Yale University Press.

Seabrook, J. (1994) *Victims of development, resistance and alternatives*. London: Verso.

Seagrave, S. (1996) *Lords of the Rim*. London: Corgi Books.

Seers, D (1979) 'The birth, life and death of development economics', *Development and Change*, 10 (4): 707-19.

Sen, A. (1985) *Commodities and capabilities*. Oxford: Oxford University Press.

Sen, A. and J.D. Wolfensohn (1999) 'Let's respect both sides of the development coin', *International Herald Tribune*, 5 May.

Sen, G. (1997) 'Globalization in the 21st century: challenges for civil society', Amsterdam: University of Amsterdam.

Senge, P.M. (1990) *The fifth discipline: the art and practice of the learning organization*. New York: Doubleday.

Shack, W.A. and E.P. Skinner (eds) (1979) *Strangers in African societies*. Berkeley: University of California Press.

Sheffield Group (eds) (1989) *The social economy and the democratic state*. London: Lawrence and Wishart.

Sheth, D.L. (1987) 'Alternative development as political practice', *Alternatives*, 12 (2): 155-71.

Shils, E. (1966) *Political development in the new states*. The Hague: Mouton.

Shiva, V. (1988a) 'Reductionist science as epistemological violence', in Nandy (ed.), pp. 232-56.

Shiva, V. (1988b) *Staying alive: women, ecology and development*. London: Zed.

Shiva, V. (1991) 'Problems with the Enlightenment', in A. Dobson (ed.) *The Green reader*. London: Zed.

Shiviah, M. (1994) 'New realities, new utopia: a perspective on convergence of "radicalisms",' *Economic and Political Weekly*, 5 February: 305-12.

Shweder, R.A. (1993) '"Why do men barbecue?" and other postmodern ironies of growing up in the decade of ethnicity', *Daedalus*, Winter: 279-308.

Singer, H.W. (1989) 'When pursuit of surplus ends', *India International Centre Quarterly*, Spring.

Singer, H.W. (1996) 'How relevant is Keynesianism today for understanding problems of development?' Paper presented at EADI conference, Vienna.

Singer, H.W. and R. Jolly (eds) (1995) 'Fifty years on: the UN and economic and social development', *IDS Bulletin*, 26 (4).

Singh, Y. (1989) *Essays on modernization in India*. New Delhi: Manohar.

Siu, R.G.H. (1957) *The Tao of science: an essay on Western knowledge and Eastern wisdom*. Cambridge, MA: MIT Press.

Skocpol, T. (1979) *States and social revolutions*. Cambridge: Cambridge University Press.

Skocpol, T. (ed.) (1984) *Vision and method in historical sociology*. Cambridge: Cambridge University Press.

Skolimowski, H. (1994) *The participatory mind*. London: Penguin/Arkana.

Slater, D. (1992) 'Theories of development and politics of the post-modern – exploring a border zone', in J. Nederveen Pieterse (ed.), *Emancipations, modern and postmodern*. London: Sage, pp. 283-319.

Slater, D. (1995) 'Challenging western visions of the global', *European Journal of Development Research*, 7 (2): 366-88.

Smelser, N.J. and R. Swedberg (eds) (1994) *The handbook of economic sociology*. Princeton, NJ: Princeton University Press.

Smillie, I. (1997) 'Let them eat paradigms: public attitudes and the long, slow decline of development cooperation', *Development*, 40 (4): 59-65.

Smith, R. (1993) 'The Chinese road to capitalism', *New Left Review*, 199: 55-99.

So, A.Y. (1990) *Social change and development*. London: Sage.

Sobhan, R. (1989) 'The state and development of capitalism: the Third World perspective', in K. Bharadwaj and S. Kaviraj (eds), *Perspectives on capitalism*. New Delhi: Sage, pp. 247-58.

Sogge, D. (ed.) (1996) *Compassion and calculation: the business of private foreign aid*. London: Pluto.

Somjee, A.H. (1991) *Development theory*. London: Macmillan.

Soros, G. (1997) 'The capitalist threat', *Atlantic Monthly*, February.

Soros, G. (1998) *The crisis of global capitalism*. New York: Public Affairs.

Soto, H. de (1989) *The other path: the invisible revolution in the Third World*. New York: Harper and Row.

Sousa Santos, B. de (1995) *Toward a new common sense*. London: Routledge.

South Centre (ed.) (1993) *Facing the challenge: responses to the Report of the South Commission*. London: Zed.

Stallings, B. (ed.) (1995) *Global change, regional response: the new international context of development*. Cambridge: Cambridge University Press.

Stavenhagen, R. (1986) 'Ethnodevelopment: a neglected dimension in development thinking', in R. Apthorpe and A. Kráhl (eds) *Development studies: critique and renewal*. Leiden: Brill.

Stavrianos, L.S. (1981) *Global rift: the Third World comes of age*. New York: Morrow.

Stent, G.S. (1978) *Paradoxes of progress*. San Francisco: WH Freeman.

Sternberg, E. (1993) 'Transformations: the eight new ages of capitalism', *Futures*, 25 (10): 1019-40.

Stewart, F. (1996) 'Groups for good or ill', *Oxford Development Studies*, 24 (1): 9-25.

Stewart, F., S. Lall, S. Wangwe (1993) *Alternative development strategies in sub-Saharan Africa*. New York: St Martin's Press.

Stiefel, M. and M. Wolfe (1994) *A voice for the excluded: popular participation in development*. London and Geneva: Zed and UNRISD.

Stiglitz, J. (1998) 'More instruments and broader goals: moving toward the post Washington Consensus', Helsinki, WIDER annual lecture 2.

Stocking, G.W. (1987) *Victorian anthropology*. New York: Free Press.

Straaten, F. van (1996) 'Sociaal paradijs Kerala vergat zijn economie', *NRC Handelsblad*, 24 August.

Strange, S. (1996) *The retreat of the state*. Cambridge: Cambridge University Press.

Subrahmanyam, K. (1998) 'Nuclear India in global politics', *World Affairs*, 2 (3): 12-40.

Sundaram, K.V. (1994) 'Development from within: a rethinking on an alternative development path', *Asia-Pacific Journal of Rural Development*, 4 (1 & 2): 52-67.

Swaan, A. de (ed.) (1994) *Social policy beyond borders*. Amsterdam: Amsterdam University Press.

Taussig, M. (1980) *The devil and commodity fetishism in South America*. Chapel Hill: University of North Carolina Press.

Taylor, C. (1989) *Sources of the self*. Cambridge, MA: Harvard University Press.

Taylor, L. and U. Pieper (1996) 'Reconciling economic reform and sustainable human development: social consequences of neo-liberalism', New York: UNDP, Office of Development Studies (discussion paper).

Teilhard de Chardin, P. (1955) *Le phénomène humain*. Paris: Editions du Seuil.

Temple, J. and P. Johnson (1996) 'Social capability and economic development', unpublished paper.

Tenkasi, R.V. and S.A. Mohrman (1999) 'Global change as contextual collaborative knowledge creation', in Cooperrider and Dutton (eds), pp. 114-36.

Terhal, P. (1987) *World inequality and evolutionary convergence*. Delft: Eburon.

Tharamangalam, J. (1998) 'The perils of social development without economic growth: the development debacle of Kerala, India', *Bulletin of Concerned Asian Scholars*, 30 (1): 23-34.

Therborn, G. (1995) *European modernity and beyond: the trajectory of European societies 1945-2000*. London: Sage.

Thomas, C. and P. Wilkin (eds) (1997) *Globalization and the South*. London: Macmillan.

Thornton, R.J. (1988) 'The rhetoric of ethnographic holism', *Cultural Anthropology*, 3 (3): 285-303.

Thrift, N. and A. Amin (1995) *Holding down the global*. Oxford: Oxford University Press.

Tilly, C. (1984) *Big structures, large processes, huge comparisons*. New York: Russell Sage.

Tipps, D.C. (1973) 'Modernization theory and the comparative study of societies: a critical perspective', *Comparative Studies in Society and History*, 15: 199-226.

Tiryakian, E.A. (1991) 'Modernization: exhumetur in pace (Rethinking macrosociology in the 1990s)', *International Sociology*, 6 (2): 165-80.

Tiryakian, E.A. (1992) 'Pathways to metatheory: rethinking the presuppositions of macrosociology', in G. Ritzer (ed.), *Metatheorizing*. London: Sage, pp. 69-87.

Tiryakian, E.A. (1996) 'Three cultures of modernity: Christian, Gnostic, Chthonic', *Theory, Culture & Society*, 13 (1): 99-118.

Todd, S. (1997) 'Actualizing personal and collective health: questioning how development policy meets innate human needs', MA research paper, The Hague: Institute of Social Studies.

Tomlinson, J. (1991) *Cultural imperialism*. Baltimore, MD: Johns Hopkins University Press.

Toulmin, S. (1990) *Cosmopolis: the hidden agenda of modernity*. Chicago: University of Chicago Press.

Toye, J. (1987) *Dilemmas of development: reflections on the counterrevolution in development theory and policy*. Oxford: Blackwell.

Trainer, T. 1989 *Developed to death: rethinking third world development*. London: Green Print.

Truong, T.-D. (1999) 'The underbelly of the tiger: gender and the demystification of the Asian miracle', *Review of International Political Economy*, 6 (2): 133-65.

Tucker, V. (1996a) 'Critical holism: towards a new health model', Cork University College.

Tucker, V. (ed.) (1996b) *Cultural perspectives on development*. London: Frank Cass.

Tucker, V. (1996c) 'Health, medicine and development: a field of cultural struggle', in Tucker (ed.), pp. 110-28.

Tucker, V. (1997) 'From biomedicine to holistic health: towards a new health model', in A. Cleary and M.P. Treacy (eds) *The sociology of health and illness in Ireland*. Dublin: University College Dublin Press, pp. 30-50.

Tucker, V. (1999) 'The myth of development: a critique of Eurocentric discourse', in Munck and O'Hearn (eds), pp. 1-26.

Tvedt, T. (1998) *Angels of mercy or development diplomats? NGOs and foreign aid*. Oxford and Trenton, NJ: James Currey and Africa World Press.

ul Haq, M. (1995) *Reflections on human development*. New York: Oxford University Press.

ul Haq, M., I. Kaul and I. Grunberg (1996) *The Tobin tax: coping with financial volatility*. New York: Oxford University Press.

ul Haq, M. and K. Haq (1998) *Human development in South Asia: the education challenge*. Karachi: Oxford University Press.

UNDP (1996) (1997) (1998) *Human Development Report*. New York: Oxford University Press.
UNRISD (1995) *After the Social Summit: implementing the programme of action*. Geneva: UN Research Institute for Social Development.
Vail, L. (ed.) (1989) *The creation of tribalism in Southern Africa*. London: James Currey.
Vattimo, G. (1988) *The end of modernity*. Cambridge: Polity.
Verhelst, T.G. (1990) *No life without roots: culture and development*. London: Zed.
Visvanathan, S. (1988) 'On the annals of the laboratory state', in Nandy (ed.), pp. 257–88.
Vries, J. de (1963) *Etymologisch woordenboek*. Utrecht: Spectrum.
Wade, R. (1990) *Governing the market: economic theory and the role of government intervention in East Asian industrialization*. Princeton, NJ: Princeton University Press.
Wade, R. (1996) 'Japan, the World Bank and the art of paradigm maintenance: the East Asian Miracle in political perspective', *New Left Review*, 217: 3-36.
Wade, R. and F. Veneroso (1998) 'The Asian crisis: the high debt model versus the Wall Street-Treasury-IMF Complex', *New Left Review*, 228: 3-24.
Waldinger, R. et al. (1990) *Ethnic entrepreneurs: immigrant business in industrial societies*. Newbury Park, CA: Sage.
Wallace, M. (1992) 'Negative images: towards a black feminist cultural criticism', in L. Grossberg, C. Nelson and P. Treichler (eds), *Cultural studies*. London: Routledge, pp. 654-71.
Wallerstein, I. (1979) *The politics of the world economy*. Cambridge: Cambridge University Press.
Warde, I. (1998) 'Crony capitalism in the West: the banking system in turmoil', *Le Monde diplomatique*, November.
Waters, M. (1995) *Globalization*. London: Routledge.
Weber, R. (1982) '*The Tao of Physics* revisited: a conversation with Fritjof Capra', in Wilber (ed.), pp. 215-48.
Webster, A. (1984) *Introduction to the sociology of development*. London: Macmillan.
Wei-Ming, T. (1979) *Humanity and self-cultivation: essays in Confucian thought*. Berkeley, CA: Asian Humanities Press.
Weiss, L. (1996) 'Sources of the East Asian advantage: an institutional analysis', in R. Robison (ed.), *Pathways to Asia: the politics of engagement*. St Leonard's: Allen and Unwin, pp. 171-201.
Wertheim, W.F. (1974) *Evolution and revolution*. Harmondsworth: Penguin.
White, G. (ed.) (1988) *Developmental states in East Asia*. London: Macmillan.
Whitmyer, C. (ed.) (1995) *Mindfulness and meaningful work: explorations in right livelihood*. Berkeley, CA: Parallax Press.
Wignaraja, P. (1992) 'People's participation: reconciling growth with equity', in P. Ekins and M. Max-Neef (eds) *Real-life economics: understanding wealth creation*. London: Routledge, pp. 392-401.
Wignaraja, P. (ed.) (1993) *New social movements in the South: empowering the people*. London: Zed.
Wilber, K. (ed.) (1982) *The holographic paradigm and other paradoxes*. Boulder, CO: Shambala.
Wilber, K. (1982) 'Physics, mysticism and the new holographic paradigm: a critical appraisal', in idem (ed.), pp. 157-86.
Willett, C. (1998) 'Introduction', in idem (ed.), *Theorizing multiculturalism*. Oxford: Blackwell.
Williams, R. (1976) *Keywords*. Glasgow: Fontana/Croom Helm.
Wolfe, M. (1981) *Elusive development*. Geneva: UNRISD/UNECLA.
Wolferen, K. van (1990) *The enigma of Japanese power*, 2nd edn. London: Macmillan.
Wood, B. (1984) *E.F. Schumacher: his life and thought*. New York: Harper and Row.
Woost, M. (1997) 'Alternative vocabularies of development? "Community" and "participation" in development discourse in Sri Lanka', in Grillo and Stirrat (eds), pp. 229-54.
World Bank (1995) *Advancing social development*. Washington, DC: World Bank.
World Bank (1996) *The World Bank Participation Sourcebook*. Washington, DC: World Bank.
World Bank (1997) *The state in a changing world: World Development Report 1997*. New York: Oxford University Press.
World Bank (1998) *Knowledge for development: World Development Report 1998/99*. New York: Oxford University Press.
World Commission on Culture and Development (1996) *Our creative diversity* (report). Paris: UNESCO Publishing.

World Commission on Environment and Development (1987) *Our common future* (report). Oxford: Oxford University Press.

Worsley, P. (1984) *The three worlds*. London: Weidenfeld and Nicolson.

Wuyts, M., M. Mackintosh and T. Hewitt (eds) (1992) *Development policy and public action*. Oxford: Oxford University Press.

Yoshihara, K. (1988) *The rise of ersatz capitalism in South-East Asia*. Singapore: Oxford University Press.

Young, I.M. (1991) *Justice and the politics of difference*. Princeton, NJ: Princeton University Press.

Young, J. (1999) *The exclusive society: social exclusion, crime and difference in late modernity*. London: Sage.

Yurick, S. (1985) *Behold Metatron the recording angel*. New York: Semiotext(e).

Zachariah, M. and R. Sooryamoorthy (1994) *Science for social revolution? Achievements and dilemmas of a development movement: the case of Kerala*. London: Zed.

INDEX